The All-Star ★ BATHROOM SAMPLER

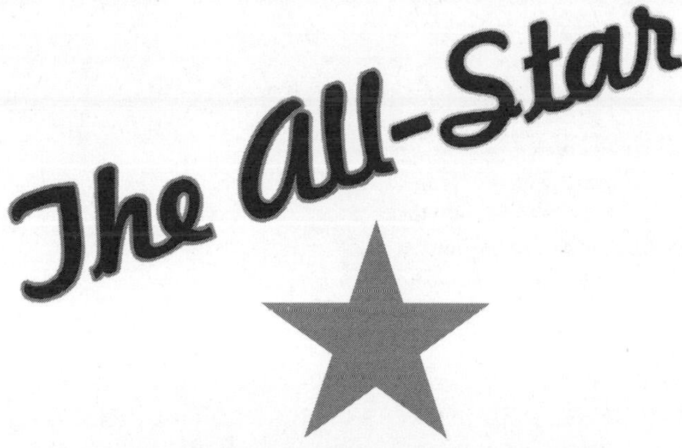

BATHROOM SAMPLER

A Sports Fan's Collection of Easily Digestible Lists, Facts, Stories, and Anecdotes

MAX BRALLIER

THE LYONS PRESS
Guilford, Connecticut
An imprint of Globe Pequot Press

To my Mom. How'd I get so lucky?
Thanks for being the greatest.

To buy books in quantity for corporate use
or incentives, call **(800) 962–0973**
or e-mail **premiums@GlobePequot.com.**

The Lyons Press is an imprint of Globe Pequot Press.

Project Manager: David Legere
Layout Artist: Mary Ballachino
Contributor credits: Abby Wolff, Geoff Baker, Aaron Winik, Justin Kirkpatrick, Dan DeStefano, Ben Murphy, Russell Trakhtenberg, Nancy Trypuc, Jess M. Brallier
Illustrator credit: Mike Mandolese

Library of Congress Cataloging-in-Publication Data is available on file.
ISBN 978-1-59921-476-4

Printed in the United States of America

10 9 8 7 6 5 4 3 2 1

Contents

Name Crazy

Other Sports We Love Too

Quotabily Quoatious Quoations

Sex, Scandals, and Screw-Ups

Superstitions and Such

Quizzes!

INTRODUCTION

To all the sports fans, benchwarmers, and backups that populate the bathrooms of this great world—here is your bathroom bible. Facts, quotes, jokes, anecdotes, trivia, history, and more, we've got a little something for everyone.

If you're ambitious, read it all in one sitting, front to back. Or back to front. Or upside down. It doesn't matter. Pick a page and dive in. Flip around—that's the whole idea.

Sure, you'd probably rather be watching *SportsCenter* or *Caddyshack* while you're sitting on the john, but installing a flat-screen TV in your bathroom costs thousands of bucks. This book'll only run you a very reasonable number of bucks. So skip the plasma and enjoy the next best thing: *The All-Star Bathroom Sampler.*

When it comes to sports, it's not always easy determining what's fact, what's exaggerated, what's spun, what's fictional legend, and what's just simply not true. Take, for example, my own grandfather, John K. Brallier Sr. For over 60 years he was recognized by the National Football League, the Pro Football Hall of Fame, and the established sports media as the first professional football player. But then, documentation later surfaced that proved otherwise. (My poor great-granddaddy went to his grave assuming he "was the guy.") Anyway, if I turn to trusted resources, many still list a Brallier as first having played football for pay.

So help me out here. If you spot something wrong, let me know, drop me an e-mail. And we'll get it fixed on the next printing. Or better yet, if you'd like to contribute something to the next edition of *The All-Star Sports Fan's Bathroom Sampler,* just let me know. We'll be sure to acknowledge your contribution. Again, an e-mail will do the trick.

Just use: AllStarBathroomSampler@gmail.com

OK, now, sit back, do your business, and enjoy the best, worst, oddest, funniest, and most inspiring of sports.

Max Brallier
New York City
September 2009

THE DOCK ELLIS EXPERIENCE

Bean balls, the longest home run ever, and one amazing no-hitter.

Dock Ellis pitched from 1968 to 1979, was an All-Star in '71, and won a World Series with the Pirates that same year. He pitched in 345 career games but is probably best remembered for three distinct incidents.

Reggie Jackson's Kisser and the Longest Home Run Ever Hit

Dock was on the mound against Reggie Jackson in the 1971 All-Star Game when Reggie, a Yankee at the time, crushed a fastball to right field. It was a monstrous shot. Wayne State University once did a study and determined that had the ball not been impeded by a light tower on the roof of Tiger Stadium, it would have traveled 650 feet, making it the longest home run ever hit. Jackson did a little showboating after the homer and, apparently, Doc held a grudge. Five years later, Doc faced Jackson again and promptly beaned him in the face. Jackson was carried off the field on a stretcher. Years later, he claimed that his face was still numb.

Hit Batsman Aplenty

In 1974, Dock had grown unhappy with his Pirates teammates. They had lost their guts, he felt, grown lackadaisical after three straight division titles. Worse, they were acting like they were afraid of division rival Cincinnati's Big Red Machine. Dock's solution? Jump-start his Pirates club by beaning every batter in the Cincy lineup.

Dock faced leadoff batter Pete Rose first: He plunked him in the ribs. Next was Joe Morgan: He drilled him in the side. Dock loaded the bases by beaning Dan Driessen in the back. Cleanup batter Tony Perez was next. Perez managed to dodge every one of Dock's beanball attempts, so Dock walked him, bringing in a run. The next hitter was Johnny Bench. "I tried to deck him twice,"

Dock later said. "I threw at his jaw, and he moved. I threw at the back of his head, and he moved."

Finally, Pirates manager Danny Murtaugh had had enough and he yanked Dock from the mound.

Strangest. No-Hitter. Ever.

Records are made to be broken. Do something crazy in sports, someone will probably do it again. Hit a bunch of homers, someone else will hit more. Run really fast, someone else will run faster. Dock Ellis, however, did something on the baseball field that, most likely, no one will ever do again. He threw a no-hitter while tripping on LSD.

It was June 12, 1970. Dock was hanging out in Los Angeles with his girlfriend, Mitzy, and some friends. Around noon, he took a hit of Purple Haze LSD. Hallucinogens were nothing new to Dock. Hell, this is a guy who had a special room in his basement called The Dungeon where'd he lock himself up and get high.

Then Mitzy opened up the newspaper. "Dock," she said, "You're supposed to pitch today."

Doc thought hard. No, he said, he wasn't pitching until Friday. That's when Mitzy told him it was Friday and that he had, in fact, slept right through Thursday.

Doc caught a 22-minute flight from Los Angeles to San Diego, hopped in a cab, and told the driver "get to the fu#@ing stadium. I got to play."

"I can only remember bits and pieces of the game," Doc would later say. "I was psyched. I had a feeling of euphoria. I was zeroed in on the [catcher's] glove, but I didn't hit the glove too much. I remember hitting a couple of batters and the bases were loaded two or three times.

"The ball was small sometimes, the ball was large sometimes, sometimes I saw the catcher, sometimes I didn't. Sometimes I tried to stare the hitter down and throw while I was looking at him. I chewed my gum until it turned to powder. They say I had about three to four fielding chances. I remember diving out of the way of a ball I thought was a line drive. I jumped, but the ball wasn't hit hard and never reached me."

It was an ugly no-hitter—the ball was moving everywhere and Dock walked eight batters. But the Pirates won, 2–0, and he got the no-hitter . . . on acid.

In 1975 Japan's Junko Tabei became the first woman to reach the top of Mt. Everest.

THE LEGEND OF THE OCTOPUS (AND OTHER AIRBORNE ITEMS)

The story behind the slippery, slimy, eight-legged tradition.

Squid Story

The Legend of the Octopus is a Detroit Red Wings tradition whereby fans throw octopuses onto the ice for good luck, particularly when in the midst of a playoff run. It all started during the 1952 playoffs, when NHL teams played two best-of-seven series on the way to winning the Stanley Cup. The octopus, with its eight "arms," represented the number of wins needed for the Red Wings to bring home the Stanley Cup.

Toss Like a Champ

Not a Detroit native? New to the octopus-tossing game? For best results, follow these instructions:

Boil your octopus for at least 20 minutes—then add a little white wine and lemon juice. The wine and lemon work to mask the octopus's nasty scent, plus it helps to preserve it. Raw octopuses stink to high heaven and when thrown, they stick to the ice and leave a big inky splotch. A cooked octopus, on the other hand, will roll and slide across the ice juuuust right.

It's against the law to throw anything onto the ice during a game, so you'll have to sneak your octopus into the stadium. Do like the local fans and wrap the octopus in a trash bag and tape it to your gut. Luckily, this is Detroit, and your beer belly will blend right in.

Choose your tossing time. Launch it either right after the national anthem or after the Red Wings score a goal. Be sure to throw it clear of any players—even opposing ones.

If you get caught, you'll be the one getting tossed. Ask surrounding fans to stand up and hide you.

All right, toss time: Grab the octopus around the middle part of the tentacles, so that the head hangs down by your knees.

Major League Baseball goes through roughly 850,000 balls per season.

Begin swinging in an overarm, cattle-roping motion, then let 'er rip. Be careful not to swing it by the very end of its tentacles—they'll just rip off and the head will go flying off on its own.

Clean up. Even though you boiled the thing in wine and lemon, it's still going to leave a stink on your hands. Bring a Wet-Nap or two.

We Want to Play Too!

Octopus tossing is pretty awesome. So, naturally, other teams and fans decided to get in on the action.

During the 1996 Stanley Cup playoffs, Florida Panthers winger Scott Mellanby used his stick to kill a rat in the locker room—and then scored two goals later in the game. Fans loved Mellanby's "rat trick," as it came to be called. Figuring the rat must have been good luck, they began showering the ice with plastic rats whenever the team scored a big goal—at times covering the ice with thousands of the toy rodents and forcing the goalies to take cover in their nets! Unfortunately for Florida's plastic rat industry, the NHL put a stop to the practice.

During a 2006 playoff series between the Red Wings and the Edmonton Oilers, Edmonton fans bombarded the ice with Alberta beef as an answer to Detroit's octopuses.

Nashville Predators fans began throwing catfish onto the ice during the 2002–2003 season. Said a stadium employee: "They are so gross. They're huge, they're heavy, they stink, and they leave this slimy trail on the ice. But, hey, if it's good for the team, I guess we can deal with it."

Hey, It Ain't Just Hockey

No matter the sport, stuff's going to wind up on the field of play. Some of the more interesting projectiles:

A pig's head: Soccer great Luís Figo became a star playing for Barcelona, then took more money to play for rival Real Madrid. When Figo returned to Barcelona in 2002, angry Barcelona fans threw all sorts of stuff onto the field, including a pig's head.

Motorized scooter: In 2001, Inter Milan fans somehow managed to sneak a motorized scooter, stolen from a rival fan during the pregame festivities, into the stadium. They then tossed it from the upper deck. Fortunately it crashed harmlessly into an empty section below—though it did catch fire.

Carpet samples: In the late '80s, western basketball fans taunted bad-toupee-wearing Illini coach Lou Henson by hurling pieces of rug onto the court.

Coins in marshmallows: Wisconsin football fans have been known to stuff quarters into marshmallows, dip them in water, and then hurl them at opposing players—hoping to get the 25-cent marshmallow to stick to a player's helmet.

Soviet gymnast Larissa Latynina has won more Olympic medals, 18, than anyone else.

AWFUL GOLF JOKES

So bad they're good.

Hot Damn!

First guy: "I just got a new set of golf clubs for my wife."

Second guy: "Great trade!"

Well Prepared

Q: Why did the golfer always bring an extra pair of pants when he went out on the golf course?

A: Just in case he got a hole in one.

Some Husband

Birthing coach: "All you mommies-to-be should know that walking and staying active while you're pregnant is quite beneficial. And you husbands, be good and take the time to go walking with your lovely wives."

Husband: "Is it OK if she carries a golf bag?"

He's a Shark in Bed Too!

Q: Why do women like making love to Australian golf great Greg Norman?

A: Because he always finishes second!

Ouch

Q: What's the difference between a golfer and a skydiver?

A: The golfer goes, whack! . . . Damn! A skydiver goes, Damn! . . . whack!

Planning Ahead

A husband and wife were golfing when the woman asked, "Honey, if I died would you get married again?"

"No, dear," the man said.

"I'm sure you would," the wife said.

So the man said, "OK, fine, I would"

Then the woman asked, "Would you let her sleep in our bed?"

And the man replied, "Yeah, I guess so."

Then the woman asked, "Would you let her use my golf clubs?"

And the man replied, "No, she's left-handed."

Holy One

Jesus and Moses are playing a round of golf. Moses shanks the ball and it heads straight for a pond, but just before the ball hits the water hazard, Moses raises his hands to the sky, the pond parts, and the ball rolls up onto the green.

Jesus sets up his shot, but it rolls left, headed for the pond. Jesus extends his arms, closes his eyes, and his ball hits the water and simply skips across onto the green.

Then, suddenly, lightning flashes and a ball drops from the sky into the pond. A fish swallows the ball, then a huge eagle swoops down, picks up the fish and drops the ball into the mouth of a turtle. The turtle slowly walks over to the hole and drops it in.

Moses turns to Jesus and says, "I hate it when your dad plays!"

BERMANISMS

Sportscaster Chris Berman is known for the colorful nicknames he gives players. Here are a few of our favorites. Can you figure out what he's referencing?

Rollie "Chicken" Fingers

Chuck "Baby, You Can Drive My" Carr

Rick "See Ya Later" Aguilera

Chuck "New Kids On" Knoblauch

Nomar "Mr. Nice Guy" Garciaparra

Rich "Protect Your Car With" Amaral

Ricky Ledee "The Earth Stood Still"

Carlos "One if by Land, Two if by Sea, Three if" Baerga

Ken "Good Evening Mister" Phelps

Jeff "Brown Paper" Bagwell

Oddibe "Young Again" McDowell

Lance "You Sunk My" Blankenship

Todd "Which Hand Does He" Frohwirth

Bert "Be Home" Blyleven

John "I Am Not a" Kruk

Greg "Crocodile" Brock

Volleyball was invented in 1895 by William George Morgan in Holyoke, Massachusetts.

Scott "Supercalifragilisticexpiali" Brosius

Jay "Ferris" Buhner

Mark Carreon "My Wayward Son"

Pat "OK" Corrales

Omar "Barbie" Daal

Damion "It Don't Come" Easley

Karim "Of the Crop" Garcia

Jesus "Skip to My" Alou

Scott "Rock the" Kazmir

Eddie "Eat, Drink, and Be" Murray

Terry "Pit and the" Pendleton

Royce "a Roni" Clayton

BEST OF THE BEST: *NORTH DALLAS FORTY*

So here's the deal. We pick the best flick for each sport. There are a lot of good football movies out there, but none of them gets to the heart of the game like this classic. A gritty, satirical look at pro football.

The Stats

Released: 1979
Director: Ted Kotcheff (he also directed *Weekend at Bernie's* . . . Yeah, he's a god as far as we're concerned.)
Starring: Nick Nolte, Mac Davis, Charles Durning, Dayle Haddon, Bo Svenson, John Matuszak, Steve Forrest, G. D. Spradlin, Dabney Coleman
Box Office Haul: $26 million

Tagline

"They pay you and they pay you well. On one condition: You play the game their way, even if you're forced to break every bone in your body."

The Basics

Nick Nolte stars as Phillip Elliot, a wide receiver for the fictional North Dallas Bulls professional football team (a not-so-thinly-veiled representation of the Dallas Cowboys). To stay competitive on the field, the aging Elliot is forced to rely on painkillers. It's a darkly comic look at the sex-, drugs-, and alcohol-fueled state of 1970s pro football, and it's still eye-opening, applicable, and entertaining today.

The first modern Olympic Games were held in Athens, Greece, in 1896.

Loyal Fans

Variety magazine: "The production is a most realistic, hard-hitting, and perceptive look at the seamy side of pro football."

Memorable Moment

The opening scene. Nolte's aging receiver lies in bed, blood soaking his pillow, beer cans and pill bottles littering his bedside, as he replays every brutal hit of the previous night's game over in his head. You can feel the pain.

Classic Quotes

Seth Maxwell: "You had better learn how to play the game, and I don't mean just the game of football."
Phillip Elliott: "Hell, Coach, I love needles."
Coach Johnson: "This is national TV. So don't pick your noses or scratch your nuts."
Elliott: "Jo Bob is here to remind us that the biggest and the baddest get to make all the rules."
Charlotte Caulder: "Well I don't agree with that."
Elliott: "Agreeing doesn't play into it."
Conrad Hunter: "People who confuse brains and luck can get in a whole lot of trouble. Seeing through the game is not the same as winning the game."
Elliot, to the team's owner: "We're not the team. You're the team! We're only the equipment—like the jockstraps and the helmets."

In the Know

Next time you're watching the movie with your buddies, look smart by tossing out these facts.

Watch carefully: During the game with Chicago, all the seats in the stadium are empty.

The NFL didn't like the movie, and they made it clear. After the film's release, the Raiders cut all ties with receiver Fred Biletnikoff, who coached Nolte on how to act like a receiver. Tom Fears was an advisor on the film and an NFL scout, but was fired once the movie opened. NFL commissioner Pete Rozelle denied any sort of league-wide agenda, but did say, "I can't say that some clubs in their own judgment [did not make] decisions based on many factors, including that they did not like the movie."

And Second Place Goes to . . .

The Longest Yard. Burt Reynolds is machismo personified, and there aren't many lines better than, "You could have robbed banks, sold dope, or stole your grandmother's pension checks and none of us would have minded. But shaving points off of a football game, man, that's un-American."

CASEY AT THE BAT

The classic baseball poem by Ernest Lawrence Thayer. First published June 3, 1888, in the San Francisco Examiner.

Casey at the Bat:
A Ballad of the Republic Sung in the Year 1888
Ernest Lawrence Thayer

The outlook wasn't brilliant for the Mudville nine that day:
The score stood four to two, with but one inning more to play.
And then when Cooney died at first, and Barrows did the same,
A sickly silence fell upon the patrons of the game.

A straggling few got up to go in deep despair. The rest
Clung to that hope which springs eternal in the human breast;
They thought, if only Casey could get but a whack at that—
We'd put up even money, now, with Casey at the bat.

But Flynn preceded Casey, as did also Jimmy Blake,
And the former was a lulu and the latter was a cake;
So upon that stricken multitude grim melancholy sat,
For there seemed but little chance of Casey's getting to the bat.

But Flynn let drive a single, to the wonderment of all,
And Blake, the much despised, tore the cover off the ball;
And when the dust had lifted, and the men saw
what had occurred,
There was Jimmy safe at second and Flynn a-hugging third.

Then from 5,000 throats and more there rose a lusty yell;
It rumbled through the valley, it rattled in the dell;
It knocked upon the mountain and recoiled upon the flat,
For Casey, mighty Casey, was advancing to the bat.

There was ease in Casey's manner as he stepped into his place;
There was pride in Casey's bearing and a smile on Casey's face.
And when, responding to the cheers, he lightly doffed his hat,
No stranger in the crowd could doubt 'twas Casey at the bat.

Ten thousand eyes were on him as he rubbed his hands with dirt;
Five thousand tongues applauded when he wiped them on his shirt.
Then while the writhing pitcher ground the ball into his hip,
Defiance gleamed in Casey's eye, a sneer curled Casey's lip.

And now the leather-covered sphere came hurtling through the air,
And Casey stood a-watching it in haughty grandeur there.
Close by the sturdy batsman the ball unheeded sped—
"That ain't my style," said Casey. "Strike one," the umpire said.

From the benches, black with people, there went up a muffled roar,
Like the beating of the storm waves on a stern and distant shore.
"Kill him! Kill the umpire!" shouted someone on the stand;
And its likely they'd a-killed him had not Casey raised his hand.

With a smile of Christian charity great Casey's visage shone;
He stilled the rising tumult; he bade the game go on;
He signaled to the pitcher, and once more the spheroid flew;
But Casey still ignored it, and the umpire said, "Strike two."

"Fraud!" cried the maddened thousands, and echo answered fraud;
But one scornful look from Casey and the audience was awed.
They saw his face grow stern and cold, they saw his muscles strain,
And they knew that Casey wouldn't let that ball go by again.

The sneer is gone from Casey's lip, his teeth are clenched in hate;
He pounds with cruel violence his bat upon the plate.
And now the pitcher holds the ball, and now he lets it go,
And now the air is shattered by the force of Casey's blow.

Oh, somewhere in this favored land the sun is shining bright;
The band is playing somewhere, and somewhere hearts are light,
And somewhere men are laughing, and somewhere children shout;
But there is no joy in Mudville—mighty Casey has struck out.

A bowling pin needs to tilt 7.5 degrees to fall down.

TOP 10 TERRIBLE CALLS

Referee regrets and umpire uncertainties. In our opinion, the 10 worst calls ever, in order from bad to worse.

10. "I said tails."

Certain blown calls are understandable. Things happen fast on the field of play. But a coin flip—no ref could blow that, right? Wrong. The Steelers were playing the Lions on Thanksgiving Day, 1999, and the game went into overtime. The Steelers called the toss and Jerome Bettis clearly and audibly said "tails." Referee Phil Luckett, however, heard "heads." A stunned Bettis said, "I called tails." A mistaken Luckett said, "No, you didn't."

As the network cut to commercial break, announcer Greg Gumble sarcastically said, "When we come back, the Lions—*we think* — have won this coin toss and will receive."

9. The Long Count

On September 27, 1927, boxers Gene Tunney and Jack Dempsey met at Chicago's Soldier Field, with Dempsey attempting to reclaim his heavyweight title. Tunney led through six rounds and Dempsey needed a knockout if he was going to win. In the seventh round he got what he needed . . . almost. Dempsey landed a wicked combo that sent Tunney to the mat. Dempsey, likely unaware of a new rule that required the other fighter to go to his corner after a knockdown, hovered over the downed Tunney. Thus, referee Dave Barry waited the six seconds it took to move Dempsey to his corner before beginning the count. When Tunney rose at the count of 9, he had really been down on the mat for 15 seconds. Tunney regained his wits and went on to win the bout in a 10-round decision.

Tunney later claimed he was aware of the miscount and could have gotten up at any moment but, as he asked reporters, "Why would anyone want to get up early in the same ring as Jack Dempsey?"

It takes 3,000 cows to supply the NFL with enough leather for one season's supply of footballs.

8. Scottie Pippin Phantom Foul on Hubert Davis

It was Game 5 of the 1994 NBA Eastern Conference finals and, with time expiring, the Bulls were clinging to a slim lead against the Knicks. Scottie Pippin played perfect, no-contact D on a 3-point attempt by the Knicks' Hubert Davis—but ref Hue Hollins saw something else and called a foul where there was none. Davis went to the line, made his free throws, and the Knicks went on to steal the game and win the series.

7. No Interference on Jeter Home Run

Twelve-year-old Yankees fan Jeffrey Maier had more than a little to do with the Yankees 5–4 win over the Orioles in Game 1 of the 1996 American League Championship Series. Maier, sitting along the right field wall, reached over the fence and yanked a Jeter fly ball away from Baltimore rightfielder Tony Tarasco. Umpire Rich Garcia failed to call fan interference and ruled it a home run, tying the game. The Yankees then won it in the 11th and the series in 5 games. Maier became a local celebrity—New York mayor Rudy Giuliani even awarded him the key to the city!

6. Colorado's Fifth Down

With time winding down, the Colorado Buffaloes trailed the Missouri Tigers 27–31 in a 1990 early-season NCAA football conference game. As Colorado neared the end zone, they spiked the ball to stop the clock—but the refs forgot to count it as a down! On the final play of the game, the "fifth down," Colorado scored, capping a 33–31 comeback. Once the mistake was revealed, Colorado coach Bill McCartney refused to forfeit the game, saying "the field was lousy." The botched call's impact was far-reaching—had Colorado not won the game, they most likely would not have been crowned the AP's National Champion.

5. "No goal!"

The city of Buffalo is still groaning about this one. Dallas Star Brett Hull scored hockey's most controversial goal against Buffalo Sabres goalie Dominik Hasek in Game 6 of the 1999 Stanley Cup finals. The score gave the Stars the win and the championship.

Pittsburgh is the only U.S. city with three sports teams that wear the same colors: black and gold.

Replays showed that Hull's skate crossed the crease before the puck, which should have voided the goal. That's not how the refs saw it though: Since Hull had already been inside the crease with the puck earlier during the possession, they viewed the entire thing as one play.

4. The "Hand of God"

In Argentina, they call this play the "Hand of God." It was the 1986 FIFA World Cup quarterfinals. Diego Maradona split two defenders and, using his hand, punched the ball into the goal. The refs completely missed the handball and Argentina defeated England 2–1. As Maradona later said, the goal was scored "partly by the hand of God and partly by the head of Mara Dona."

3. Roy Jones Jr. Somehow Loses to Park Si Hun

Referees are swayed by the home crowd; it happens, and, on a minor level, it's to be expected. But sometimes home-field advantage goes too far. At the 1988 Summer Olympics in Seoul, three boxing judges awarded hometown boy Park Si Hun a gold-medal victory over Roy Jones Jr., despite the fact that Jones Jr. had spent three rounds absolutely abusing Hun in the ring. Jones Jr. landed 54 more punches than Hun, and if the fight hadn't been stopped, he most likely would have knocked Park out. Officials suspected bribery. The three judges were suspended, but ultimately no evidence was found.

2. Soviet Union Gets Precious Extra Seconds in 1972 Olympic Basketball

In 1972, the Soviet Union handed the U.S. Men's basketball team its first Olympic loss when officials twice mistakenly put extra time on the clock in the final seconds of the game, allowing the Soviets to score at the buzzer and walk away with a 51–50 victory and the gold medal. Team USA appealed but lost. All U.S. players refused their silver medals and several team members have stated in their wills that, even after their deaths, their heirs are never to accept the medals.

1. Denkinger Calls Orta Safe

The most controversial call in World Series history. Game 6. Ninth inning. 1985 World series. Umpire Don Denkinger calls the Royals' Jorge Orta safe at first base. Controversy erupts when replays show St. Louis Cardinals pitcher Todd Worrell clearly beating Orta to the bag. The non-out allows the Royals to stage a two-run rally, taking the game 2–1, and go on to win the series in seven games. Denkinger quickly became the most hated man in St. Louis, receiving death threats and even a letter from one irate fan saying if he ever saw him in person, he'd "blow him away" with a .357 Magnum.

Most track records are broken late in the day, when the athletes' body temperatures are highest.

CHANKO NABE

Eat like a sumo wrester!

You might be surprised, but sumo wrestlers have a very strict diet. They pretty much eat only one thing: *chanko nabe.* This chicken-based stew isn't all that unhealthy on its own—sumo wrestlers just happen to eat it constantly and in massive quantities. It's also quite tasty—so next time you're in the mood to cook . . .

First, you'll need to cook up some chicken stock.

What You Need

3 pounds chicken parts—wings, thighs, necks, etc. (leave a little meat and skin on the bone)
1 small carrot, sliced
1½ onions, chopped
1 clove garlic, crushed
parsley
1 teaspoon pepper
½ teaspoon salt

1. Dump everything into a large pot and fill ¾ of the way with water.
2. Bring to a slow boil, lower heat to a simmer, and cook, covered, for 2 hours.
3. Remove cover, simmer for an hour and a half.
4. That's it! Congrats, you've got chicken stock.

Now that you've got your chicken stock, it's time to cook the real thing.

What You Need (serves 4 to 6)

1 pack udon noodles
1 sliced radish
1 sllced potato
4 boneless chicken breast halves, chopped into chunks

2 chopped onions
1 sliced carrot
10 chopped shiitake mushrooms or white mushrooms (be sure to remove the stems)
2 cakes chopped "cotton" tofu, fried in butter
1½ cups chopped broccoli
½ cup soy sauce
2 teaspoons salt
1 teaspoon pepper
½ cup white wine and sugar to taste
Garnish: ginger and chili pepper to taste

Cook the udon noodles, following the directions on the package. Strain and set aside.

Bring water to boil, add the sliced radish and potato and partially boil for a few minutes. Drain, splash with cold water, and set aside.

Cook the chicken over a skillet, being careful not to overcook (or undercook, obviously . . . pink chicken = no good).

Get out that chicken stock you made earlier and bring it to a boil. Add the onions, carrots, mushrooms, and fried tofu, and simmer for 10 to 12 minutes or until the vegetables are cooked through. Add the radish, potato, and broccoli and simmer for 5 more minutes.

Dump your cooked chicken into the pot and season with soy sauce, salt, pepper, white wine, and sugar. Let simmer for 3 more minutes.

Put cooked udon noodles in bowls, and scoop the soup over them.

Garnish with ginger and chili pepper.

Serve steaming hot.

Enjoy!

The average lifespan of a major league baseball is six pitches.

PHILOSOPHY OF FISHING

Deep thoughts on aquatic hunting.

"You must lose a fly to catch a trout."
—GEORGE HERBERT

"Fishing is much more than fish. It is the great occasion when we may return to the fine simplicity of our forefathers."
—HERBERT HOOVER

"The charm of fishing is that it is the pursuit of what is elusive but attainable, a perpetual series of occasions for hope."
—JOHN BUCHAN

"I love fishing. You put that line in the water and you don't know what's on the other end. Your imagination is under there."
—ROBERT ALTMAN

"Bragging may not bring happiness, but no man having caught a large fish goes home through an alley."
—CHRISTOPHER J. AMARU

"Many men go fishing all of their lives without knowing that it is not fish they are after."
—HENRY DAVID THOREAU

"There is certainly something in angling that tends to produce a serenity of the mind."
—WASHINGTON IRVING

A hockey puck weighs .38 pounds.

"SOMEBODY JUST BACK OF YOU WHILE YOU ARE FISHING IS AS BAD AS SOMEONE LOOKING OVER YOUR SHOULDER WHILE YOU WRITE A LETTER TO YOUR GIRL."
—ERNEST HEMINGWAY

"THE GODS DO NOT DEDUCT FROM MAN'S ALLOTTED SPAN THE HOURS SPENT IN FISHING."
—BABYLONIAN PROVERB

"NOTHING MAKES A FISH BIGGER THAN ALMOST BEING CAUGHT."
—ALEXANDER DESTEFANO

"THIS PLANET IS COVERED WITH SORDID MEN WHO DEMAND THAT HE WHO SPENDS TIME FISHING SHALL SHOW RETURNS IN FISH."
—LEONIDAS HUBBARD JR.

"SCHOLARS HAVE LONG KNOWN THAT FISHING EVENTUALLY TURNS MEN INTO PHILOSOPHERS. UNFORTUNATELY, IT IS ALMOST IMPOSSIBLE TO BUY DECENT TACKLE ON A PHILOSOPHER'S SALARY."
—PATRICK F. MCMANUS

"SOME GO TO CHURCH AND THINK ABOUT FISHING, OTHERS GO FISHING AND THINK ABOUT GOD."
—TONY BLAKE

"RIVERS AND THE INHABITANTS OF THE WATERY ELEMENTS ARE MADE FOR WISE MEN TO CONTEMPLATE AND FOR FOOLS TO PASS BY WITHOUT CONSIDERATION."
—IZAAK WALTON

"A BAD DAY OF FISHING IS BETTER THAN A GOOD DAY OF WORK."
—WESLEY RYAN

Golf balls can reach speeds of 170 mph.

THE BAT AND THE BALL

The basics . . .

What's Inside a Baseball?

Since 1872, the dimensions of the baseball haven't changed: five ounces heavy, nine inches in circumference, 108 stitches holding it all together. At the center is a small cork sphere, about the size of a grape. Surrounding that cork sphere is a thin black layer of compressed rubber and around that is a layer of red rubber. Tightly wrapped around this elastic, bouncy-ball-like core are several layers of tightly wound twine—this is the meat of the ball. That's all wrapped in a thin layer of tweed and the famous white leather casing. The tighter the yarn, the more elastic the ball. In other words, tighter winding = more homers.

How Are Bats Made?

A baseball bat begins at the lumber mill when splits of wood (usually ash, sometimes bamboo, hickory, or maple) are run through a lathe that shaves off the tree's rough edges; resulting in smooth chunks of wood called billets. At this point, they're still considered "green" because they contain gum and sap, so they're put through an air-dryer—a process that takes up to two years.

Once dried, the billets are weighed, inspected, and run through another, more precise lathe that shapes the billet into the rough shape of a bat. Finally, this almost-bat is turned over to plant workers known as bat turners. Bat turners are artists of a sort; it's a delicate operation and they're highly skilled. They choose a billet of the appropriate length, based on the model bat they're making. The bat turner carefully sands the bat, measuring and weighing it until it's perfect.

Finally, the bat is branded with the company logo and the signature of the player who first requested the model. The signature is always located one-quarter turn from the bat's sweet spot (that perfect spot high on the bat that produces the best hit). The bat is then varnished and sent off to the team.

On average, women take three times longer in the bathroom than men.

When Bat Meets Ball

OK, time for physics class. When the ball meets the bat, the bat recoils; the more recoil, the more energy is lost in the transaction. The heavier the bat, the less recoil. But the bat can't be too heavy—then the hitter sacrifices speed. The speed of the pitch has little to do with the distance the ball flies—it's the speed of the bat that determines the hit. A-Rod would hit a Roger Clemens fastball just as far as he would hit a Johan Santana changeup. A successful hitter uses a bat that's heavy enough to provide enough force to put a hurting on the ball, but light enough that he can quickly move it through the air.

Mmm, donuts . . .

Relax, Homer, we're talking batting donuts, not Krispy Kremes. Y'know, the circular weights batters place around their bats while taking practice swings in the on-deck circle? The weight makes the bat lighter and easier to swing when they step up to the plate. Old-time ballplayer Elston Howard, a Negro league star before becoming the first African-American to play for the Yankees, is credited with inventing the batting donut.

Holy Oversize Bat, Batman!

The world's largest baseball bat rests against the Louisville Slugger museum in Louisville, Kentucky. The 120-foot carbon steel bat, erected in 1995, weighs 34 tons. It's a replica of the bat Babe Ruth used in the '20s—just 117 feet longer.

WILT CHAMBERLAIN AND THE 20,000 LADIES

Promiscuity on a Hall of Fame level.

Wilt Chamberlain's stats are beyond impressive: 13-time All-Star, four-time NBA MVP, two-time NBA Champion, 1972 Finals MVP, 1960 All-Star Game MVP, fourth all-time in points scored. And, of course, the big one—the last player to score 100 points in a game.

To many people, though, Wilt's best remembered for one number: 20,000, the number of different women he claimed to have slept with.

He made the claim in his 1991 autobiography, *A View From Above.* "Yes, that's correct," he wrote, "twenty thousand different ladies. At my age, that equals out to having sex with 1.2 women a day, every day since I was 15 years old."

Response and Defense

People were disgusted. Wilt was a national punch line. He defended himself, saying "I was just doing what was natural—chasing good-looking ladies, whoever they were and wherever they were available," adding that he never chased after a married woman.

As his lawyer "Sy" Goldberg said, "Some people collect stamps, Wilt collected women."

Wilt vs. Ashe

African-American tennis star Arthur Ashe condemned Wilt's comments, along with the behavior of HIV-positive Magic Johnson, saying their actions produced "a certain amount of racial embarrassment."

In his 1993 memoir, Ashe wrote "African-Americans have spent decades denying that we are sexual primitives by nature, as racists have argued since the days of slavery. These two college-trained black men of international fame and immense personal wealth do their best to reinforce the stereotype."

Ashe went on to say he "felt more pity than sorrow for Wilt as his macho accounting backfired on him in the form of a wave of public criticism."

Wilt the Romantic

In an interview shortly before his death, Wilt said, "With all of you men out there who think that having a thousand different ladies is pretty cool, I have learned in my life . . . I've found out that having one woman a thousand different times is much more satisfying."

The Wall of Wilt

In a skit from a 1993 episode of *In Living Color* a mother and daughter visit a Vietnam Wall-like monument to the 20,000 women Wilt had slept with, and both of them joyfully point out their names. According to friends, Wilt had seen the skit and loved it.

20,000 . . . Now, Let's See, That's . . .

- ✓ .78 ladies slept-with for every million box-office dollars taken in by the universally panned *Conan the Destroyer,* in which Wilt, in some of the most bizarre casting of all time, co-starred as the villainous Bombaata
- ✓ One lady slept-with for every league that Captain Nemo descended under the sea. We heard they're working on a sequel: 20,000 Deeds Under the Sheets (sorry, sorry)
- ✓ 66.6 ladies slept-with for every pound Wilt weighed as a Laker, when he topped 300 on the scale
- ✓ 1,333 women slept-with for every year Wilt played in the NBA
- ✓ 4,000 ladies slept-with for every Emmy teenage heartthrob Richard Chamberlain (unrelated) was nominated

SCI-FI SPORTS

Ever wonder what sports we'll be playing in the future? Or what sport might be being played right now, in some alternate universe or on some distant planet? For a fun guess at the answer to that question, just turn on your TV or pick up a book.

DEJARIK

Played in: *Star Wars*

What it is: Similar to chess, Dejarik is played on a holographic board with a black-and-white checkerboard pattern. Playing pieces are holographic representations of creatures from throughout the galaxy. If you ever find yourself in the middle of a game, just remember one thing: Let the Wookie win.

GERMAN BATBALL

Played in: Kurt Vonnegut's *The Sirens of Titan*

What it is: The most popular game on the human-colonized Mars, German Batball is similar to baseball, but features only three bases. The ball is a "flabby ball the size of a big honeydew melon. The ball is no more lively than a 10-gallon hat filled with rain water." There's no pitching involved—instead, the player at bat places the ball in one fist and punches it with the other, then players in the field do their best to peg the runner with the ball.

BROCKIAN ULTRA-CRICKET

Played in: Douglas Adams's *The Hitchhiker's Guide to the Galaxy* series

What it is: As described in *Life, the Universe, and Everything,* Brockian Ultra-Cricket is "a curious game which involve[s] suddenly hitting people for no readily apparent reason and then

Americans use an average of seven sheets of toilet paper per bathroom visit—more than any other country.

running away." A parody of real cricket, the rules include growing three extra legs (just to keep the crowd amused) and a common strategy is to find a good player, then clone him, to save training time. "The winning team shall be the first team that wins." Ah, but of course.

FUTURESPORT

Played in: *Futuresport,* made-for-TV-movie
What it is: In 2025, a new game called Futuresport (part basketball, part baseball, part hockey, with hoverboards and rollerblades) is created in an attempt to eliminate gang warfare. As the tagline says, "In 2025, a revolutionary sport is the only way to stop a revolution." Badass.

SKY-SURFING

Played in: *Judge Dredd* comic series
What it is: Also known as powerboarding, this highly dangerous sport is played on an antigravity surfboard that floats in the air. The surfer controls his or her speed with foot controls on the surface of the board. In championship sky-surfing events, surfers fly through everyday obstacles, such as the rigging of a sailing ship.

QUIDDITCH

Played in: *Harry Potter* series
What it is: The most popular sport in the wizard world, Quidditch is comparable to a mid-air game of soccer. Two teams compete, battling in the sky while chasing after a tiny buzzing ball called the golden snitch. There's some scoring that goes on, but, basically, whichever team grabs the snitch first wins. Shh . . . don't tell *Harry Potter* fans, but the whole scoring system pretty much doesn't make any sense.

Leave It to Beaver **was the first TV program to show a toilet.**

AARGROOHA

Played in: Terry Pratchett's *Discworld* series

What it is: It's a lot like soccer, only it's played by trolls and they use a human head as ball.

ROLLERBALL

Played in: *Rollerball* (1975)

What it is: Similar to Roller Derby, but way more awesome. Rollerball is the sport of the future where two teams skate around a circular, banked track, trying to score points by throwing a softball-size steel ball through a circular goal on the arena's wall. Whichever team has the ball does whatever they can to get it through the goal while the other team does everything they can to stop them. It's an ultraviolent, full-contact sport.

EARL MORRALL

The gridiron's most spectacular second stringer

Earl Morrall spent 21 years in the NFL as a starting QB, backup QB, and, on occasion, a punter. Though he never excelled as a starter, he did earn one distinction: greatest backup in NFL history.

A Slow Start

Morrall's pro career got off to a rocky start. After leading his Michigan State Spartans to a Rose Bowl victory, he was drafted in the first round of the 1956 draft by the 49ers. The 49ers soon passed him off to the Steelers, however, and less than a year later the Steelers sent him to the Lions for future Hall of Famer Bobby Lane (setting off Detroit's Curse of Bobby Lane). Morrall spent six years with the Lions—his best was 1963, when he threw for 24 touchdowns and 2,600 yards. But a shoulder injury set him back, and the Lions shipped him to the Giants. He started for a few years in New York, admirably guiding them through a shaky rebuilding period before being traded to the Colts for a draft pick. Up to that point, his career had been remarkable only for how truly unremarkable it was.

Running with the Colts

Morrall started the 1968 season riding pine behind Johnny Unitas. It looked like another average year for Morrall—until Unitas went down with an injury. Morrall was superb, leading the Colts to a 13-1 record and winning two playoff games on the way to being named league MVP. But in the Super Bowl, Morrall and his Colts ran headlong into the Jets and Joe Namath's legendary guarantee and, in one of the greatest upsets ever, the Jets defeated the Colts 16–7.

The first Olympic race was won by Corubus, a chef, in 776 B.C.

Morrall (once again replacing an injured Johnny Unitas) redeemed himself in Super Bowl V, however, leading the Colts to a 16–13 victory over the Cowboys.

A Part of History

After the 1971 season, Morrall was claimed off of waivers by the Miami Dolphins for just $100. Miami coach Don Shula, who had coached Morrall as a Colt, said "I happen to have a good memory. I remember what Earl did for me in 1968."

Shula knew what he was doing. Dolphins starting QB Bob Griese went down with an injury during the fifth game of the season and Morrall stepped in, guiding the Dolphins into the playoffs and keeping them undefeated along the way. Though Morrall didn't start for much of the Dolphins' successful Super Bowl run, he was still named AFC Player of the Year as well as NFL Comeback Player of the Year—the first time the award was given out. Most important, Morrall proved himself an integral part of the historic undefeated 1972 Dolphins—the last NFL team to go undefeated.

Morrall remained the Dolphins backup QB for the next four seasons, announcing his retirement in 1977. His career stats are impressive:

✓ Two-time Pro Bowl selection (1957, 1968)

✓ Three-time Super Bowl champion (V, VII, VIII)

✓ 1968 AP NFL MVP

✓ 1972 NFL Comeback Player of the Year

✓ TD-INT: 161-148

✓ 20,809 yards passing

THE SPORTS NUMERIST 0–20

The games. By the numbers. Zero through twenty.

On October 7, 1916, the Cumberland College Bulldogs scored **0** points against the Georgia Tech Engineers. The final score was 222–0—the most lopsided game in college football history.

"In case of a thunderstorm, stand in the middle of the fairway and hold up a **1**-iron. Not even God can hit a 1-iron."—Lee Trevino

On October **2**, 1978, Bucky Dent hit his famous homer, propelling the Yankees on to their 22nd World Series victory and sparking 26 more years of Boston bitching.

On January **3**, 1920, the Yankees purchased Babe Ruth from the Red Sox, marking the start of the Curse of the Bambino.

Craig Morton completed **4** passes in Super Bowl XII—the fewest ever in an NFL championship game.

Former Yankees manager Billy Martin was hired and fired **5** times by George "The Boss" Steinbrenner.

On April **6**, 1973, Ron Blomberg of the New York Yankees became the first designated hitter in Major League Baseball history. Purists everywhere shed a tear.

Kansas City Quarterback Len Dawson fumbled **7** times in a 1964 game against San Diego, a record.

8 Chicago White Sox players were banned for life from baseball after throwing the 1919 World Series.

The Detroit Tigers went through 220 bottles of champagne celebrating when they clinched a playoff birth in 2006.

On July **9**, 2003, Pittsburgh Pirates first baseman Randall Simon was arrested, and fined and suspended by Major League Baseball for tapping the Italian Sausage with a bat during the Milwaukee Brewers' famous mascot sausage race, knocking Mandy Block, the woman inside the costume, to the ground. She didn't press charges, asking only for the offending bat—autographed, of course.

Little Leaguer Danny Almonte, pitching "phenom," was supposedly **10** years old when he led his Bronx, New York, team to third place in the 2001 Little League World Series. It was later revealed that he was actually 12.

Pete Rose's son, Pete Rose Jr., played in just **11** major-league games.

Babe Ruth allegedly downed **12** hot dogs in between games of a doubleheader.

"Till I was **13**, I thought my name was Shut Up!"

—Joe Namath

As a Cincinnati Red, Pete Rose wore jersey No.**14**. His number was unofficially retired by the Reds and officially retired by the Cincinnati Cyclones of the East Coast Hockey League.

In the **15** years between 1991 and 2006, John Daly claims to have lost between $50 and $60 million dollars gambling.

The average Wonderlic score for an NFL halfback is **16**—the lowest at any NFL position.

Floyd Landis's stage-**17** victory in the Tour de France was described as "one of the most epic days of cycling ever seen"—until it was discovered he was 'roided up for the whole thing.

William "Refrigerator" Perry's Super Bowl XX ring is the largest ever made—size 25.

Jean Van de Velde was the clear leader heading into the **18**th hole of the 1999 British Open and needed only a double-bogey six to take the tournament. Then, in possibly the greatest collapse professional golf has ever seen, Van de Velde proceeded to choke mightily, putting the ball everywhere but in the hole.

On April **19**, 1951, the St. Louis Browns baseball club trotted out three-foot, seven-inch Eddie Gadel as a batter. The little guy, with only a 1.5-inch strike zone, walked.

The 1899 Cleveland Spiders, the worst baseball team in history, won only **20** games to go along with their 134 losses.

SPORTS ILLUSTRATED COVER JINX

It couldn't be true . . . could it?

Sports Illustrated has a long history of putting athletes and teams on their covers, only to see those same cover stars suffer injuries, major losses, or worse. In 2002, the magazine even dedicated a cover to the phenomenon, complete with black cat and the headline THE COVER THAT NO ONE WOULD POSE FOR. Here's a timeline of just a few of the magazine's major cover catastrophes.

August 16, 1954
Eddie Matthews was both the first *SI* cover subject and the first to fall victim to the jinx. Just one week after the magazine's release, Matthews injured his hand and missed seven games.

January 31, 1955
Skier Jill Kinmont struck a tree and was left paralyzed from the neck down the same week her issue hit the stands.

March 7, 1955
Joe Alston, FBI agent and badminton star, was about to go undercover when his cover issue hit the stands. The publicity forced the FBI to keep him on desk duty for the rest of his career.

October 29, 1956
Notre Dame football was in good shape until *SI* did a cover story on them. Oklahoma blew them out 40–0 the Saturday after their cover hit the stands. They followed that with losses to Navy and Pitt.

May 26, 1958
Pat O'Conner, featured on the cover of *SI*'s Indianapolis 500 preview, was killed in a 15-car crash during the race's first lap.

April 18, 1960
Carin Cone was undefeated for four years in the 100-meter backstroke. Then, just weeks after she graced the cover, she finished second and failed to qualify for the summer games.

July 11, 1960
Just one week after runner Jim Beatty's cover, the U.S. record holder in the 5,000-meter injured his foot and failed to make the finals at the summer games.

October 3, 1960
Washington QB Bob Schloredt was riding high, heavily favored to defeat Navy. But the week after his cover (featuring him taking a shotgun snap) hit the stands, Washington lost to Navy 15–14. It was a botched shotgun snap that led to the loss.

February 13, 1961
Two days after *SI* described Laurence Owen as "America's Most Exciting Girl Skater," she and the rest of the U.S. skating team lost their lives in the Sabena Flight 548 plane crash in Belgium.

March 26, 1962
SI's cover featured a grinning shot of Formula 1 racer Ricardo Rodriguez and the caption "Mexico's Young Fireball." Later that year he died when his car crashed and went up in a blaze.

March 22, 1965
Light heavyweight Willie Pastrano is featured on the cover for his upcoming title defense. He is knocked out in the 9th round and never fights again.

December 14, 1970
The Texas Longhorns were riding a 30-game win streak until their cover hit the stands. They lost 24–11 to Notre Dame in the Cotton Bowl, fumbling an unbelievable nine times.

The International Golf Club in Massachusetts is the world's longest golf course—8,325 yards from the tiger tees.

June 26, 1978

Poor Andy North got it twice. In '78 he graced the cover after winning his first tournament, the U.S. Open. It took him seven years to win another event on the PGA tour. When he finally did, in '85, he made his second cover appearance. He never won another PGA tournament.

November 30, 1978

Bill Rodgers was just asking for it. He'd won seven marathons in a row. He got his cover; next marathon he finished sixth.

November 19, 1984

The Dolphins were 11-0, threatening to go undefeated again. One *SI* cover later (and one loss later), all that talk is put to rest.

May 24, 1993

Barry Bonds had an unstoppable bat in 1993—until he made his cover appearance. In two weeks his batting average plummeted 40 points.

August 16, 1993

In 1993 Nike ruled the world. In the weeks after CEO Phil Knight graced the cover, Nike's stock plummeted. High school players that Nike sponsored saw their eligibility endangered, and hundreds of employees lost their jobs.

March 5, 2001

Red Sox star shortstop Nomar Garciaparra received his first *SI* cover—days later he split a tendon in his wrist, the first major injury in a career that was eventually derailed by injuries.

The average age for a professional BMX biker is 20.

WHAT'S IN AN (MLB) NAME?

The names are probably familiar.
The history behind them might not be.

New York Yankees

The Bronx Bombers didn't always play in the Bronx. They started off as the original Baltimore Orioles in 1901, but made the move to New York in 1903 and were renamed the Highlanders—after Hilltop Park, where they played their games. The name Highlanders was a little too long for sportswriter Mark Roth—he started calling them the Yankees in 1913 and the name stuck.

Detroit Tigers

The Tigers, formed in 1901, derive their name from the striped stockings that are part of their uniform. Stripes, tigers—get it?

Atlanta Braves

Around the turn of the century, when the Braves played in Boston, they went by the name Doves because of their owners, the Dovey Brothers. They also went by Beaneaters and the Redcaps for a time until John Montgomery Ward and James E. Gaffney took over the team in 1912. The name Braves was then chosen because co-owner James E. Gaffney was known as the "Brave of Tammany Hall." Tammany Hall's symbol was an Indian chief, and that provided for the logo.

Kansas City Royals

The name was chosen from fan suggestions after the team joined the AL in 1969. It draws from the American Royal Livestock and Horse show, a yearly Kansas City event.

L.A. Dodgers

During the team's early years in Brooklyn they were known as the Bridegrooms because so many of their players were married. They then took their names from their managers for a while—first Ward's Wonders after manager Montgomery Ward and then Foutz's Fillies for manager Dave Foutz. In the 1890s they earned the name Trolley Dodgers because fans and players were forced to dodge Brooklyn's many trolley cars on their way to the ballpark. Trolley Dodgers was soon shortened to Dodgers.

Montreal Expos

The Expos joined the league in 1969 and took their name from the famous world exposition held there two years earlier, Expo67.

Milwaukee Brewers

Originally the Seattle Pilots, the franchise moved to Milwaukee in 1970 and changed their name as a nod to the city's dominant industry: brewskies.

The Tactu Golf Club in Morococha, Peru, is 14,335 feet above sea level, making it the world's highest golf course.

MAGIC ON BIRD, BIRD ON MAGIC

"And the rivalry has pushed us on to new heights . . . Great athletes in the past have always been part of a great rivalry.

—Swimmer Ryk Neethling

Magic on Bird

"WHEN I PLAYED, LARRY BIRD WAS THE ONLY ONE I FEARED."

"LARRY, YOU ONLY TOLD ME ONE LIE. YOU SAID THERE WILL BE ANOTHER LARRY BIRD. LARRY, THERE WILL NEVER, EVER, EVER BE ANOTHER LARRY BIRD."

"WHEN THE NEW SCHEDULE WOULD COME OUT EACH YEAR, I'D GRAB IT AND CIRCLE THE BOSTON GAMES. TO ME, IT WAS THE TWO AND THE OTHER 80."

"A LOT OF BLACK GUYS ALWAYS ASK ME, COULD LARRY BIRD REALLY PLAY THAT GOOD? I WOULD SAY, 'MAN, LARRY BIRD WAS SO GOOD . . . IT WAS FRIGHTENING.' "

More than 70 million decks of cards are sold in the United States each year.

Bird on Magic

"HE'S JUST A GREAT BASKETBALL PLAYER. THE BEST I'VE EVER SEEN. UNBELIEVABLE."

"THERE'S NO QUESTION ABOUT MAGIC—WE HAD A GREAT TIME."

"I KNEW HE WAS WATCHING ME BECAUSE I WAS WATCHING HIM. I WAS MAKING SURE I KNEW WHAT HE WAS DOING EVERY NIGHT."

"THERE'S ONE THING WE CAN AGREE UPON THAT WE'RE RETIRED NOW. PROBABLY WILL NEVER COME BACK AGAIN. BUT—I WANNA ASK YOU. THEN WILL YOU GET THE HELL OUT OF MY DREAMS?"

The longest golf hole in the world is the 7th hole (par 7) of the Sano Course at the Satsuki Golf Club in Japan. It's 909 yards.

FOR RICHER OR POORER OR, MICHAEL VICK VERSUS MY UNCLE VIC

Michael Vick's legal troubles forced him to sell his Georgia mansion. While perusing the real estate listing, we couldn't help but think of our Uncle Vic . . .

Michael Vick's house	**My Uncle Vic's trailer**
8 bedrooms	1 pull-out sofa
8.5 baths	1 bath, two trees out back
4-car garage	one blue tarp
swimming pool	old bathtub out back
water view	interstate overpass view
buried on property: 8 dogs	buried on property: 2 goldfish, 4,000-plus Marlboro butts, possibly gold
wet bar	wet spot
tennis court	court summons posted on screen door
central air-conditioning	sister's old fan
whirlpool tub	sister's old fan in old bathtub out back
central vacuum	broken dustbuster
professional landscaping	two plastic pink flamingos
security booth	Louisville slugger
intercom system	ham radio
bidet	no comment

The world's largest green is the 695-yard 5th hole at the International Golf Club in Massachusetts.

RUN, ROSIE, RUN!

How Rosie Ruiz (almost) stole the Boston Marathon.

In 1980 Rosie Ruiz was the first-place female finisher in the 84th annual Boston Marathon. But days later it was revealed that she had cheated; she didn't actually run the race, she simply jumped into the pack at the end and sprinted to the victory line. Here's how it went down.

Twenty-three-year-old Rosie recorded a time of 2:31:56—a record for a female runner. But certain people were immediately suspicious. Checkpoint officials didn't remember seeing her and Rosie wasn't in particularly good shape for a runner. When asked why she'd barely broken a sweat, she simply said "I got up with a lot of energy this morning."

After a little investigation it was discovered that Rosie had cheated in the New York marathon that qualified her for Boston. She simply hopped on the subway, got off near the finish line, and claimed to have been injured during the race—and the "injury" automatically qualified her for Boston.

Rosie the Celeb

Rosie was immediately the butt of national jokes. A late-night headline. Some of the best:

"ONE DISGRUNTLED RUNNER TOLD ROSIE RUIZ THAT SHE DIDN'T LOOK TIRED ENOUGH TO HAVE RUN 26 MILES—SO SHE HIT HIM WITH HER ROLLER SKATE!"

—MARK RUSSELL, WRC RADIO

"ROSIE RUIZ WAS DISQUALIFIED FROM THE BOSTON MARATHON TODAY. OFFICIALS BECAME SUSPICIOUS WHEN SHE CROSSED THE FINISH LINE OF THE 26.2-MILE EVENT WEARING OPEN-TOED SANDALS AND SMOKING A CIGARETTE."

—ABC TV "FRIDAY" SHOW

Early volleyball nets were only 6 feet, 6 inches high!

"Rosie Ruiz is taking this too seriously. Instead of crying on national TV, she could have written a book, Shortcuts to Fame. It would start on chapter 20."
—DAVID KINDRED, THE *WASHINGTON POST*

Why, Rosie, Why?

There are a number of theories about why exactly Rosie attempted to bamboozle her way to a Boston Marathon victory. The most popular being that Rosie never actually intended to win the race—she just wanted to cross the line with a half-decent finish time. After cheating her way through the New York City Marathon, she was too embarrassed to tell her boss at work, who was so impressed by her qualifying that he paid her expenses to Boston. So, on the day of the Boston marathon, she simply threw on some sweats and jumped into the race—unfortunately for her, a bit too early.

Aftermath

Soon after Rosie's deceit was discovered, a press conference was held and second-place finisher Jacqueline Gareau was awarded a first-place medal of her own. Today, Rosie's scheme seems almost laughably simple. The incident prompted the Boston Marathon and many other races to institute a number of safeguards. In the modern race world, full of cameras and digital checkpoints, it would be nearly impossible to duplicate Rosie's scam.

Rosie's post-race life hasn't been particularly pretty. In 1982, she was put on probation for stealing $60,000 in checks from the Manhattan real estate firm for which she worked. Two years later she was arrested and accused of conspiring to sell 4.4 pounds of cocaine to undercover agents in Miami.

Rosie claims to have been approached by book publishers offering big chunks of money to write her story, but she has refused. To this day she denies any cheating, insisting she ran both races honestly and flat-out refusing to return her first-place medal.

FOOTBALL MYTHS . . . DEBUNKED!

The truth behind some of the NFL's most enduring rumors and legends.

Myth: Each season, when the league's last remaining undefeated team loses, the undefeated 1972 Dolphins pop open a bottle of champagne and celebrate.

Don Shula, coach of the '72 Dolphins, put the kibosh on this one, saying: "That's probably the most talked about thing that just doesn't happen. We've got players scattered all over the country. Nick Buoniconti, Bob Griese, and Dick Anderson all live in Coral Gables, and they'll go to a parking lot and open a bottle of champagne, but those three are too cheap to invite the rest of us down there."

Myth: Bad officiating killed Minnesota Vikings QB Fran Tarkenton's father.

The 1975 NFC divisional playoff game between the Minnesota Vikings and the Dallas Cowboys was a doozy. With 5½ minutes left, the Vikings took a 14–10 lead; all they had to do was hang on. But with 44 seconds left, Dallas QB Roger Staubach completed a controversial, fourth-and-16 pass to convert the first down. The Vikings protested—but the call stood. Then Staubach let loose a 50-yard Hail Mary and connected with Drew Pearson for the TD that gave the Cowboys the win.

Shortly afterward, Tarkenton's day got a lot worse: He learned that his 63-year-old father had suffered a heart attack and passed away while watching the game. Immediately, a rumor spread that the infamous call on fourth-and-16 and Roger Staubach's Hail Mary pass had induced the heart attack. The facts don't support the claim, however, as Tarkenton's father died during the third quarter.

Myth: Jimmy Hoffa is buried in the end zone at Giants Stadium.

Teamster boss Jimmy Hoffa disappeared from a Michigan restaurant parking lot in 1975 and the location of his body has been a mystery ever since. Urban legend long claimed he was buried in the end zone at Giants Stadium, but it could never be proved. In a 2004 episode of the TV show *Mythbusters*, hosts Adam Savage and Jamie Hyneman used a radar device to examine several of the rumored Giants Stadium burial locations. They found no traces consistent with the remains of a rotted body.

BLAME IT ON THE LAWYERS

Bizarre lawsuits and outrageous litigation from the wide world of sports.

Yogi Berra vs. Turner Broadcasting System

Yogi Berra was less than pleased when he caught a glimpse of the new ads TBS was running to promote its syndicated *Sex & the City* repeats. One spot, plastered all over the NYC transit system, asked for the definition of *Yogasm,* with the possible answers being (a) a type of yo-yo; (b) sex with Yogi Berra; or (c) what Samantha has with a guy from yoga class. Berra described the ads as "hurtful" and sued TBS for $10 million. The case was settled out of court. The answer was C, by the way.

Allen Heckard vs. Michael Jordan and Nike

Apparently, this is the one guy who doesn't want to be like Mike. In 2006, Allen Heckard of Portland, Oregon, sued Michael Jordan and Nike for a total of $832 million because he felt Jordan looked too much like him. Heckard claimed defamation, permanent injury, and emotional pain and suffering. Said the Jordan look-alike, "I'm constantly being accused of looking like Michael and it makes it very uncomfortable for me." Heckard dropped the suit.

Bryan Fortay vs. the University of Miami

In 1993, heavily recruited prep school QB Bryan Fortay filed a $10 million federal lawsuit against the Miami Hurricanes, charging that then-coach Dennis Erickson had promised Fortay if he came to Miami he would be the starter. Instead, redshirt junior Gino Torretta beat out Fortay for the starting spot (it's safe to say Miami went with the right guy: Torretta went on to win the Heisman). Said Coach Erickson, "All I promised Bryan Fortay is the opportunity to compete for the starting job. I think I gave Bryan more than a fair chance to win the job, and he didn't." Fortay and Miami settled in 1996 for an undisclosed amount.

Professional table-tennis players are required to wear socks.

Cole Bartiromo vs. Trabuco Hills High School

Cole Bartiromo was only 17 years old when the Securities and Exchange Commission charged him with scamming online investors out of nearly $1 million through a "risk-free" gambling site that was anything but. Bartiromo pleaded guilty, but not before suing his former high school for $50 million for cutting him from the varsity baseball team. He claimed that the Blue Jays and Rangers had showed interest in him and that his high school's decision to cut him ended his pro baseball career before it even started (he was destined to be a Hall of Famer, for sure).

Terri Carlin versus Janet Jackson, Justin Timberlake, along with MTV, CBS, and Viacom

Janet Jackson's infamous Super Bowl XXVII "wardrobe malfunction" shocked a lot of people. But Knoxville resident Terri Carlin was more than shocked, and she let it be known in a billion dollar class-action lawsuit. Carlin claimed that she, as well as "all Americans," had been made to "suffer outrage, anger, embarrassment, and serious injury" as a result of the nipple slip. Just a week later, Carlin dropped the suit, saying that her point had been made. Some claim her point was that she was nuts.

The World Adult Kickball Association (WAKA) vs. DCKickball

In 2006, The World Adult Kickball Association sued rival DCKickball founder and former WAKA employee Carter Rabasa for $356,000 in punitive and compensatory damages. WAKA claimed that Rabasa had stolen rules from WAKA and that WAKA had been defamed when Rabasa called the organization the "Microsoft of kickball." Doesn't make much sense to us, since the rules of kickball have been around for a long, long time . . . unfortunately, lawyers and frivolous lawsuits have been around even longer.

Mark Guthrie vs. the Tribune Co.

In 2003, the Tribune Co., owner of the Cubs, deposited a total of $301,102.50 into the checking account of Mark Guthrie. One problem, it was the checking account of Mark Guthrie, newspaper

Because of the American football's resemblance to an olive, the Chinese often call the game "olive ball."

deliveryman, not Mark Guthrie, Cubs relief pitcher. Not surprisingly, Guthrie the deliveryman wasn't too eager to return the cash. The Tribune seized $275,000 before Guthrie was able to freeze his account, then filed a suit to get back the rest. They ultimately came to an undisclosed agreement.

Lynn Rubin vs. New Haven Unified School District

In 2003, California dad Lynn Rubin sued the local school district for $1.5 million after his 15-year-old son was busted down from the varsity basketball team to the JV team. Last reported, the case was still pending.

BASEBALL LETTER EQUATIONS

Can you bear using your brain?
Just for a few minutes, we swear . . .

Letter Equations are facts and phrases where the important words have been replaced with the first letter of that word. They're often displayed in the form of an equation, with a number followed by an equal sign, with the rest of the phrase disguised.

Here's an example: 4 B = W

Solution: 4 balls = walk

Get it? See if you can decipher these.

1. 3 S and Y O
2. B R = F P to H 700 H R in a M L B C
3. 6 = O in 1 I of B
4. 162 G = in a M L B R S
5. 4 = B on a B D
6. 108 = S in a B
7. C R J = P 2,632 C M L B G
8. 90 F = D B B on a R B D

Turn to page 351 for answers.

A third of the TV commercial spots aired during the 2000 Super Bowl were for dot-com companies.

WIDE WORLD OF WHEATIES

All about the orange box.

A Happy Accident

America's favorite whole-grain cereal was birthed in 1922 when a Minneapolis doctor spilled a batch of wheat bran over a hot stove. The bran crisped and crackled into tiny, tasty flakes. The doctor got his crisped bran in front of George Cormack, the head of the Washburn Crosby Company (General Mills's predecessor) and, 36 different wheat combos later, Wheaties were born!

Wheat's in a Name?

Wheaties originally went by a much less memorable name: Washburn's Gold Medal Whole Wheat Flakes. Someone at Washburn was smart enough to realize that wasn't exactly the catchiest of names. An employees-only contest was held and the name Wheaties was selected. The No. 2 vote-getter? Nutties.

Wheaties and Sports: Best of Buddies

Wheaties' long affiliation with the world of sports began in 1933 with an ad on the wall of minor league baseball's Nicollet Park in Minneapolis. The billboard depicted their brand new logo WHEATIES: THE BREAKFAST OF CHAMPIONS. Soon, Wheaties presence in baseball was so strong that of the 51 players selected for the 1939 All-Star Game, 46 were on the Wheaties payroll, including greats Babe Ruth, Jackie Robinson, Joe DiMaggio, and Mickey Mantle.

Wheaties Firsts

First athlete to appear anywhere on a Wheaties box: Lou Gehrig, 1934

First female athlete to appear anywhere on a Wheaties box: golfer Babe Didrikson, 1935

Q: Why is basketball such a gross sport? A: Because they dribble all over the court!

First athlete to grace the full cover of a Wheaties box: pole vaulter Bob Richards, 1958

First male golfer to grace the full cover of a Wheaties box: Lee Trevino, 1969

First female athlete to grace the full cover of a Wheaties box: Gymnast Mary Lou Retton, 1984

First football player to appear on the front of a Wheaties box: Walter Payton, 1986

First team to appear on the front on a Wheaties box: 1987 World Series Champion Minnesota Twins

First hockey team depicted on a Wheaties box: 1991 Stanley Cup Champion Pittsburgh Penguins

First nonorange Wheaties box: red and black package in honor of the Chicago Bulls, 1992

First race-car driver to appear on the front of a Wheaties box: Dale Earnhardt, 1997

First professional women's sports team to appear on a Wheaties box: Sacramento Monarchs, 2005

First college football rivalry to appear on a Wheaties Box: Texas and Texas A&M: 2006

Wheaties Facts

✓ Michael Jordan has appeared on a Wheaties box 18 times, more than any other athlete. Tiger Woods is second with 14 covers.

✓ Number of calories in a single, 1½-cup serving of Wheaties? 200. Number of calories in a single Dunkin' Donut? 200. Your choice . . .

✓ U.S. pennies minted from 1909 through 1958 are known as "Wheaties" because they feature wheat ears on one side.

✓ Kurt Vonnegut's 1973 novel *Breakfast of Champions* borrowed its title from the Wheaties slogan—though in the book, the phrase refers to a martini, not cereal.

Cheech and Chong parodied ABC's *Wide World of Sports* in 1973 but changed the opening to "Welcome to the 'White' World of Sports, brought to you by Budweiser—Breakfast of Champions!"

Does It Really Work?

In 1950, a 22-year-old New Jersey man lifted a 2,700-pound elephant on his back in front of 300 people. Afterward he said, "I guess there's only one thing I eat every day—Wheaties." According to General Mills, he was not paid for the quote.

Americans spend more than $630 million a year on golf balls.

NASCAR ABSURDITY

Wild happenings on the circular track.

Monkeying Around

In 1953 driver Tim Flock raced for much of the season with his pet monkey Jocko Flocko on board. The simian co-pilot sat in a safety seat next to him. Things were all good until he got loose in the middle of a race and began jumping around the car. The poor monkey was scared to death and Flock, with the monkey around his neck, was forced to make a pit stop and let the little guy loose.

Bad Parenting

As a boy Richard Petty worked on the pit crew cleaning his racer father Lee Petty's windshield during stops. During one race, the rest of the pit crew finished before Richard was done—and Lee Petty took off with Richard still on the hood! Papa Petty allegedly went a full lap before making another pit stop so Richard could get off. According to reports, the window was clean.

Speedway Robbery

Near the end of a 1970 race at Bristol, driver Jabe Thomas was down nearly a hundred laps. With no chance of victory, he pulled into the pit of race leader Donnie Allison and asked the car's owner how much he would pay him not to spin Donnie out. The owner held up a sign that read FIFTY CENTS. During the next lap, Jabe pulled back in to the pit, collected his 50 cents, and Allison went on to win the race, unharmed.

Petty Argument

The 1976 Daytona 500 ended with probably the strangest and greatest finish in NASCAR history. During the final lap David Pearson and Richard Petty were neck and neck, battling for first

While in the slammer, John Dillinger was a star on the penitentiary baseball team.

place. While jockeying for the first spot their cars collided and they both spun out, crashing into the sidewall and sliding onto the grass. Petty's pit crew ran out to push the car to the finish line—but to no avail. Pearson was able to restart his car and crawl to a slim victory.

DUIdiot

At Talladega Superspeedway in 1986, a seriously inebriated man found the keys to the pace car (can you see where this is going?). As any good drunk would do, he hopped in and went for a joy ride. Police cruisers pursued him as he whizzed around the track before finally being pulled over and arrested.

Just Rolling Along

During the last lap of the 1990 DieHard 500 at Talladega, drivers Michael Waltrip and Kenny Schrader crashed on the back straightway. Trailing place driver Jimmy Spencer hit his breaks, trying to avoid sliding into the wreck. His car flipped, became airborne, went into a barrel roll, then landed right side up. Spencer continued on driving and finished the race.

A Beer in the Headlights

At the 1993 Winston Cup race at Pocono, a drunken man, spurred on by a dare from his friends, hopped the infield fence and ran across the track, hoping to touch the outside wall. Halfway across, he stopped, frozen with fear, as cars whizzed by him. He made it back unharmed.

Monday Night Football's original booth crew consisted of Keith Jackson, Don Meredith, and Howard Cosell.

KICKOFF WEEKEND DRINKS—AFC

Kick off the NFL season right. If you're an AFC fan, we've got the perfect opening-day drink for you. *NFC fan? See page 314.*

Cognac
Baltimore Ravens

Cognac

Any brand of cognac will do, but it's nice to go expensive in honor of the yearly bottle left at the grave of onetime Baltimore resident Edgar Allen Poe, whose poem "The Raven" inspired the football team's name.

1. Sip at room temperature from a tulip-shaped wine glass.

Buffalo Sweat
Buffalo Bills

1 shot tequila
2 drops Tabasco sauce

1. Pour shot of tequila.

2. Squeeze two drops Tabasco sauce in shot.

3. Take shot.

4. Run to the bathroom: You're probably going to puke. If you can keep it down, though, it'll warm you right up. A few liters of tequila and a bottle of Tabasco sauce should keep you warm through that oh-so-long Buffalo winter.

Roughly 42,000 tennis balls are used in the Wimbledon Championship. That's an average of 65 balls a match.

Tiger Beer
Cincinnati Bengals

Asia Pacific Breweries Tiger Beer

This China-brewed beer can be tough to find, so you might have to head online. Stock up, it's a damn good beer and has won its fair share of awards.

1. Pop open. Drink until you're able to forget about that Steelers-Bengals 2005 wild card game. We know it still hurts and we know you're still pissed. And we don't blame you.

Jim Brown's Badass Bourbon and Water
Cleveland Browns

2 ounces bourbon
4 ounces water

1. Pour bourbon and water into old-fashioned, ice-filled glass.

2. Add two slices of orange, twisting them along the top of the glass—an ode to the Browns' not-so-brown helmets.

Mile High Maker's Mark
Denver Broncos

Maker's Mark Bourbon

1. Serve over ice with a splash of water.

2. Drink five or six of these. Hard to stand? That ain't the altitude . . .

More pizza is eaten during Super Bowl week than any other time of year.

Fire Water Fit
Kansas City Chiefs

1 ounce Fire Water Cinnamon Schnapps
3 dashes Tabasco sauce

1. Serve in shot glass.

2. Add the Tabasco first, then fill with Fire Water Cinnamon Schnapps.

3. Drink. Cough heavily.

Jägermeister
Houston Texans

One bottle Jägermeister (we recommend you don't drink the entire thing by yourself)

1. Serve in shot glass.

2. Observe the liquor's oily look and texture. Drink. Reminisce on the good ol' days of Earl Campbell, Warren Moon, and the Houston Oilers.

White Russian
Indianapolis Colts

2 ounces vodka
1 ounce coffee liqueur
milk

1. Pour vodka and coffee liqueur over ice in an old-fashioned glass.

2. Fill with milk, in honor of the post-victory celebratory tradition at Indianapolis's most famous sporting event, the Indy 500, and serve.

During the 1905 football season, 19 players died in college and high school games.

The Jaguar
Jacksonville Jaguars

1 part vodka
3 parts soda (7-up, Sprite, or Fresca)
1 part banana syrup

1. Mix. Add ice if desired.

2. Serve in highball glass.

Marino's Miami Vice
Miami Dolphins

5 ounces Bacardi 151 rum
piña colada mix
strawberry daiquiri mix

1. Combine piña colada mix with 2.5 ounces of rum and ice.

2. Combine strawberry daiquiri mix with 2.5 ounces of rum and ice.

3. Pour your piña colada into a cocktail glass, then pour your daiquiri on top. Do it slowly and they'll stay separated.

4. Serve. Drink. Reminisce about the Dan Marino days.

Sam Adams Boston Lager
New England Patriots

Sam Adams Boston Lager

1. Head to the market, pick up a case. Avoid the flavored ales and stick with the classic.

2. Serve colder than a New England winter.

The Volleyball Hall of Fame is located in Holyoke, Mass.

Gang Green Iguana
New York Jets

1 part tequila
1 part Midori melon liqueur
2 parts sweet-and-sour mix

1. Mix together and serve in a cocktail glass with a little salt sprinkled around rim. Once mixed, it'll have a nice Jets-green color.

2. Drink 6 of these, try to kiss Suzy Kolber.

Raider Rum and Coke
Oakland Raiders

4 ounces Captain Morgan's spiced rum
8 ounces Coca-Cola

1. Mix. Serve in an old-fashioned glass.

2. Add a lime.

3. As you drink, pretend to be a pirate. Add eye patch for full effect.

Black & Gold Martini
Pittsburgh Steelers

2 ounces Blavod vodka
1 ounces Goldschläger

1. Pour Blavod vodka into ice-filled cocktail shaker.

2. Shake well.

3. Strain into a chilled martini glass.

4. Top off with Goldschläger.

5. Look at your drink. It's black and gold! Just like the team! Get it?

58 percent of all major football injuries involve the knee.

Blue Lightning
San Diego Chargers

⅓ ounce Southern Comfort
⅓ ounce Blue Curacao
⅓ ounce bourbon
½ ounce lime mix

1. Pour liquors into an ice-filled highball glass.

2. Fill with lime mix.

3. Arts and crafts time. Get out a good, serrated knife and slice a piece of lemon into a lightning-bolt shape (not unlike the Chargers logo). Place on the rim of the glass.

Tennessee Mud
Tennessee Titans

1 cup of coffee
½ ounce Jack Daniel's whiskey
½ ounce amaretto
whipped cream

1. Mix coffee, Jack Daniel's, and amaretto.

2. Shoot it up with whipped cream.

3. Serve in a coffee mug.

The average height of an NBA player is 6 feet, 7 inches.

YOGIISMS

Yogi Berra: the master of the malapropism. Over the years a million different quotes have been attributed to him. Did he definitely say all of these? Probably not. But that doesn't make them any less entertaining. As Yogi himself said, "I didn't really say everything I said."

"A NICKEL AIN'T WORTH A DIME ANYMORE."

"IF THE WORLD WERE PERFECT, IT WOULDN'T BE."

"ALWAYS GO TO OTHER PEOPLE'S FUNERALS—OTHERWISE, THEY WON'T GO TO YOURS."

"IF YOU CAN'T IMITATE HIM, DON'T COPY HIM."

"WHEN YOU GET TO A FORK IN THE ROAD, TAKE IT."

"NO ONE GOES THERE ANY MORE, IT'S TOO CROWDED."

"I'D GIVE MY RIGHT ARM TO BE AMBIDEXTROUS."

"I COULDN'T TELL IF THE STREAKER WAS A MAN OR A WOMAN BECAUSE IT HAD A BAG ON ITS HEAD."

"I USUALLY TAKE A TWO-HOUR NAP FROM ONE TO FOUR."

"IT'S TOUGH TO MAKE PREDICTIONS, ESPECIALLY ABOUT THE FUTURE."

"PITCHING ALWAYS BEATS BATTING—AND VICE-VERSA."

"YOU HAVE TO GIVE 100 PERCENT IN THE FIRST HALF OF THE GAME. IF THAT ISN'T ENOUGH, IN THE SECOND HALF, YOU HAVE TO GIVE WHAT'S LEFT."

"THIS IS LIKE DÉJÀ VU ALL OVER AGAIN."

The original Stanley Cup was only 7 inches high.

HOCKEY GOONS

All about the rink's ruffians—including why they're being left out in the cold.

What's a Goon?

The Hockey Goon—aka the Enforcer, the Fighter, or the Tough Guy—the baddest guys on the rink. For years they patrolled the ice, serving out frontier justice. Heck, half of these guys could barely skate—but they didn't have to. The enforcer's job was simple: beat the hell out of the opponent. Check him, deck him, and wreck him.

Where'd They All Go?

The NHL enforcer is a dying breed. The 2004–2005 NHL lockout brought about major changes in the way the game is played. New rules designed to increase scoring and the speed of the game led to a dramatic decrease in on-ice fighting and left teams less than eager to devote a roster spot to a one-dimensional player who can't score and plays turnstile defense.

Goons Never Say Die

One former enforcer, Tony Twist, isn't convinced that the goons will ever be entirely run out of the league. When asked about the sad disappearance of these beats o' the ice, he commented, "Men will be men. You mark your territory and I'm going to mark mine."

Best of the Brawlers

In honor of this endangered species, we take a look back at a few of the greats.

Bob Probert: Probert spent the majority of his career as a Detroit Red Wing in the '80s and '90s and is widely

Jim Thorpe, Ace Parker, George Halas, and Ernie Nevers are the only NFL Hall of Famers to have played major league baseball.

recognized as the greatest hockey enforcer of all time. Besides being able to rumble, Probert could score—racking up 62 points in 1987 (to go with an absurd 398 penalty infraction minutes) and making the All-Star squad. Probert got into as much trouble off the ice as he did on—in 1989 he was suspended by the league and did three months in jail for cocaine possession.

Dave "The Hammer" Schultz: Schultz was the lead enforcer and most physical member of the "Broad Street Bullies," the '70s era Philadelphia Flyers team that bruised, battled, and bullied their way to two straight Stanley Cup championships. After that, he played the role of mercenary, traveling from the Los Angeles Kings to the Pittsburgh Penguins to the Buffalo Sabers, kicking ass and taking names. Whenever a GM needed to add a little toughness to his team, Schultz was the first guy they'd call. He was the first fighter to wear boxing wrap-ons on his wrists, starting a trend among enforcers that ended when the league enacted the "Schultz Rule," banning all boxing wraps in professional hockey.

Dave Semenko: Semenko's battles rarely lasted long—he was as quick as he was strong and usually dropped his opponents in seconds. As an Edmonton Oiler, Semenko played the role of bodyguard, using his particular skill set to protect all-time greats Wayne Gretzky and Mark Messier: His muscle allowed them to do their thing. The man known as Cementhead was so tough he even went toe-to-toe with Muhammad Ali in an exhibition match in 1983.

MASCOT MADNESS, PART I

A timeline of mascots causing problems, getting into trouble, and generally acting ridiculous.

August 1988: Dodgers manager Tommy Lasorda attacks the Philly Phanatic after the mascot beats up a doll of Lasorda. Lasorda lands a few punches before wrestling the effigy free.

August 1989: Clearly, Tommy Lasorda and mascots don't mix. Just one year after the Philly Phanatic incident, Montreal Expos mascot, Youppi, becomes the first mascot to be ejected from a Major League Baseball game after Lasorda complains about him dancing atop the Dodgers' dugout.

September 1989: University of Miami's Sebastian the Ibis carries a fire extinguisher onto the football field, planning to soak the flaming spear of the Florida State Seminoles' Chief Osceola. Instead, cops besiege Sebastian and empty the fire extinguisher.

January 1991: The San Diego Chicken grabs a Chicago Bulls cheerleader and does a little dance with her that ends with her sprawled out on the floor. She sues for $317,000, and wins.

October 1992: A brawl breaks out between Northwestern State University's Vic the Demon and Northeast Louisiana's Chief Brave Spirit. Vic the Demon loses his head, literally, before pummeling Chief Brave Spirit.

April 1994: During a Final Four game, the University of Arizona's Wilbur Wildcat shreds his knee tackling the Arkansas Razorback.

May 1994: The overly friendly Philly Phanatic injures a fan's back while giving out hugs at the opening of a local paint store. The man sues for damages and is awarded $2.5 million.

The most common score in a World Cup finals match is 1–0.

August 1994: During a game, Colorado Rockies mascot Dinger the Dinosaur slips down a flight of steps and bumps into broadcaster Jeff Kingery. Kingery is not pleased and lets it be known, swearing at Dinger and giving him a shove.

October 1994: The Miami Heat's Burnie drags a female fan on to the court by her legs at an exhibition game in Puerto Rico. Unfortunately for Burnie, the woman's husband is a local Supreme Court justice and has Burnie brought up on charges of aggravated assault. The couple sue for $1 million. Said Burnie, "I pull people out of the stands all the time at our place to dance. I picked the wrong person."

February 1995: Don Jackson, coach of the International Hockey League's Cincinnati Cyclones, is fined $1,000 and suspended 10 games after scaling the rink-side glass and pummeling Atlanta Knights mascot Sir Slapshot for hitting the glass while Jackson was leaning against it.

February 1995: The University of California's Oski the Bear gets into a brawl with the Stanford Tree during an ESPN-televised timeout. Police step in, but not before the Tree manages to rip off Oski's headpiece, nearly ending Cal's 60-year tradition of keeping the mascot's identity a secret.

April 1995: In what would soon become a well-publicized, good-natured feud, Denver Nuggets mascot Rocky the Mountain Lion challenges Charles Barkley to a boxing match. Barkley promptly punches Rocky in the face.

October 1995: Seattle's Mariner Moose breaks his ankle after smashing into the Kingdome's outfield wall while being towed on roller skates behind an ATV—all on national TV.

October 1995: The Cleveland Indians' Slider blows out his knee after falling six feet from the outfield wall during the ALCS.

October 1995: The Anaheim Mighty Ducks' Wild Wing attempts to impress the crowd by jumping over a wall of fire. Can you see where this is going? He doesn't quite make it and collapses atop the fire, legs ablaze.

1995: It was a bad year for Oregon's Benny Beaver. First the mascot—portrayed by a 5-foot-9, 135-pound woman—hits Cal offensive tackle Tarik Glenn on the shoulder with an inflatable hammer and in response gets punched by the 6-6, 330-pound lineman. A few games later, the mascot takes another shot to the head—this time from 305-pound Arizona offensive lineman Frank Middleton.

Kresimir Cosic is the only non-American player in the NBA Hall of Fame.

THE IMMACULATE RECEPTION

The football gods bless the Steelers.

Besides being one of the most spectacular plays in NFL history, the Immaculate Reception is also one of the game's most controversial. It was the AFC divisional playoffs, Steelers versus Raiders at Three Rivers Stadium in Pittsburgh, on December 23, 1972.

How It Happened

The Steelers trailed the Raiders 7–6. With 22 seconds left in the game and no time-outs, the Steelers were staring at fourth-and-10 from their own 40-yard line. Steelers coach Chuck Noll called a pass play, 66 Circle Option, intended for rookie receiver Barry Pearson. Steelers quarterback Terry Bradshaw, under pressure and out of the pocket, couldn't find Pearson and instead slung the ball in the direction of Steelers running back John "Frenchy" Fuqua near the Raiders' 35-yard line. Just as the ball arrived, Raiders safety Jack Tatum collided with Fuqua, knocking him to the ground and sending the ball sailing backward, end over end. Steelers running back Franco Harris, who was initially blocking on the play, had run downfield to give Bradshaw another target. Harris scooped up the ball just before it hit the ground, off the tops of his shoes, and ran downfield for the touchdown that gave the Steelers a 12–7 lead and the victory.

Controversy

But was it even a touchdown? The answer hinged on two points. First, who did the ball bounce off of first in the Fuqua-Tatum collision? If it hit off Fuqua first, then the reception was illegal because two offensive players could not touch a pass in succession (a rule that was changed in 1978), meaning the Raiders would gain possession and the game would be theirs. If the ball bounced off Tatum first, then the reception was legal and the play was clean.

Before 1850 golf balls were made of leather and stuffed with feathers.

Second, it was unclear whether or not the ball had been caught cleanly by Harris. The sideline cameras were of no help—Harris had caught the ball out of frame. The only other live video was an end-zone shot from above and behind the goal posts—and one of the posts perfectly blocked the ball at the moment Harris caught it. The most famous and most clear clip is an NFL Films one from the end zone that shows Harris snagging the ball—appropriately, his feet and the ground are just out of frame.

The on-field officials didn't immediately make a call. Instead, referee Fred Swearingen (no relation to the *Deadwood* pimp) headed to the side of the field and called up to the NFL's supervisor of officials, Art McNally, who was in the press box. Seconds later Swearingen hung up the phone and signaled touchdown, stating that Tatum and Fuqua made contact with the ball simultaneously and that Franco Harris legally caught the ball prior to it making contact with the ground. This was the first use of television replay to confirm a call. Some people (i.e., Raiders fans) claimed that Swearingen was scared of backlash from the Steelers fans (a full stadium worth of 'em) if he didn't rule in their favor.

Steeler fans swarmed the field. It took 15 minutes to clear them so the extra point could be kicked, ending the game and giving the Steelers the win.

Stuck in the Elevator

Poor Art Rooney, the Steelers owner and founder, had been waiting years for a great Steelers moment to celebrate—and he missed it! Thinking the Steelers were done for, Rooney was riding the elevator down to the locker room to give his boys a consolation speech—all the while, history was being made outside on the field!

Still Angry

The play continues to be disputed by fans as well as by those involved. Jack Tatum swears up and down that the ball did not bounce off him. Fuqua has said he knows exactly what happened that day but will never tell. John Madden, coach of the 1972 Raiders, continues to be bothered by the play, though he has more of a problem with the dubious delay between the end

Boston Celtic Chris Ford scored the NBA's first three-point shot.

of the play and the referee's signal of touchdown than by which player the ball truly hit or whether or not Harris actually caught the ball cleanly.

Aftermath

The Steelers' luck ended there. The next week they lost the AFC Championship game to the Miami Dolphins, who went on to win the Super Bowl, capping off their historic undefeated season. The play did, however, mark a turnaround for the Steelers franchise: They went on to reverse 40 years of failure, winning four Super Bowls with Hall of Famers Terry Bradshaw, Franco Harris, Lynn Swann, and John Stallworth battling alongside Jack Lambert, Jack Ham, "Mean" Joe Green, and the Steel Curtain defense.

To Coin a Phrase . . .

The phrase the "Immaculate Reception" is often credited to longtime Steelers radio announcer Myron Cope—but he was always quick to admit that he didn't come up with it on his own. Minutes before he was to go on air to report on the historic victory he received a phone call from fan Sharon Levosky, who said her friend had just come up with a perfect name for the amazing play—the "Immaculate Reception." Cope loved it, used it on the air, and the rest is history.

At the Hawaiian Open in 1982, Wayne Levi became the first PGA player to win a tournament using a colored ball (it was orange).

JUST RICKEY BEING RICKEY

There's no doubt Rickey Henderson was the greatest leadoff hitter of all time. There's also no doubt that he was one of the oddest ducks to ever play the game of baseball.

There are dozens of Rickey Henderson stories floating around, so we won't vouch for the veracity of all these. But they're entertaining (and pretty likely) nonetheless.

Rickey the Agent

When calling Padres GM Kevin Towers to speak about contract, Rickey left the following message: "This is Rickey, calling on behalf of Rickey. Rickey wants to play baseball."

Rickey's Millions

This one occurred while Rickey was playing for the Oakland A's. The team's accountants discovered a $1 million discrepancy in the books. The cash was eventually traced to Rickey, who had received the one million in the form of a signing bonus. There are two different stories about why the check remained uncashed. In one, instead of cashing the check, Rickey had it framed and hung it on his wall. In the other, Rickey was waiting for interest rates to go up before cashing it. Either way, awesome.

Rickey without a Ride

One night, after a late game, Rickey couldn't find his transportation. He was heard yelling out to no one in particular, "Rickey don't like it when Rickey can't find Rickey's limo!"

Mark McGwire's record 70 home runs during the 1998 season traveled a total distance of 29,598 feet.

Rickey, Self Motivator

During his playing years, Rickey stood stark naked in front of a full-length locker room mirror before game time, repeating "Ricky's the best. Rickey's the best. Rickey's the best."

Rickey and Seating

On the team bus another player offered Rickey his seat, saying Rickey had "tenure." Rickey replied, "Ten years? What are you talking about? Rickey got 16, 17 years."

Rickey and His Bats

When stuck in a slump Rickey would sometimes speak to his bats, asking them which one has the next big hit inside it.

Rickey's Shoddy Memory

This one has often been disputed—but it's a classic nonetheless. Rickey once saw John Olerud playing first base while wearing a batting helmet, so he said "Hey, Rickey used to have a teammate with the Mets who played first with a helmet." Olerud then informed Rickey that they had been teammates with the Mets and that it was indeed him who played first while wearing a batting helmet.

Rickey, Manhattanite

As a Yankee, Rickey bragged to his teammates that his new Manhattan condo had such a great view that he could see the "Entire" State Building.

Jackie Robinson was the first person to letter in four sports at UCLA.

THE XFL

A swing and a miss.

When it comes to giant, unmitigated, unquestionable disasters in the world of sports, not much tops the XFL. Founded by Vince McMahon, the mastermind behind the WWE, the XFL was intended as a league that could rival the NFL. Instead, it folded after just one season.

The Rules

There were a few major differences between the NFL and the XFL that significantly altered the play of the game.

Scoring: There were no extra points. Instead, teams ran a single offensive play from the 2-yard line. If they got into the end zone, they got a point. Teams also had the option to go for a two-point or three-point conversion by moving further back from the end zone.

The Kickoff: No coin flips. Not "Xtreme" enough. Instead, two opposing players would sprint toward a ball placed on the 50-yard line and wrestle until one player had full possession (not surprisingly, this resulted in the league's first injury).

Punts: Every punt over 25 yards was considered live and there were no fair catches. Defenders were only required to give a 5-yard "halo" to the receiver. This is standard in the CFL and the AFL—the only problem was, very few XFL players had actually played in the CFL and the AFL. Their inexperience with the rule resulted in penalties galore—taking all of the intended excitement out of the punt-return game.

Defensive contact: Unlike the NFL, defensive backs were allowed to hit wide receivers any time before the QB released the ball, as long as the hit didn't come from behind. This didn't work at all and resulted in a lack of

The last NASCAR driver to do jail time for running moonshine was Buddy Arrington.

offensive production. The rule was scrapped during the fourth week of the season for the more traditional limited bump-and-run rules used in the NFL.

Overtime: Similar to college football, each team got one possession starting from the opponent's 20-yard line. However, there were no first downs—teams had to score within four downs and couldn't attempt a field goal until fourth down. If they scored in less than four downs, the other team had the same number of downs to do the same.

Ownership and Cash

The XFL was a single entity league wherein each team was owned by the league and they all operated as one single business unit. Unlike the NFL, the XFL paid players standard salaries across the board. QBs received $5,000 a week, kickers and punters received $3,500, and everyone else got $4,000 a week. Slick L.A. Extreme receiver Matt Malloy had himself listed as a third-string QB in order to squeeze an extra $1,000 a week out of the league.

Fans Hate You

The XFL's plan was to grab hold of professional wrestling fans as well as football fans. As such, players were encouraged to wear nicknames on the backs of their jerseys (Chad Johnson would have been in heaven). Las Vegas running back Ron Smart's jersey had HE HATE ME printed on the back of his jersey. Smart wanted to put THEY HATE ME on the back—but it wouldn't fit. Smart went on to play in the NFL for the Carolina Panthers, where quarterback Jake Delhomme named his horse "She Hate Me."

The Million-Dollar Game

The XFL's version of the Super Bowl. Originally given the cutesy name of "The Big Game at the End of the Season," the league later named it the Million Dollar Game (the amount of money awarded to the champion team). In the sole Million Dollar Game, the L.A. Xtreme defeated the San Francisco Demons 38–6.

Mini-helmets were given out as fan souvenirs, and in an ironic, fitting twist, "Million Dollar Game" was actually misspelled as "Million Dollar Gave" on all helmets.

No Fans League

The league was an immediate disaster. NFL fans were suspect of the league's ties to pro wrestling and stayed away in droves. Scoring was so low that gamblers couldn't set a low enough over/under total. Unders of 20 became commonplace throughout the season—a number absurdly low for pro football. Most devastating of all, newspapers didn't report scores, completely robbing the league of any sense of validity.

Legacy

It wasn't all for nothing. The league popularized "in-game" interviews, which are now used by Major League Baseball and the NHL. The XFL was also the first football league to feature the Skycam—a camera on wires that hangs above the field and allows viewers at home to see behind the offense. The Skycam is now used in nearly all NFL broadcasts. A few players caught on with the NFL once the league went under, most famously Tommy Maddox, who was the XFL's only MVP. Maddox was the Steelers starting quarterback in 2002 and 2003, taking them to the playoffs and winning the 2002 NFL Comeback Player of the Year Award.

Not So Fast, Arnold

The first scene in the 2000 Arnold Schwarzenegger near-future sci-fi flick *The 6th Day* takes place in an XFL stadium, with XFL logos and gear everywhere.

Cal Hubbard is the only person to be elected to both the baseball and football Hall of Fame.

SHAQ QUOTES

The big guy makes for a helluva quote.

Because the world revolves around him?

"I would like to be referred to as the Big Aristotle."

On Breakfast (We Think)

"They shot the ball well early. What comes out of the microwave hot doesn't always stay hot. I know, because I eat bagels in the morning."

On the NBA Dress Code and Mama O'Neal

"David Stern should get with the mothers of the NBA and let the moms decide what the dress code should be. I asked my mother if I could wear a chain, and she told me yeah. So I do stuff that my parents allow me to do."

Shaq, Rapper

"I am aware that most people only see me as Shaq, the guy on the court. But there is another side to who I am, Shaquille O'Neal. And Shaquille O'Neal wants to explore every part of life. He wants the opportunity to pursue all of his desires. That includes being a part of the music industry as an emcee. Music is and will always be a part of who I am."

Shaq, Spokesman

"I'm tired of hearing about money, money, money, money, money. I just want to play the game, drink Pepsi, wear Reebok."

Saint Bernard is the patron saint of skiers.

Karate Man Shaq

"I am the number-one Ninja and I have killed all the shoguns in front of me."

Shaq and the Almighty

"Me shooting 40 percent at the foul line is just God's way to say nobody's perfect."

Shaq, Purina

"I knew I was dog meat. Luckily, I'm the high-priced dog meat that everybody wants. I'm the good-quality dog meat. I'm the Alpo of the NBA."

Shaq and the Rest of Us Bums

"Someday I might have to put down a basketball and have a regular nine-to-five like everybody else."

Shaq on Why?

"Some things you just can't question. Like you can't question why two plus two is four. So don't question it, don't try to look it up. I don't know who made it, all I know is it was put in my head that two plus two is four. So certain things happen. Why does it rain? Why am I so sexy? I don't know."

Shaq on Being a Man

"When you flop, that's just another message that you don't know how to play me. Stand up and take your medicine like a man."

Shaq on Your Face

"Why don't you bring your face up here and let me punch it? Then you can tell me [if I'm stronger]."

Gatorade was named for the University of Florida Gators where it was created.

NFL REFEREE SIGNALS

Do you recognize these?

Touchdown

Ball Illegally Touched, Kicked, or Batted

Facemask

When the University of Nebraska Cornhuskers play football at home, the stadium becomes the state's third-largest city.

Illegal Motion

Invalid Fair-Catch Signal

Illegal Crackback

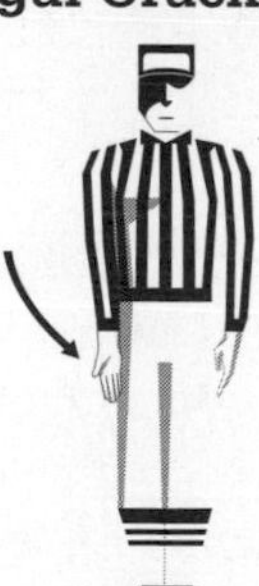

The Yale Crew team, started in 1843, was the first college sports team.

THE BLACK SOX SCANDAL

The best team money could buy.

The mother of all sports scandals: The 1919 World Series. Here's the story behind The Chicago White Sox, the Cincinnati Reds, and the throwing of the World Series.

The Scheme

It all started with two men: William Thomas "Sleepy Bill" Burns and Billy Maharg. Burns was a former major league pitcher with connections to the White Sox. Maharg was a small-time gambler with a few loose ties to organized crime. Together these two managed to do the unthinkable: fix the World Series.

The duo approached two White Sox players, first baseman Arnold "Chick" Gandil and pitcher Ed Cicotte, who agreed to the scheme. But in baseball it takes more than two players to ensure a proper fix. So Cicotte and Gandil recruited six other White Sox: pitcher Lefty Williams, centerfielder Happy Felsch, shortstop Swede Risberg, third baseman Buck Weaver, utility man Fred McMullin, and beloved leftfielder "Shoeless" Joe Jackson. To guarantee a fix the players demanded to be paid upfront: $100,000 to be split among the bunch. A helluva lot of cash, especially in those days—and Burns and Maharg needed help. So they brought their scheme to mega mobster Arnold "Mr. Big" Rothstein. Rothstein agreed to fund the scam.

Cheapo Comiskey?

It's often been said that Cubs owner Charles Comiskey and his infamously tight wallet may have been indirectly responsible for the players' involvement, particularly in regard to pitcher Ed Cicotte. Cicotte had a clause in his contract that would have earned him an extra $10,000 if he won 30 games. In the book, *Eight Men Out,* author Eliot Asinof claims that Comiskey forced Cicotte to sit out the last two weeks of the season after Cicotte earned his 29th win, thereby screwing him out of his bonus.

Cheap as Comiskey was, however, this likely never happened. Cicotte won his 29th game on September 19th, the same day he agreed to the fix and before he could have known of any attempt by Comiskey to deny him the opportunity to win his 30th and cash in. Sorry Cicotte, no excuses.

Word Gets Around

At the time, the World Series was a nine game affair. Leading up to it, the White Sox were 5–1 favorites. As the game drew closer, however, rumors of a fix began to spread. Friends told friends, gamblers told gamblers, and the word got around. Everyone in the know poured money on the Reds. By the start of Game 1, the Reds were favored 8–5.

The Series

The day before the series started, Ed Cicotte found his $10,000 under his pillow. With his second pitch of the opening game he beaned batter Morrie Rath. That was the signal, the fix was in. Backed by some awful Cicotte pitching, the Reds took Game 1. Game 2 wasn't much different, 2–0 Reds. Dickie Kerr, Chicago's starter for Game 3, wasn't in on the fix—he pitched admirably and the Sox won to put the series at 2–1 Reds. The next day, backed by Cicotte errors, the Sox lost again.

Then things got a little close. Chicago took Game 6 in extra innings and, backed by a strong Cicotte pitching performance, took Game 7 as well. The Sox were only down 3–4.

Lefty Williams, who was in on the scheme, was due to pitch Game 8. But Rothstein was nervous, the series was too close for comfort, so he sent an associate to Williams's place, letting him know he better do his job, or he and his wife would be in danger. Williams got the message and blew the game.

It was done. The White Sox had thrown the World Series.

The Trial

In September 1920, a Chicago grand jury was investigating rumors that the Cubs had thrown a game earlier that season, and, in the process of digging around, they unearthed the Series

Rookie surfers are known as "hodads."

fix—or as it came to be known, the Black Sox scandal. Cicotte and Jackson readily admitted their role in the scheme; Gandil never confessed to anything. Evidence began to pour in. Despite being in the middle of a pennant race, Comiskey suspended all seven White Sox in on the fix, effectively ending the team's season. Hey, maybe Comiskey wasn't so bad after all!

The players confessed—but prior to the trial, the confessions went missing (only to turn up years later with Comiskey's lawyer—boy, Comiskey's a tough one to figure out . . .).

Said Rothstein, "The whole thing started when [Abe] Attell [a boxer and suspected associate of Rothstein's] and some other cheap gamblers decided to frame the series and make a killing. The world knows I was asked in on the deal and my friends know how I turned it down flat. I don't doubt that Attell used my name to put it over. That's been done by smarter men than Abe. But I was not in on it, would not have gone into it under any circumstances, and did not bet a cent on the series after I found out what was under way."

The jury bought it. Rothstein walked. The players didn't get off so easy.

Aftermath

The public was shocked—their faith in the game had lost. To battle this, the owners appointed the League's first commissioner—Federal Judge Kenesaw Mountain Landis. Landis' verdict:

> "Regardless of the verdict of juries, no player who throws a ball game, no player who undertakes or promises to throw a ball game, no player who sits in confidence with a bunch of crooked ballplayers and gamblers, where the ways and means of throwing a game are discussed and does not promptly tell his club about it, will ever play professional baseball."

And with that, all eight implicated White Sox were banned from baseball for life.

Bobby Abreu holds the record for most homers in the Home Run Derby with 41.

"Shoeless" Joe Jackson

Most controversial of all was Shoeless Joe Jackson's involvement in the fix. Jackson's performance in the series was largely impressive, recording a .375 batting average, throwing out five base runners, and making zero errors in the field. In the games the White Sox lost, Jackson performed poorly—hitting only .268 and putting up runs only once the games were securely in the Reds' hands. In the games the Sox won, however, Jackson came to bat with runners in scoring position only five times, and twice he advanced them.

According to some reports, Jackson apparently told Comiskey of the fix and asked that he be benched for the series. Comiskey refused in an attempt to cover up the entire thing.

Joe maintained his innocence until his death. His dying words were, "I'm about to face the greatest umpire of all, and he knows I am innocent."

Bodacious is the highest ranking rodeo bull of all time.

BEST OF THE BEST: *CADDYSHACK*

There's not much room for debate—
Caddyshack is THE golf movie.

The Stats

Released: 1980
Director: Harold Ramis
Starring: Chevy Chase, Bill Murray, Rodney Dangerfield, Ted Knight, Michael O'Keefe
Box Office Haul: $39,846,344

Tagline

The Snobs Against the Slobs!

The Basics

Michael O' Keefe plays Danny Noonan, a young caddy at Bushwood Country Club, aka snob central. He's doing his best suck-up job to earn a caddy scholarship from Judge Smails (Ted Knight), while learning a few life lessons from laid-back golf natural Ty Webb (Chevy Chase). Meanwhile, rude and crude millionaire Al Czervik (Rodney Dangerfield) is thinking about buying the club. And then there's Carl Spackler (Bill Murray), the lazy, high-out-of-his-mind groundskeeper, doing his best to catch the godforsaken gopher that's tearing up the course.

Die-Hard Fans

Tiger Woods. He's such a big fan that he played Carl Spackler in an American Express commercial that referenced the movie.

Memorable Moment

Bill Murray's Carl Spackler, clad in a stained shirt and ridiculous hat, whacking away at flowers with a putter delivers every time.

Skis over 4,000 years old have been discovered in Scandinavia.

"Cinderella story. Outta nowhere. A former greens keeper, now, about to become the Masters champion. It looks like a mirac . . . It's in the hole! It's in the hole! It's in the hole!"

Best of all, Murray completely improvised the whole thing!

The Quotes

Al Czervik: Oh, this your wife, huh? A lovely lady. Hey, baby, you must've been something before electricity.

Ty Webb: You've got to win this hole.
Danny Noonan: I kinda thought winning wasn't important.
Ty Webb: Me winning isn't. You do.
Danny Noonan: Great grammar.

Judge Smails: Danny, I'm having a party this weekend.
[pauses a moment]
How would you like to come over and mow my lawn?

Danny Noonan: I gotta go to college.
Ty Webb: You don't have to go to college. This isn't Russia. Is this Russia? This isn't Russia.

Carl Spackler: So I jump ship in Hong Kong and make my way over to Tibet, and I get on as a looper at a course over in the Himalayas. A looper, you know, a caddy, a looper, a jock. So, I tell them I'm a pro jock, and who do you think they give me? The Dalai Lama himself. Twelfth son of the Lama. The flowing robes, the grace, bald . . . striking. So, I'm on the first tee with him. I give him the driver. He hauls off and whacks one—big hitter, the Lama—long, into a 10-thousand-foot crevasse, right at the base of this glacier. Do you know what the Lama says? *Gunga galunga . . . gunga, gunga-galunga*. So we finish the eighteenth and he's gonna stiff me. And I say, "Hey, Lama, hey, how about a little something, you know, for the effort, you know." And he says, "Oh, uh, there won't be any money, but when you die, on your deathbed, you will receive total consciousness." So I got that goin' for me, which is nice.

Spalding Smails: I want a hamburger . . . no, a cheeseburger. I want a hot dog. I want a milkshake . . .
Judge Smails: You'll get nothing and like it!

Carl Spackler: This is a hybrid. This is a cross, ah, of Bluegrass, Kentucky Bluegrass, Featherbed Bent, and Northern California Sensemilia. The amazing stuff about this is that you can play 36 holes on it in the afternoon, take it home, and just get stoned to the bejesus-belt that night on this stuff.

Al Czervik: Last time I saw a mouth like that, it had a hook in it.

In the Know

The gopher sound effects are actually dolphin noises—the same sound effects that were used for Flipper.

Those are actual club members watching the filming of the pool scene. You can see them at the fence, cracking up.

And Second Place Goes to . . .

Tin Cup. Kevin Costner's never been better; Don Johnson's never been more obnoxious.

The first recorded swimming competition in the United States took place in 1883 at the New York Athletic Club.

PROSTARS

Saturday-morning cartoons at their finest.

"*ProStars* . . . It's all about helping kids."

Buried among the clutter of early '90s licensed, product-driven, Saturday morning cartoons was *ProStars,* a short-lived series featuring animated versions of Michael Jordan, Wayne Gretzky, and Bo Jackson as a superhero team fighting crime, helping kids, and working to protect the environment. Need a laugh? Just read that last part again: animated versions of Michael Jordan, Wayne Gretzky, and Bo Jackson as a superhero team fighting crime, helping kids, and working to protect the environment. It's almost too good to be true. Each episode was bookended by a live action bit whereby the ProStars (usually just Wayne and Bo) would introduce the day's episode and answer questions from viewers.

The Team

Michael "Air" Jordan: No. 23 is the leader of the bunch. The Leonardo, if you will, in '90s cartoon terms. MJ is supersmart and an excellent mechanic—he can often be seen fiddling with complicated contraptions. Besides whupping supervillain rear end, it's Michael's job to encourage children to study hard at science and math.

Bo "Bo Knows" Jackson: The gruff and tough Bo is the group's designated slugger. He's superpowerful; in the opening credit he's shown batting an evil robot using a gigantic tree trunk as a bat. Of course, every episode had Bo in some situation where he'd say "Bo knows such-and-such!"

Wayne "The Great One" Gretzky: Wayne Gretzky provides the comic relief. His mind is constantly on food . . . a little odd, since Gretzky probably maxed out about 190 pounds—soaking wet, in his pads, with skates on.

East Germany's Manfred Wold set the world record for longest ski jump in 1969, traveling 541.3 feet through the air.

But whatever, every '90s cartoon needed a character who was constantly hungry. Coincidentally, the guy who did Gretzky's voice also voiced the perpetually starving Michelangelo on *Teenage Mutant Ninja Turtles.*

Combining all these Cartoon Character 101 personality traits, you might get an exchange like this:

Jordan: "Come gather around, kids, I'm going to teach you about subtraction!"

Wayne: "But MJ, I'm starving! I need to eat first. Where can I get some chips?!"

Bo: "Bo knows chips! Try the pantry . . . "

Rounding Out the Roster

Mom: An absurd stereotype of a Jewish mother, Mom plays a role similar to that of Q in the James Bond movies. She provides the guys with equipment and gadgets; for example, MJ can often be seen flying around in a pair of Mom's rocket-powered basketball shoes. The ProStars spend their spare time working out in "Mom's Gym" and apparently live there as well.

Denise: Denise is the lively gal that tags along on missions, doing what she can to do help. She usually just ends up getting kidnapped by the bad guys and waiting around until the gang can save her.

The Bad Guys

Every episode began with the crew getting a video message from a child detailing the need for the ProStars help—for example, a young boy from the South Seas asking for help getting back his village's stolen treasures. In another episode, a mad scientist kidnaps a child, demanding the ProStars play a game against his robot athletes.

Until 1859 baseball umps sat behind the catcher in a padded rocking chair.

ProStars for Breakfast!

Couldn't get enough of your *ProStars?* Luckily, there was a comic book and a breakfast cereal to keep you entertained. Head to eBay to get your unopened box of *ProStars* official licensed cereal—starting at just 45 bucks! It's the supersugary, way-past-expiration-date, breakfast of champions.

The first hockey puck was a chunk of frozen cow dung.

BOWLING IN BRIEF

The history of rolling balls and knocking stuff over

Knock Down Pagans

Rolling a ball to knock down targets is the sort of thing that bored humans most anywhere might come up with. And they did; in Egypt thousands of years ago and in Polynesia hundreds of years ago. In Germany around A.D. 300, German peasants carried a club-like stick for protection. When the peasants showed up at church, it became their custom to stand up their clubs and attempt to knock them down with a rolled stone. The clubs symbolized the pagans. So, the successful roller (bowler) was considered free of sin.

This custom eventually grew into a sport that spread across Europe. Drinkers especially enjoyed the excitement and pretty soon lanes made of wood were being built next to taverns.

On to the USA

By 1650 the Dutch had picked up the game and played it like this: nine pins arranged like a diamond (a 1-2-3-2-1 pattern.) Because the diamond sat at the end of a 90-foot plank, "gutter" balls were common. The Dutch settlers brought their nine-pin game to Connecticut and New York, where the sport was often banned because of the gambling associated with it. Despite that, by 1850 there were more than 400 alleys in New York City. But like pool halls, bowling alleys were, at best, barely respectable.

Know Your ABCs

The American Bowling Congress was founded in 1895 to standardize rules and eliminate gambling from the sport. In 1901, teams from 17 cities competed in the congress's first National Bowling Championship. The ABC eliminated gambling and brought respectability to the sport by offering prize money and holding sanctioned tournaments throughout the country.

In the 1920s Bulgaria became the first country in the world with a governing body of volleyball.

Pin Monkey Revolution

The sport's popularity soared in the 1950s with the introduction of the automated pin-setting machine and an extensive industry-marketing campaign. The campaign's highlights were advertisements featuring pretty society ladies happily bowling away. Shows like *Bowling for Dollars, Celebrity Bowling,* and *Make that Spare* brought the sport directly into America's living rooms. By the early 1960s, Americans were spending nearly $44 million a year on bowling balls and rolling them down more than 10,000 lanes.

And Now . . .

Bowling is truly a global sport with over 100 million bowlers spread throughout 90 countries. With the exception of soccer, it's the most played sport in the world. No matter in what country you end up playing it, always remember this bowling superstition: Never change your clothes during a hot streak. Hmm . . . maybe that's where that distinctly dirty, bowling-alley smell comes from?

ON DRINKING

Sports and drinking bump into each other often enough. Here's some commentary from those in the know.

"I HAD MY BAD DAYS ON THE FIELD, BUT I DIDN'T TAKE THEM HOME WITH ME. I LEFT THEM IN A BAR ALONG THE WAY."
—BOB LEMON, PITCHER

"I SEE THREE BASEBALLS, BUT I ONLY SWING AT THE MIDDLE ONE."
—PAUL WANER, OUTFIELDER, ON HITTING WELL AFTER A BENDER

"WHEN I REALIZED THAT WHAT I HAD TURNED OUT TO BE WAS A LOUSY, TWO-BIT POOL HUSTLER AND DRUNK, I WASN'T DEPRESSED AT ALL. I WAS GLAD TO HAVE A PROFESSION."
—DANNY MCGOORTY, POOL HUSTLER

"IF YOU DRINK, DON'T DRIVE. DON'T EVEN PUTT."
—DEAN MARTIN

"THERE IS MUCH LESS DRINKING NOW THAN THERE WAS BEFORE 1927, BECAUSE I QUIT DRINKING ON MAY 24, 1927."
—RABBIT MARANVILLE, BOSTON BRAVES SHORTSTOP

"DRINK THE FIRST. SIP THE SECOND SLOWLY. SKIP THE THIRD."
—KNUTE ROCKNE, NOTRE DAME COACH

Q: Why are spiders good baseball players? A: Because they're great at catching flies.

"They say some of my stars drink whiskey, but I have found that the ones who drink milkshakes don't win many ball games."
—Casey Stengel, outfielder and manager

"You can't be a true bleacher creature drinking this kind of beer."
—Stan Johnson, on light beer being sold at the Detroit Tigers stadium

A soccer ball is composed of 32 leather panels, held together by 642 stitches.

WHAT'S IN AN (NBA) NAME?

You know the names—
now find out where they come from.

Boston Celtics

Founded in 1946, team owner Walter Brown bounced around a number of ideas, including the Whirlwinds, the Olympics, and the Unicorns. Brown then had an epiphany "Wait, I've got it—the Celtics! We'll call them the Boston Celtics. The name has a great basketball tradition from the old Original Celtics in New York. And, Boston is full of Irishmen. We'll put them in green uniforms and call them the Boston Celtics." And they did.

Houston Rockets

Surprisingly, the name Rockets has nothing to do with the NASA Space Center in Houston. The moniker was actually chosen in 1967 when the franchise played in San Diego. The name was selected because it echoed the rapid growth of modern industry in the city.

Washington Wizards

The franchise known as the Wizards entered the league as the Chicago Packers in the 1961. In 1963 the franchise moved to Baltimore and became the Baltimore Bullets, borrowing the name from an earlier Baltimore-era basketball team (those Bullets got their name from a local ammunition factory). In 1996 owner Abe Pollin announced the franchise would be changing its name to avoid the violent overtones of "bullets," a sensible move considering D.C. was home to one of the country's highest murder rates at the time. Washington Wizards was the winning entry in a fan contest.

In poker a player who antes himself broke is known as "Broomcorn's Uncle."

Indianapolis Pacers

When Indianapolis entered the ABA in 1967, the name Pacers was chosen for its dual meaning—it's both a nod to Indiana's historical ties to the harness-racing pacers as well as a reference to the pace car used for the city's most famous sporting event, the Indianapolis 500.

Chicago Bulls

When the team joined the NBA in 1966, Richard Klein, the club's first owner, wanted a name that implied strength and power but also referenced the city's meatpacking history. Said Klein: "We were the meat capital of the world. At first, I was thinking of names like Matadors or Toreadors . . . I was sitting around the house, kicking these names around with my wife and three sons, when my little son Mark said, 'Dad, that's a bunch of bull!' I said, 'That's it! We'll call them the Bulls!' "

Minnesota Timberwolves

Like many team names, Timberwolves was the winning entry in a fan contest. It's a fitting name—Minnesota lays claim to the largest population of timber wolves in the lower 48 states.

Floors used in gymnastic routines have special springs hidden underneath to give the gymnast extra launch.

THE MADDEN CURSE

It couldn't be true . . . could it?

Being asked to be on the cover of the newest Madden videogame is an honor—well, at least it used to be. Players need to be careful because something keeps happening to those cover boys.

Madden '99: Garrison Hearst, San Francisco 49ers

Hearst was the first player to appear on a Madden cover. Prior to 1999, the game art featured only a picture of a grinning John Madden. Apparently, someone decided that young, athletic superstars would sell more copies of the game than an aging, overweight John Madden. Hearst's season was fantastic—until the playoffs, when he broke his leg. He didn't play again until 2001—and he was never the same.

Madden 2000: Barry Sanders, Detroit Lions

Barry Sanders announced his retirement just prior to the season's start, so his involvement with the curse is a little up in the air. However, Dorsey Levens appeared on editions released in PAL regions (Europe, Australia, etc.). He put up so-so numbers before aggravating a knee injury and his career was downhill from there.

Madden 2001: Eddie George, Tennessee Titans

Eddie George's cover year was fantastic, until the Titans' divisional playoff loss to the Baltimore Ravens in which George bobbled a pass that was returned for a touchdown, ending the Titans season. The next season he was hampered by injuries and never quite returned to form.

On July 29, 2003, Bill Mueller became the first player ever to hit a grand slam from both sides of the plate in the same game.

Madden 2002: Daunte Culpepper, Minnesota Vikings

Culpepper threw 23 interceptions during his cover year before suffering a back injury during Game 11 and missing the rest of the season. Minnesota finished 5-11, their worst record since 1984.

Madden 2003: Marshall Faulk, St. Louis Rams

Marshall Faulk injured his ankle, missed five games, and never rushed for more than a 1,000 yards in a season again.

Madden 2004: Michael Vick, Atlanta Falcons

Just days after the release of Madden 2004, Michael Vick suffered a fractured right fibula. He missed the first 11 games of the season, and by the time he returned, the Falcons were out of playoff contention. And then there was that whole dog fighting thing.

Madden 2005: Ray Lewis, Baltimore Ravens

Lewis, the first defensive player to be featured on the Madden box, followed his cover year with one of his worst seasons as a pro. He failed to record a single interception and the Ravens missed the playoffs.

Madden 2006: Donovan McNabb, Philadelphia Eagles

McNabb suffered a sports hernia during the first game of the season, attempted to play though it, aggravated it, and was forced into season-ending knee surgery. He's been plagued by injuries since.

Madden 2007: Shaun Alexander, Seattle Seahawks

Alexander earned his cover with a fabulous 2005–2006 season when he scored a record 27 rushing touchdowns. The next year, he fractured a bone in his foot, failed to rush for 1,000 yards for the first time since 2000, and saw his previous year's touchdown record broken by LaDainian Tomlinson.

Madden 2008: Vince Young, Tennessee Titans

Young threw 17 interceptions and just 9 touchdowns, but he did lead his Titans into the playoffs.

Madden 2009: Brett Favre, Green Bay Packers/New York Jets

Favre was signed up as cover athlete after he announced his official retirement from the NFL. Then, just a week before the game's release, Favre returned as a New York Jet. The game hit stores with Favre in his Packer jersey. Favre failed to lead his new Jets team to the playoffs.

ALI THE PHILOSOPHER

Muhammad Ali was more than the best boxer of all time; he was a civil rights activist, a pioneer, and a thinker. Here are a few words of wisdom from the man known simply as the Greatest.

"A man who views the world the same at 50 as he did at 20 has wasted 30 years of his life."

"Friendship is the hardest thing in the world to explain. It's not something you learn in school. But if you haven't learned the meaning of friendship, you really haven't learned anything."

"He who is not courageous enough to take risks will accomplish nothing in life."

"Hating people because of their color is wrong. And it doesn't matter which color does the hating. It's just plain wrong."

"It isn't the mountains ahead to climb that wear you out; it's the pebble in your shoe."

"It's the repetition of affirmations that leads to belief. And once that belief becomes a deep conviction, things begin to happen."

"Only a man who knows what it is like to be defeated can reach down to the bottom of his soul and come up with the extra ounce of power it takes to win when the match is even."

"AGE IS WHATEVER YOU THINK IT IS. YOU ARE AS OLD AS YOU THINK YOU ARE."

"AT HOME I AM A NICE GUY—BUT I DON'T WANT THE WORLD TO KNOW. HUMBLE PEOPLE, I'VE FOUND, DON'T GET VERY FAR."

"IT'S LACK OF FAITH THAT MAKES PEOPLE AFRAID OF MEETING CHALLENGES, AND I BELIEVED IN MYSELF."

"IT'S NOT BRAGGING IF YOU CAN BACK IT UP."

"LIFE IS A GAMBLE. YOU CAN GET HURT, BUT PEOPLE DIE IN PLANE CRASHES, LOSE THEIR ARMS AND LEGS IN CAR ACCIDENTS; PEOPLE DIE EVERY DAY. SAME WITH FIGHTERS: SOME DIE, SOME GET HURT, SOME GO ON. YOU JUST DON'T LET YOURSELF BELIEVE IT WILL HAPPEN TO YOU."

"OLD AGE IS JUST A RECORD OF ONE'S WHOLE LIFE."

"RIVERS, PONDS, LAKES, AND STREAMS—THEY ALL HAVE DIFFERENT NAMES, BUT THEY ALL CONTAIN WATER. JUST AS RELIGIONS DO—THEY ALL CONTAIN TRUTHS."

"SERVICE TO OTHERS IS THE RENT YOU PAY FOR YOUR ROOM HERE ON EARTH."

Tom Seaver is the only Hall of Famer to be enshrined with a Mets cap on his plaque.

STREAKIN'!!!

No, not the naked kind. Listed here are the 10 greatest individual streaks in sports (in our not-so-humble opinion).

1. Joe DiMaggio's 56-game hitting streak (1941)

The Rolls Royce of streaks. As soon as the streak ended, DiMaggio started up another one—this one a 17-gamer—so had it not been for two fantastic defensive plays by Ken Keltner, the streak would have lasted an astonishing 75 games. To put that in perspective, Pete Rose has the second longest streak in the modern era with 44. In today's game, with starters rarely going beyond 100 pitches and set-up men and closers working effectively in the late innings, there's a good chance this record will never be touched.

2. Edwin Moses's 107 straight victories in 400-meter hurdle finals (1977 to 1987)

For almost a decade Edwin Moses was unbeatable, winning 107 straight finals in the 400-meter intermediate hurdles and setting a new world record of 47.02 seconds. For a period of time, he held the 11 fastest times in the event. He went nearly 10 years without losing a race and his record 47.02 seconds still ranks as the second best of all time. Said former U.S. Olympic track-and-field coach Leroy Walker, "Extraordinary talent is obvious. We're in the rarefied presence of an immortal here. Edwin's a crowd unto himself."

3. Cal Ripken Jr.'s 2,632 straight games played (1982 to 1998)

Sixteen years—zero games missed. Cal Ripken is the very definition of an iron man. And when his streak finally ended, it had nothing to do with injury or exhaustion. No, Ripken went out on his own terms, telling his manager, Ray Miller, "I think the time is right." Rookie third baseman Ryan Minor started in Ripken's

Romanian driver Ferenc Szisz won the first Formula I Grand Prix at Le Mans, France, in 1906. He drove a Renault.

place: When the crowd realized the streak was ending, the fans, his teammates, and the entire visiting Yankee dugout gave Ripken a standing ovation.

4. Glenn Hall's 506 straight games played (1955 to 1962)

Playing 506 straight games is impressive for any position, any sport. The fact that Glenn Hall did it as a goalie—one of the toughest and most grueling positions in sports—makes it flat-out ridiculous. And, oh yeah, he did it all during the time before goalies wore masks.

5. Byron Nelson's 11 straight tournament wins (1945)

Byron Nelson's 1945 season may be the greatest season in the history of golf. He won 11 straight tournaments on his way to 18 total victories. To be fair, it must be mentioned that the sport's talent was somewhat watered down that year because of the war—but many of the game's best players still competed. Said Arnold Palmer, "I don't think that anyone will ever exceed the things that Byron did by winning 11 tournaments in a row in one year."

6. Brett Favre's 275-plus consecutive games starting as quarterback (1992 to 2008)

Favre started his first game as Green Bay Packers quarterback on September 27, 1992, against the Steelers—and he never missed a game after that, starting every contest until his retirement as a Packer and through his return as a New York Jet. His 275 consecutive games and counting shattered Ron Jaworski's previous record of 110. Eleven different QBs were stuck riding the bench behind Favre during his iron-man streak, none ever getting a start.

7. Alexander Karelin's 13-year winning streak (1987 to 2000)

Few athletes have ever dominated a sport like wrestler Alexander Karelin. From 1987 to 2000, he didn't lose a single match, earning gold medals in three separate Olympics during that stretch. Karelin's streak came to a shocking end at the 2000 Summer Olympics when he was upset by a relative unknown, U.S. wrestler Rulon Gardner.

8. Johnny Unitas's 47 straight games throwing a TD pass (1956 to 1960)

From 1956 to 1960—five seasons—Johnny Unitas threw a TD in 47 straight games. Hell, these days a QB playing in 47 straight games is impressive. Unitas's streak is 7 games longer than the next-closest QB, Dan Marino with 40. Unitas, the ultimate man's man, paid the streak no mind, saying, "Records don't mean a thing to me. Nothing is as important as winning. . . . I imagine if I was record-hungry, the thing wouldn't have been extended this far. It makes no difference to me when it stops."

9. Orel Hershiser's 59 consecutive scoreless innings (1988)

Hershiser's 1988 season was the stuff of legend: 23 wins, 15 complete games, 2.26 ERA, Gold Glove, NLCS MVP, World Series MVP, Unanimous Cy Young Award. Most impressive though, is the 59 consecutive scoreless innings. He threw six complete-game shutouts in a row before finally letting up a run in the first game of the NLCS—and that wasn't until the ninth inning. The closest another starter has come was Greg Maddux in 2000, with 39 scoreless innings.

10. Johnny Vander Meer's two straight no-hitters (1938)

Vander Meer's streak is far and away the shortest on the list—hell, we're not even sure two counts as a "streak." But it's also one of the most untouchable on this list. Vander Meer was a rookie when he no-hit the Boston Braves and then, four days later in Brooklyn, walked eight and struck out seven on the way to no-hitting the Dodgers in the first-ever night game at Ebbets Field. Breaking this record would require a pitcher to throw three straight no-hitters. Not happening.

Originating over 2,500 years ago as a war game in Pakistan, polo is considered the oldest sport in the world.

TENNIS TRIVIA

If you love the game like we do, you'll be an ace at these. Get a few wrong—we won't fault you.

1. Who defeated Bobby Riggs in 1973's historic Battle of the Sexes match?

a. Chris Evert
b. Billie Jean King
c. Margaret Court
d. Martina Navratilova

2. What year was tennis first introduced as an Olympic sport?

a. 1896
b. 1924
c. 1962
d. 1988

3. What nationality is Anna Kournikova?

a. Russian
b. Yugoslavian
c. Belgian
d. Swiss

4. What famous tennis player died of AIDS on February 6, 1993?

a. Rod Laver
b. Bjorn Borg
c. Arthur Ashe
d. Stefan Edberg

5. What is the name for the left side of the tennis court for the receiving player or team?

a. Ad court
b. Odd court
c. Deuce court
d. Base court

Barry Bonds was once intentionally walked with the bases loaded.

6. **Who did John McEnroe defeat in the finals to win his first Wimbledon singles title?**
   a. Jimmy Connors
   b. Bjorn Borg
   c. Chris Lewis
   d. Kevin Curren

7. **Who was the first professional tennis player to host *Saturday Night Live?***
   a. Roger Federer
   b. Anna Kournikova
   c. John McEnroe
   d. Chris Evert

8. **Who is the only tennis player to have won the U.S. Open on three different surfaces?**
   a. Chris Evert
   b. Arthur Ashe
   c. Jimmy Connors
   d. Guillermo Vilas

9. **Where do the Maleeva sisters hail from?**
   a. Romania
   b. Croatia
   c. Slovakia
   d. Bulgaria

10. **Who was the first unseeded player to win a Wimbledon singles title?**
    a. Michael Chang
    b. Bjorn Borg
    c. Boris Becker
    d. Guillermo Vilas

Turn to page 351 for answers.

With the exception of a bullet, the tip of a fencing weapon is the fastest moving object in sports.

STRANGER THAN FICTION

Weird stuff—straight from the news.

Nuts About the Sooners

When talking college football, be careful what you say to Allen Beckett. As his lawyer said, Mr. Beckett is "not necessarily an overboard die-hard OU fan, but he certainly admits he said something in a joking fashion to the guy about his Texas T-shirt. The guy got offended. He said he was sorry." What exactly was said isn't clear, but what is clear is that one minute Beckett was hassling the guy about his T-shirt and the next minute Beckett was tearing the guy's scrotal sack. Ow. Beckett was charged with aggravated assault. Best part of the story? Allen Beckett is a church deacon.

Whopper of a Bad Idea

Two employees working the overnight shift at an Idaho skating rink got a little hungry, so, y'know, they did the same thing anyone else would do. Hit up the vending machine? No—take the rink's Zamboni for a little spin to the local Burger King. FYI, Zambonis have a top speed of 5 mph. Both men lost their jobs. That's one expensive hamburger.

Lady, Just Let It Slide . . .

Little Leaguer Martin Gonzalez got his first hit of the season . . . but tried to stretch his single into a double, slid, and suffered "serious bodily injury" that led to "permanent scarring and disability." So the boy's mom does the American thing and, three years later, sues the coach and the local Little League for not teaching Martin the "skills needed to avoid and/or minimize the risks of injury" while sliding.

Ridiculous, No Matter How You Slice It

According to police reports, Sherri Ferns was working the food and drink stand during the local Little League all-star game. Her son's team lost 10–9 after his teammate was tagged out at third and then ejected for throwing his helmet. A number of parents, who may or may not have been drinking, heckled the umpire. Ferns took it a step further—she dug into her concession stand's arsenal and pelted the umpire with a slice of pizza. Not only that, the slice managed to ricochet off of the ump and hit another parent—à la the *Seinfeld* "magic loogie, second spitter" incident. Ferns was charged with two counts of simple assault.

Charity Case

In an attempt to draw bigger crowds to the 2004 Pineapple Open to benefit the Muscular Dystrophy Association, Arizona's Club West Golf Club in Ahwatukee promised to pay $1 million to any golfer who could manage a hole-in-one on the 178-yard sixth hole. Only problem—Keith Schott actually got a hole-in-one on the sixth hole and claims 11 people saw it happen. Schott was of course disappointed to learn that the only way he'd see the money was if he was to "re-perform that miracle feat yet one more time in a videotaped shootout." Considering the odds of hitting a hole-in-one range from one in 20,000 to one in 33,000, Schott decided to just sue the Muscular Dystrophy Association instead.

Gymnasium comes from the Greek word *gymnazein*, which means to "exercise naked."

THE STEVE BARTMAN BALL

A foul ball turns one poor guy's life upside down.

The Setting

It was Game 6 of the National League Championship Series between the Chicago Cubs and the Florida Marlins at Wrigley Filed. Mark Prior had pitched the Cubs to a 3–0, eighth-inning lead. Cubs fans were ecstatic: They led the series three games to two and were just five outs from reaching the World Series for the first time since 1945 (and a shot at winning the thing for the first time since 1908).

Do the Bartman

Steve Bartman, a Chicago native, was in a front-row box seat along the leftfield corner wall—just behind the bullpen (aisle 4, row 8, seat 113 to be exact). Luis Castillo popped a foul ball toward Bartman. Cubs leftfielder Moises Alou ran over, hoping for a shot at a catch, but it was Bartman, who had his eyes on the ball, who got his hands on the ball first. A furious Alou slammed his glove to the ground and screamed at Bartman. Alou barely had a shot at catching the ball, but his reaction was enough. In the fans' eyes, Bartman had cost his team an out. The crowd screamed, "Kill him!" as security stepped in and escorted Bartman from the game for his own protection.

The Marlins went on to score 8 runs and win the game. They won the next day as well, winning the series and moving onto the World Series. As far as Cubs fans were concerned, Bartman had just cost them the World Series.

Statement

To set the record clear, Bartman released a statement:

> "There are few words to describe how awful I feel and what I have experienced within these last 24 hours.

Men's water polo was the first team sport added to the 1900 modern Olympics.

I've been a Cub fan all my life and fully understand the relationship between my actions and the outcome of the game. I had my eyes glued on the approaching ball the entire time and was so caught up in the moment that I did not even see Moises Alou, much less that he may have had a play.

Had I thought for one second that the ball was playable or had I seen Alou approaching I would have done whatever I could to get out of the way and give Alou a chance to make the catch.

To Moises Alou, the Chicago Cubs organization, Ron Santo, Ernie Banks, and Cub fans everywhere, I am so truly sorry from the bottom of this Cubs fan's broken heart.

I ask that Cub fans everywhere redirect the negative energy that has been vented towards my family, my friends, and myself into the usual positive support for our beloved team on their way to being National League champs."

Afterward

Sadly, the statement wasn't enough. When the *Chicago Sun-Times* released Bartman's name and address he became nationally infamous—the butt of countless late-night jokes by the Lettermans and Lenos of the world. At home he was hounded by reporters. At work he received death threats. "Death to Bartman" message boards popped up on the Internet. Cartoons depicted him hiding out with Osama Bin Laden and Saddam Hussein. The Governor of Illinois at the time, Rod Blagojevich, even went so far as to tell the *Chicago Sun-Times* that Bartman "better join the witness protection program."

Jeb Bush, Governor of Florida, offered Bartman asylum—why not, Florida fans loved him. The Marlins even offered him a job with the club.

During the course of a single water-polo match, players can swim up to a mile and half.

Now

Bartman continues to live in the Chicago area and continues to root for the Cubs—from home, not from the stadium.

The Execution

In the midst of the fracas following the Bartman incident, a Chicago lawyer had grabbed the ball. That's right, Bartman never actually even caught the damn thing, poor guy. Months later, it was sold at an auction to restaurateur Grant DePorter for $113,824.16. DePorter, part-owner of the Chicago-area Harry Caray restaurant chain, decided to blow the ball up in an effort to put an end to the bad luck that had so long haunted their team.

The big event took place outside Harry Caray's restaurant on February 26, 2004. During its final days, the doomed ball was guarded by a squad of security men—it even received a massage and a final meal of lobster, steak, and beer. Academy Award–winning special effects man Michael Lantieri (*Jurassic Park, Who Framed Roger Rabbit?*) used his particular skill set to play the role of executioner.

On the night of February 26, an explosive charge reduced the ball to a pile of string as fans gathered around and sang "Take Me Out to the Ballgame." Money made from sales of mementoes were used to raise funds for diabetes research. A year later, DePorter was still trying to end the curse. He steamed the ball's remnants and infused them with vodka and beer to create something called Foul Ball Spaghetti. Some 4,000 diners ate it up. Yum.

Rugby balls are oval-shaped because they were originally made out of pigs' bladders, which are oval-shaped when inflated.

SUMO WRESTLING

Everything you need to know about the sport where obese men wear thongs.

Sumo, the national sport of Japan, is a centuries-old style of wrestling. Sumo wrestlers, called *rikishi,* are instantly recognizable for their huge girth and diaper-like belts, known as *mawashi.*

Starting Young

Scouts from professional sumo "stables" travel the country looking for athletic teens who are stocky but not obese. Once chosen, the wrestlers begin years of rigorous training. It can take up to 12 years to make it to the professional ranks.

The Life

Sumo is a sport defined by tradition. All professional sumo wrestlers live in communal training stables where every aspect of their life is dedicated to the sport and dictated by ritual. The youngest, lowest-level rikishi begin their training at 5 a.m. One exercise, *shiko,* consists of stomping the ground 500 times a day.

The Sumo Diet

Looking for that sumo wrestler body? Here's how they do it.

1. Don't eat breakfast. Ever. Sumo wrestlers get eight hours of sleep—but they don't eat when they wake, which helps them maintain a slow metabolism.

2. Never eat before exercising. Sumo wrestlers exercise a ton, but they don't lose weight. Because they don't have food in their bodies when they exercise, their metabolism is slowed down to conserve fuel.

Tracy Caulkins is the only swimmer to ever hold a U.S. record in every single stroke.

3. Nap after eating. This is the sumo secret—it's also pretty much the worst thing that anybody who isn't a sumo wrestler can do. As soon as sumo wrestlers finish eating, they hit the hay for at least four hours. While napping they receive massages designed to loosen the intestines and make room for more food.

4. Eat before bed. Again, if you're not a sumo wrestler, this is bad, bad, bad. Because they go to sleep with full stomachs, their bodies react to the flood of nutrients by pumping out insulin, forcing their massive bodies to store it in the cells as fat (instead of in the muscles and organs as nutrients, which is what most people aim for).

Dohyo

Sumo matches take place in a ring called a *dohyo,* a circle of rice-straw bales mounted on a clay platform. The ring, 5 yards in diameter, is covered by sand. At the center of the ring are two short, parallel white lines, which serve as the wrestler's starting marks. Surrounding the ring is a fine sand called *ja-no-me,* which is used to determine if any part of the wrestler's body touched outside the ring. A new dohyo is built for every tournament, and at the end of a tournament, fans take pieces home as souvenirs.

The Match

Each match begins with the rikishi standing behind their respective white line, crouched, fists clenched, staring each other down. This staring contest is timed; after 4 minutes, it's up. At any point during the stare-down, the rikishi may begin fighting. Fighting consists of a series of tosses, pushes, pulls, and slaps—no hair pulling, punching, eye gouging, or kicking around the groin allowed. Matches are usually short affairs with the loser being either a.) the first wrestler to step out of the ring; or b.) the first wrestler to touch the mat with any part of his body other than the bottom of his feet.

In 1922 Babe Ruth made roughly $325 per game; in 2007 Alex Rodriguez made roughly $154,320 per game.

Tapping Out

The sumo lifestyle takes a toll. Sumo wrestlers have a life expectancy of 65, 10 years less than the average Japanese male. Diabetes, cholesterol, arthritis, and heart attacks are all common, as well as liver problems stemming from the excessive amount of beer they drink to maintain their belly.

Sumo Facts

✓ The highest paid rikishi makes an annual salary of around 33,840,000 Yen (about $300,000 USD).

✓ The top knot, the sumo-wrestler's hair, is very important. Special hairdressers, called *tokoyama,* attend to the wrestler's hair. Just like the wrestlers, tokoyama are ranked according to their talent and experience. Upon retirement, wrestlers regain their civilian status through a hair-cutting ceremony.

✓ Hawaiian-born Konishiki was the first foreigner to reach the sport's second-highest rank of *ozeki*—just one below *yokozuna.* He was also the heaviest rikishi in history, weighing in at 616 pounds.

✓ The first women's sumo federation was established in April 1996.

Sumo Lingo

Toss these words around and sound like a true sumo *aikousha* (fan).

Basho: a tournament

Gyoji: referee

Aki: the sport's major tournament

Yokozuna: the highest rank a wrestler can achieve

Dohy-iri: the rituals that begin a match

FOUND ON EBAY

A few of the more bizarre oddities for sale on the world's largest online auction site.

Item: Cheetos snack shaped like deceased race-horse Barbaro (supposedly also contains Barbaro's soul)
Description: "I couldn't eat him. It wouldn't be right. Everybody loves Cheetos, but we love Barbaro even more. I don't know what made me look at this one before I ate it, know it sounds crazy, but I'm sure I heard Barbaro neighing in my ear. He sounded a little hoarse, but it was loud enough for me to stop eating and look at him. The rest is history and now we can share him with the world! Please do not bid unless you are serious about taking care of Barbaro."
Winning bid: $69.69
Worth a bid? For the serious Cheetos collector or the serious Barbaro mourner, yes, this is a once in a lifetime opportunity.

Item: Muhammad Ali Decanter from 1981
Description: "Here is a great looking decanter of the greatest boxer who ever boxed. This decanter stands 15" tall and the head comes off by the neck with the cork."
Opening bid: $200
Worth a bid? Yes! Nothing will impress your dinner guests like popping off the Greatest's head and topping off their glass of Thunderbird.

Item: Matt Holliday's game-chewed sunflower seeds
Description: "I was at the fireworks game on Friday, September 28, and seated in section 154, which allowed me to go onto the field during the fireworks show. A friend and I collected these seeds from the area where Holliday had spent a good part of the game. Of course there's the chance that some belong to the Arizona Diamondback's leftfielder . . . I suppose you could ask Matt to submit to a DNA test . . . But I'm not sure he would oblige.

Brothers Duane, Brett, Brian, Darryl, Ron, and Rich Sutter played in the NHL. In 1987 they were all in the league at the same time.

Including [*sic*] is approximately ¼ cup of slightly used sunflower seeds stored in a handy Ziploc bag. I'm also throwing in my ticket as proof that I was indeed at the game. The baggie also holds a couple stray blades of grass and a small clump of dirt, possibly kicked up by Matt Holliday's cleat."
Winning bid: $25.89
Worth a bid? Um, no. Just no.

Item: Pete Rose's 30-year-old chewed gum
Description: "You are bidding on a ONE OF A KIND lot!!! You will receive a piece of chewing gum thrown by Pete in disgust after a strikeout in a loss to the St. Louis Cardinals on 8/31/1975. The gum was thrown toward the dugout and stuck to the top wall where it was retrieved by my grandfather and stored for over 30 years. The gum is as hard as a rock but in original chewed condition."
Worth a bid? If you're a big Pete Rose fan, then yes. You should buy this, drive to Springfield, go to the Baseball of Fame, chew the gum for a little while, and stick it to a wall somewhere. It's the closest he's ever going to get.

Item: A piece of cake allegedly sampled by Tiger Woods
Description: "Not autographed in the traditional sense, but definitely a lasting item from Tiger himself! The piece of cake in question is the one that Woods himself sampled the icing from."
Opening bid: $15
Worth a bid? If you happen to actually be Tiger Woods, then go for it, have your cake and eat it too. Also, if that's the case, thanks for reading our book, Tiger.

Item: Terry Francona game-used chewing tobacco
Description: "This is an actual game-used piece of chewing tobacco chewed by Red Sox manager Terry Francona during Game 1 of the 2007 World Series at Fenway Park. The piece of tobacco is intertwined with a piece of bubble gum. This item was taken right from the seat of Terry Francona."
Winning bid: Sadly, none. The auction was nixed by eBay because of the heavy regulation of tobacco.
Worth a bid? Yes. A must for any true Sox fan's collection.

The longest-recorded volleyball marathon is 75 hours, 30 minutes.

Item: Rocky Colavito 10-piece bedroom set
Description: "No kidding! . . . .The near mint 11pc bedroom set is up for auction! And this bedroom set belongs to one of baseball's legendary players, Rocky Colavito! This lovely off-white lacquered set consists of 10 pieces, it is approx 25 yrs old with 99.5% life left in it."
Winning bid: None. No one took a shot at the $3,500 starting bid. The seller seems to have seriously overestimated the Rocky Colavito, 25-year-old-used-furniture market.
Worth a bid? If you need a new bedroom set and you're a big Rocky Colavito fan, then yes, this is a match made in heaven.

Item: Ketchup-stained Jose Reyes replica jersey that fan Matt Murphy wore while catching Barry Bonds' infamous home run number 756
Description: "This is the real Jersey I wore at the Giants game while catching the famous Barry Bonds career 756 ball . . . I have not washed the jersey. There are several ketchup stains on the front as well as back illustrated in the pictures from being on the ground of AT&T park fighting for the ball. This is the real jersey, I will be putting the hat that I wore to the game up for bid also. For me to autograph the jersey will be at the buyers request."
Winning bid: None.
Worth a bid: It's tempting. But we'd hold out for the hat.

Item: Manny Ramirez's old grill
Description: "Hi, I'm Manny Ramirez. I bought this AMAZING grill for about $4,000 and I used it once . . . but I never have the time to use it because I am always on the road. I would love to sell it and you will get an autographed ball signed by me. Enjoy it, Manny Ramirez."
Winning bid: None, eBay pulled it because no one could prove it was actually Manny's grill.
Worth a bid: Sure, get it and grill up some burgers. When the thing stops working at the worst possible time, say, "That's just Manny's grill being Manny's grill."

In 1946 Mel Ott became the first manager to get thrown out of both the first and second games of a doubleheader.

THE SPORTS NUMERIST 21–40

The games. By the numbers. Twenty-one through forty.

Charles Barkley once lost $2.5 million in a six-hour period playing blackjack, or as the kiddies call it, **21**.

On July **22**, 2005, the atrocious *Bad News Bears* remake is released. Billy Bob Thornton is no Walter Matthau.

Michael Jordan wore No. **23** with the Chicago Bulls. That was a good thing. He also wore No. 23 with the Washington Wizards. That was not as good.

"There is much less drinking now than there was before 1927, because I quit drinking on May **24**, 1927."
—Rabbit Maranville, Boston Braves shortstop

On October **25**, 1986, Bill Buckner let a ball slip through his legs and a curse continued.

26: games lost by the Tampa Bay Buccaneers in their first 26 games.

Between May 6, 1992, and July 24, 1993, pitcher Anthony Young lost a record **27** consecutive games.

John Rocker was suspended for the first **28** games of the 2000 season after making disparaging remarks about African-Americans, Asians, and homosexuals.

Boxer Luis Resto had fought **29** fights before his infamous bout against Billy Collins Jr. at Madison Square Garden. Resto defeated Collins in a 10-round unanimous decision. It was soon discovered that Resto's gloves had no padding and that his hand wraps had been soaked in plaster of Paris. The beating ended Collins's career and left him with blurred vision and a torn iris; he died soon after in a car accident that many speculate may have been a suicide.

Nolan Ryan is the only major league baseball player to have his number retired by three different teams: No. **30** by the California Angels and No. 34 by the Houston Astros and Texas Rangers.

On December **31**, 1972, Roberto Clemente perished in a plane crash while traveling to Nicaragua to deliver aid to earthquake victims.

32: arguably the most prestigious jersey number in sports. It's been worn by football greats Jim Brown, Franco Harris, and O. J. Simpson; baseball legends Sandy Koufax and Steve Carlton; and basketball stars Magic Johnson, Julius Erving, Karl Malone, Kevin McHale, Bill Walton, and Shaquille O'Neal.

33: total number of innings played in the longest game in baseball history, a 1981 game between the Pawtucket Red Sox and the Rochester Red Wings. Future Hall of Famers Cal Ripken Jr. and Wade Boggs were a combined 6-25 in the game.

A survey by University of Mississippi professor Dr. Kim Beason revealed that serious fantasy sports players spend approximately **34** minutes per day "thinking" about fantasy sports.

The late, great motorcycle wacko Evel Knievel suffered **35** total broken bones throughout his career.

36: career interceptions thrown by No. 2 overall draft pick Ryan Leaf—in comparison to 14 touchdowns.

37: players from 22 different institutions were implicated in 1962's college basketball point-shaving scandal.

In 1949 the St. Louis Cardinals were actually evicted by their stadium.

Jesse Ventura was the **38**th governor of Minnesota.

Pioneering aviator Amelia Earhart was **39** when she disappeared over the central Pacific Ocean while attempting to circumnavigate the globe.

Pat Tillman, former Arizona Cardinal who gave up a promising football career to join the army, died in combat in Afghanistan. He wore jersey No. **40**. After his death, his number was retired by the Cardinals.

The Lakers have won more NBA Finals than any other team, but the Celtics have the most championships with 17.

THE LOU GEHRIG FAREWELL SPEECH

One of the most powerful and emotional moments in baseball history, one even the vast legion of Yankee haters can respect.

After being diagnosed with amyotrophic lateral sclerosis (ALS), the great Lou Gehrig announced his retirement on June 21, 1939. That same year, July 4 was proclaimed Lou Gehrig Day at Yankee stadium. A moving, poignant ceremony was held in honor of the dying slugger. The *New York Times* described the event as "perhaps as colorful and dramatic a pageant as ever was enacted on a baseball field [as] 61,808 fans thundered a hail and farewell."

Yankees manager Joe McCarthy spoke with tears in his eyes: "Lou, what else can I say except that it was a sad day in the life of everybody who knew you when you came into my hotel room that day in Detroit and told me you were quitting as a ballplayer because you felt yourself a hindrance to the team. My God, man, you were never that."

It was then, after the speeches and presentations, that Gehrig stepped to the mic and delivered one of the most powerful speeches in the history of sports.

The Speech

"Fans, for the past two weeks you have been reading about the bad break I got. Yet today I consider myself the luckiest man on the face of this earth. I have been in ballparks for 17 years and have never received anything but kindness and encouragement from you fans.

"Look at these grand men. Which of you wouldn't consider it the highlight of his career just to associate with them for even one day? Sure, I'm lucky. Who wouldn't consider it an honor to have known Jacob Ruppert? Also, the builder of baseball's greatest empire, Ed Barrow? To have spent six years with that wonderful little fellow, Miller Huggins? Then to have spent the next nine years with that outstanding leader, that smart student of psychology, the best manager in baseball today, Joe McCarthy? Sure, I'm lucky.

"When the New York Giants, a team you would give your right arm to beat, and vice versa, sends you a gift—that's something. When everybody down to the groundskeepers and those boys in white coats remember you with trophies—that's something. When you have a wonderful mother-in-law who takes sides with you in squabbles with her own daughter—that's something. When you have a father and a mother who work all their lives so you can have an education and build your body—it's a blessing. When you have a wife who has been a tower of strength and shown more courage than you dreamed existed—that's the finest I know.

"So I close in saying that I may have had a tough break, but I have an awful lot to live for."

In 1954 Phil Cavarretta became the first manager to be fired during spring training.

KNOW YOUR NASCAR

From bootlegging to prime time.

What Exactly Is It?

NASCAR (National Association for Stock Car Auto Racing) is a sanctioning body that supervises a number of different types of racing across the U.S. (and more recently around the world), sanctioning more than 1,500 races a year. Three main race series fall under the NASCAR umbrella:

Sprint Cup Series (when people say NASCAR this is generally what they are referring to)

Nationwide Series (basically a minor league for the Sprint Cup)

Craftsman Truck Series

The Earliest Days

If you really want to go to the beginning, you have to start in 1794. Sure, there weren't cars then—but there was whiskey, and in 1794, there was the Whiskey Rebellion. Frontier farmers, unhappy with the government's new tax on whiskey, began producing the liquor in secret stills and illegally transporting it undercover.

More than a century later, there was Prohibition. Bootlegging, illegally driving liquor across the country, was back again and it was big business. To be a bootlegger, you had to be one helluva driver; running under the cover of night, outracing cops, cradling hairpin turns. These drivers were skilled. But then, prohibition ended. So, southern bootleggers used their cars for racing. Then, in 1938, a man named William France organized a race on the sandy beaches of Daytona. The bootleggers were able to show off their skills—legally. Unofficially, NASCAR had begun.

In 1964 Masanori Murakami became the first Japanese-born MLB player.

The Early Days

NASCAR was officially founded by William France Sr. and a handful of other drivers (mostly ex-moonshiners) on February 21, 1948. They jotted the points system down on a barroom napkin. Months later, the first NASCAR race was run on a three-quarter-mile dirt track in Charlotte, North Carolina; Jim Roper took the victory piloting a Lincoln.

In 1959, NASCAR had its first true photo finish. Johnny Beachcamp, Charley Griffith, and Lee Petty all crossed the Daytona 500 finish line together at the Daytona 500. It took NASCAR a full day to declare Petty the winner.

Modern Times

Things began to change in the early '70s. R. J. Reynolds Tobacco Company (maker of Winston cigarettes) signed on as sponsor and began to heavily promote the sport. The Grand National Series became the Winston Cup Series (now the Sprint Cup Series). In 1972, the season was shortened from 48 races to 31, and as such, 1972 is often recognized as the beginning of the modern era of NASCAR.

In 1979, network cameras broadcast the Daytona 500 live for the first time. It was a make-or-break moment for the league and, luckily, it was a fantastic race. Cale Yarborough and Donnie Allison led into the last lap, before crashing on the backstretch, allowing Richard Petty to pass by for the win. A fistfight broke out between Yarborough and Allison on national TV—and the fans at home loved it! NASCAR had truly arrived.

Point System and the Chase for the NEXTEL Cup

Today's scoring works like this:

5 points are awarded to any driver that leads a lap during the course of a race.

5 points are awarded to the driver that leads the most laps.

185 points are awarded for first place, 170 for second, and so on—down to 34 points for last place.

Everyone knows Jackie Robinson was the first black major league baseball player, but in 1965 he became the first black major league baseball national broadcaster as well.

As such, the most points a driver can earn in a single race is 195: 185 for winning the race, 5 for leading a lap, and 5 for leading the most laps.

After the first 26 races of the season, the top 12 point leaders are locked into the final 10 races; these 10 races are known as the Chase for the NEXTEL Cup. At that point, the 12 point leaders' point totals are reset to 5,000, plus 10 for every race they won through out the season. For example, if so-and-so finished the first 26 races in the top 12 points and that driver has won five races that season, he'd have 5,050 points. Then, for the final 10 races, points are awarded as before to determine the season's champion.

The Pits

The Pit Crew consists of seven members: front tire changer, front tire carrier, rear tire changer, rear tire carrier, gas man, gas catch can man, and jack man.

Drafting

We're not going to go too deep into the physics of drafting (because we're not that smart), but let's just say it's pretty cool. Simply put, one car rides directly behind another car, reducing the aerodynamic resistance on the trailing car. As the trailing car gets closer and closer to the first car, it pushes air forward, speeding up the first car. In the end, both cars benefit.

The "slingshot pass" is one of the most spectacular moves in racing. The trailing car uses the lead car's wake to get to maximum speed along a straightaway, then takes a high turn, passing the lead car, effectively being slingshotted ahead.

The Flags

Green signals the beginning of the race and is also used at the end of a caution period to let drivers know the track is clear.

Yellow is the caution flag, indicating that drivers must slow.

Red is used to stop the race because of a large accident or inclement weather.

Blue with a yellow stripe warns a driver to pay attention to their mirrors because faster traffic is approaching.

Black means a driver must come into the pits because of a mechanical failure or a rules infraction.

Black with a white cross lets a driver know that laps are no longer scored until they report to the pits. It's known as the consultation flag.

White indicates that one lap remains in the race.

Checkered flag means the race is over.

Fast Facts

- ✓ NASCAR cars get hot inside. Real hot. Like 140 degrees hot. It's not uncommon for drivers to shed 5 to 10 pounds during the course of a race. Fluids are a necessity.
- ✓ Racer's helmets weigh 3 pounds—but on a banked turn, where drivers pull up to 5 Gs (meaning they feel the pull of five times normal gravity), they weigh closer to 15 pounds.
- ✓ A yellow strip across the rear of a race car indicates a rookie driver.
- ✓ To protect the fans, the front grandstands along the racetrack are constructed of 15,000 tons of steel and 2 million pounds of aluminum. That's enough aluminum to produce 61 million soda cans (or Coke cans—the official soda of NASCAR).
- ✓ A single NASCAR tire can weigh up to 75 pounds.

ATHLETES AT THE MOVIES

Match the athlete with their Hollywood dialogue.

The Athlete	The Line
Dennis Rodman	"Hey, Ace, got anymore of that gum?"
Hulk Hogan	"The hell I don't. Listen, kid. I've been hearing that crap ever since I was at UCLA. I'm out there busting my buns every night. Tell your old man to drag Walton and Lanier up and down the court for 48 minutes."
Brett Favre	"Hang on! I'm contagious, outrageous, spontaneous! You can't contain this."
Brian Bosworth	"It was this girl, five-foot-nuthin'. Blocked my shot!"
Charles Barkley	"Rip 'em! Rip 'em! Rip 'em! Come on, Randy! Let's go, Charlie! We're gonna take on Jake Bullet!"
Roger Clemens	"Mongo only pawn in game of life."
Shaquille O'Neal	"You're trying to move in on my squirrel! I ought to stoot-slap your ass right now!"
Dan Marino	"The last guy that made fun of my hair is still trying to pull his head outta his ass."
Kareem Abdul-Jabbar	[after knocking around a few would-be grocery store robbers] "You better clean up on aisle four."
Alex Karras	"I'm in town to play the Dolphins, you dumbass."

Turn to page 352 for answers.

The first officially recognized save was recorded by Bill Singer in 1969.

BACKWARDS WISDOM FROM COACH BILL "PETE" PETERSON

As a coach for Florida State, Rice University, and the Houston Oilers, Coach Bill "Pete" Peterson tutored such coaching greats as Joe Gibbs, Bobby Bowden, Bill Parcells, Don James, Ken Meyer, and Dan Henning. And boy, did he have a way with words.

"MEN, I WANT YOU JUST THINKING OF ONE WORD ALL SEASON. ONE WORD AND ONE WORD ONLY: SUPER BOWL."

"LEAD US IN A FEW WORDS OF SILENT PRAYER."

"I'M THE FOOTBALL COACH AROUND HERE AND DON'T YOU REMEMBER IT."

"YOU GUYS LINE UP ALPHABETICALLY BY HEIGHT."

"YOU GUYS PAIR UP IN GROUPS OF THREE, THEN LINE UP IN A CIRCLE."

"I USED TO HAVE THIS SLIGHT SPEECH IMPLEMENT AND COULDN'T REMEMBER THINGS BEFORE I TOOK THE SAM CARNEGIE COURSE."

"JUST REMEMBER THE WORDS OF PATRICK HENRY—'KILL ME OR LET ME LIVE.' "

"THE GREATEST THING JUST HAPPENED TO ME. I JUST GOT INDICTED INTO THE FLORIDA SPORTS HALL OF FAME. THEY HAD A STANDING OBSERVATION FOR ME."

"WE CAN BEAT THIS TEAM, IF WE JUST CAPITALIZE ON OUR MISTAKES."

"I'VE GONE TO A NUTRITIONIST," HE FUMED, ADDRESSING A FEW PUDGY 290-POUNDERS, "AND I WANT TO TELL YOU GUYS SOMETHING. THREE THINGS ARE BAD FOR YOU. I CAN'T REMEMBER THE FIRST TWO, BUT THE THIRD IS DOUGHNUTS."

The first World Series night game was won by the Pittsburgh Pirates in 1971, who beat the Baltimore Orioles.

"THIS IS THE GREATEST COUNTRY IN AMERICA."

"LET SLEEPING BAGS LIE."

"DON'T LOOK A SAWHORSE IN THE MOUTH."

"DON'T BURN YOUR BRIDGES AT BOTH ENDS."

"YOU CAN OBSERVE A LOT JUST BY WATCHING."

The Olympic motto "Faster, Higher, Stronger" comes from the Latin *Citius, Altius, Fortius.*

JULEPS AND JOCKEYS

Drinking, derby style.

The Derby and the Julep

Since 1938 the mint julep has been the traditional drink of the Kentucky Derby. Well-to-do ladies and smartly dressed gentlemen sit around in their fancy hats and cheer on the horses while sipping the bourbon-based beverage. In 1990 Early Times Mint Julep Ready-to-Serve Cocktail mix was named the "official mint julep of the Kentucky Derby."

Know Your Derby

Churchill Downs opened on May 17, 1875. The first featured race's winner was three-year old colt Aristides.

The Derby was first televised nationally on May 3, 1952.

Numerous celebrities have owned Derby horses, including George Steinbrenner, Steven Spielberg, and Burt Bacharach.

Know Your Juleps

Each year, nearly 120,000 mint juleps are served at the Derby—that's 10,000 bottles of Early Times Mint Julep Mix, 1,000 pounds of mint, and 60,000 pounds of ice.

In 2006, guests at Churchill Downs were offered custom-made mint juleps in gold-plated cups with silver straws, made with Woodford Reserve bourbon, mint from Ireland, ice from the Bavarian Alps, and sugar imported from Australia. Each custom-made drink cost $1,000; all proceeds went to charity.

The 2008 Kentucky Derby featured the world's largest mint julep. Housed inside a 6-foot-tall glass (featuring a 7½-foot sprig of mint), the drink wasn't just for show—it actually pumped out

Roberto Clemente was the first Hispanic player to be enshrined in the MLB Hall of Fame.

206 gallons worth of mint juleps thanks to a complex pumping system hidden inside the drink's massive straw.

Make Your Own

You might not be able to make it down to Kentucky to watch the Derby in person, but that doesn't mean you can't still enjoy a nice julep while cheering on your favorite pony. If you want to do it all official-like, pick up a bottle of Early Times Ready-to-Serve Cocktail mix from your local store.

Or, if you're up for it, you can make it on your own from scratch. There are dozens of mint julep recipes, and everyone seems to have their own take on it. Since Early Times is the official mint julep of the Derby, we'll go with theirs:

What you need:

2 cups sugar
2 cups water
Sprigs of fresh mint
Crushed ice
Early Times Kentucky Whisky

What You Do:

1. Boil sugar and water together for five minutes, creating a syrup.

2. Place syrup in covered container with six to eight sprigs of fresh mint.

3. Refrigerate overnight.

4. Fill cup with crushed ice, then add 1 tablespoon syrup and 2 ounces Early Times Kentucky Whisky.

5. Stir rapidly to frost the cup.

6. Add a sprig of fresh mint.

In 1975 Fred Lynn became the first player to win the Rookie of the Year and MVP awards in the same year.

Do It Classy

If you want to get the true julep experience you'll need to pick up a set of silver julep cups. These aren't a necessity of course, but they do set the mood nicely. You can grab a pair of cheap-ish ones online for about $50. It's also a plus to be drinking from something that won't break: That way you don't have to worry about shattered glass when you chuck your julep against the wall after blowing your paycheck on the latest Triple Crown disappointment.

Pitcher Tom Seaver was elected to the Baseball Hall of Fame with the highest-ever percentage of votes. Of 430 ballots, 425 (98.84 percent) were cast in his favor.

THE TONYA TIMELINE

Everyone knows about Tonya Harding and Nancy Kerrigan. But for Tonya Harding, the craziness didn't stop there. Take a look at these incidents, beginning with the infamous attack.

January 6, 1994: Harding's ex-husband, Jeff Gillooly, along with her bodyguard, Shawn Eckhardt, hire a man named Shane Stant to whack rival figure skater Kerrigan on the knee. She later pleads guilty to hampering the investigation into the attack, but maintains that she knew nothing about the plan ahead of time.

September 1994: Tonya becomes an Internet celeb when a pornographic "wedding video" showing her and ex-husband Jeff Gillooly having sex surfaces. It turns out it was Gillooly who sold the tape to a tabloid show. Soon after, stills are published in *Penthouse* magazine.

May 25, 1995: Tonya calls police after tailing a Lincoln Town Car for 20 miles, convinced that it was being driven by a professional golfer who she thought was stalking her.

October 28, 1996: Tonya calls 911 and then uses mouth-to-mouth to revive 81-year-old Alison Olson, who collapsed while playing video poker at a bar in Portland, Oregon. Go, Tonya! (Seriously.)

February 12, 1997: Harding claims to have been abducted at knifepoint by a "bushy-haired man" who then forced her to drive to a secluded area. Harding says she escaped by ramming the truck into a tree then fleeing through the woods. Coincidentally, this all happened on the eve of the 1997 U.S. Figure Skating Championships. Police found no evidence of an abduction.

January 6, 2000: Exactly six years to the day after the infamous Kerrigan attack, Harding's truck spins out on an icy road and she

In 1977 Dave Kingman played for the Yankees, Padres, Mets, and Angels.

lands in a ditch. Her boyfriend at the time, Darren Silver, allegedly threatens a press photographer who arrives on the scene.

February 24, 2000: Harding is booked on fourth-degree domestic violence charges after throwing a hubcap at her boyfriend (still Darren Silver). She's sentenced to three days in jail, 10 days of community service, and ordered to stay away from alcohol.

April 20, 2002: Tonya's cited for drunk driving and violation of parole after getting into an accident while behind the wheel of her truck.

2002: Harding is evicted from the home she rents.

2002: Tonya boxes Paula Jones on a Fox TV *Celebrity Boxing* special. She wins.

February 22, 2003: Apparently inspired by her bout with Paula Jones, Tonya makes her official women's professional boxing debut as the undercard of the Mike Tyson–Clifford Etienne fight. Tonya loses.

October 23, 2005: Harding calls 911, claiming she was attacked in her home by two masked assailants. It soon becomes clear that Tonya, possibly under the influence of alcohol, got into a fight with her boyfriend, Christopher Nolan. Nolan is charged with assault.

March 11, 2007: Harding calls 911, claiming four men and a woman were attempting to break into her car and stash rifles on her property. A neighbor later said Harding was probably just seeing animals. Harding's agent attributed the bizarre behavior to a combination of medications Harding had been prescribed.

The 1992 USA men's basketball Dream Team didn't call a single time-out en route to winning the gold medal.

SUPERSTITIOUS BASEBALL

A lot of athletes are superstitious— but for some reason, baseball seems to draw the nuts more than any other sport.

It's the sport that brought us the rally cap, lucky bats, and the unwritten rule that you never discuss a no-hitter or perfect game in progress. Not surprisingly, players tend to be cut from the same mold. Here are five of the most ridiculous.

Wade Boggs

Boggs entered the batting cage at exactly 5:17 p.m. every day and ran wind sprints at exactly 7:17 p.m. He took exactly 150 ground balls before every game. During home games, he took the exact same route from his position at third base to the dugout: He was so exact that he wore down a visible path on the field. And, though not Jewish, he drew *Chai* (the Hebrew word for life) in the batter's box before every at-bat.

Mark "The Bird" Fidrych

Fidrych became an immediate fan favorite and media sensation during his rookie season with the Tigers in 1976—and not just because of his striking resemblance to the *Sesame Street* character Big Bird. Fidrych would "manicure the mound," fixing and cleaning the dirt in between pitches. He constantly strutted around the mound. He was sure certain balls "had hits in them" and refused to pitch with them, demanding they be removed from the game.

Kevin Rhomberg

Kevin may have only played 41 games in the majors, but it was enough to cement his status as a legend when it comes to superstitious ballplayers. If you touched Rhomberg, he had to touch

In 1981 Fernando Valenzuela became the first player to win the Cy Young and Rookie of the Year awards in the same season.

you back—even on the base paths. If he got tagged out at first, he'd hang around until the end of the inning, then chase down the infielder and tag him back. Pitcher Rick Sutcliffe once reached under a bathroom stall and touched Rhomberg on the toe. Rhomberg didn't know who touched him—so he proceeded to go through the clubhouse, touching every player and nonplayer in the same place. Not to mention that he positively refused to make a right turn on the diamond, on the theory that when you run the bases you're always turning left. Pitcher Rick Mahler called Rhomberg the most superstitious player he ever met. Now, we think Rhomberg sounds a little more OCD than anything else, but who are we to argue with the Mahler.

Mike Hargrove

Before stepping into the batter's box, Hargrove would go through a lengthy routine, messing with his pants and sleeves, wiping at his lips, fidgeting with his batting gloves. And this wasn't a one-and-done thing—he repeated it after every pitch! This routine earned him one of the best nicknames in baseball history: the Human Rain Delay.

Steve Finley and Darin Erstad

Lots of players have little quirks, but the Finley-Erstad duo took it a step further. They shared a small leather pouch that held a number of minerals that they believed mystically protected against injury and slumps at the plate. Finley first received the pouch from Craig Counsell in 2002 when they played together on the Arizona Diamondbacks. Finley immediately went on a hot streak, batting .350 over the next three months. Finley then passed the pouch on to Erstad, who had been plagued by injuries all season. Erstad proceeded to go on a torrid hitting streak and remained injury-free for the rest of the season. Hard to argue with those results.

THE ICE BOWL

The story behind the NFL's coldest game.

No other major sport shakes off the weather like the NFL. No matter the conditions—rain, blizzard, hurricane, the NFL plays on (OK, not counting lightning, but c'mon . . .). And no game shows off just how tough the players, fans, and refs truly are like the famed Ice Bowl did.

The Green Bay Packers were hosting the Dallas Cowboys on December 31, 1967, for the NFL Championship—the winner would go on to face the AFL in the Super Bowl. At game time the temperature was -13°F with a wind chill of -48°F—to this day the coldest game in NFL history.

Frozen Tundra

First off, the new $80,000 heating system at the Packers' Lambeau Field was busted. Instead of keeping the field clear of ice, as was intended, it did the opposite, turning the field into one giant sheet of ice.

The referees had to do away with whistles after the head ref's whistle froze to his lips during the opening kickoff. The band couldn't play at pregame or halftime because the instruments kept getting stuck to the band members' lips; seven band members were even hospitalized with hypothermia! Dallas QB Don Meredith played the entire game and was then admitted to the hospital with pneumonia. Even today many players, including Hall of Fame Packers QB Bart Starr, say they can still feel the effects of the frostbite.

Frozen Fans

50,861 frigid fans crowded the stadium to witness the historic game. Four fans had heart attacks during the game, 14 more headed for the hospital to be treated for exposure, and one elderly man died.

In 1982 shortstop Joel Youngblood had two hits while playing for two different teams in two different cities on the same day.

The Game

The Packers took an early lead on two touchdown connections from Bart Starr to Boyd Dowler, but promptly gave back 10 points off of fumbles, leaving the score 14–10 at halftime. Coming out of the locker room for the third quarter, the weather was particularly bitter and neither team could muster much offense. Then, on the first play of the fourth quarter, the Cowboys took the lead on a 50-yard pass from Dan Reeves to Lance Rentzel off the old halfback option play.

Ice in His Veins

With 4:54 remaining, starting at the Packers 32, Bart Starr put together one of the most famous drives in NFL history, completing three key passes to get the Packers into scoring range. Chuck Mercein carried the ball for 8 to the Cowboys 3-yard line. The icy turf did in running back Donny Anderson as he twice lost his footing and was stuffed on consecutive plays. With 16 seconds left Starr called the Packer's final time-out and ran to the sideline to confer with Coach Lombardi. He asked for a QB sneak. Lombardi's reply? "Well, run it and let's get the hell out of here." It worked—Starr scored and the Packers won 21–17.

Later . . .

The Packers went on to defeat the Oakland Raiders in Super Bowl II. After the season, legendary Packers coach Vince Lombardi (the guy the Super Bowl trophy is named after) retired. Perhaps he was just too damn cold to continue? Lombardi had won three consecutive NFL championships and five in seven years, as well as the first two Super Bowls. This would also mark the end of the Packers dynasty. The following year they had a losing record, which many blamed on an aging (frostbitten?) roster. It was nearly 30 years before the Packers would return to NFL glory behind Brett Favre. The Dallas Cowboys continued to be a dominant force throughout the 1970s.

Canton Aplenty

Thirty-four Hall of Famers were involved in the game—10 players, two coaches, and one general manager.

Harmon Killebrew is the batter on the MLB logo.

HOSS AND HARDBALL

The story behind baseball's love of chewing tobacco—and how to spit like a pro!

Spitting through the Years

Chewing tobacco (aka wad, quid, chaw, plug, spit, chew, tobaccy, gagger, snarl, hoss, fatty, snead, varga) and baseball go together like bees and honey, peas and carrots, or Nomar and the DL. It's a classic baseball image: the fat bulge in a player's mouth, the deliberate spitting. Sure, it's a little gross, but there's no doubting it's a unique element of the game.

Chewing tobacco first became popular with players in the 1870s because it allowed their mouths to stay moist in the dusty ballparks, plus the thick saliva helped to soften their mitts. The habit all but disappeared in the 1880s, however, when it was discovered that it could help to spread tuberculosis. Apparently chewing tobacco's good, but it's not *tuberculosis good.* It reappeared in the 1920s with the invention of the spitball but then waned again in the '50s as tobacco companies paid ballplayers to promote cigarettes. It came storming back in the '70s, though, when the full health effects of smoking were realized (although chewing isn't much healthier). By the late '80s, nearly half of all professional ballplayers were packing lips on the field.

How To

First of all, chewing tobacco is really unhealthy and you shouldn't do it. It is most definitely not a safe alternative to smoking cigarettes. But if you must, here's how you go about it.

1. Pick a brand and flavor. Red-Man Golden Blend is pretty good for a rookie.

2. Go outside! Take this book with you if you have to (please—it could use a break from your bathroom). In a

In 1935 Jesse Owens set four track-and-field world records in 45 minutes.

moment you're going to have all sorts of black stuff coming out of your mouth and you don't want that on your floor.

3. OK, here goes. Open the bag. Pull out a few leaves and stuff them in our mouth, nestling the wad between your cheek and molars.

4. Start chewing, but DO NOT SWALLOW. If you do, be prepared to puke. Be careful and chew lightly. You don't want to chew it all up.

5. Pretty soon you'll have worked up a healthy (well, not healthy . . . let's say large) amount of spit. Lean forward, purse your lips, and spit. Mind your aim—don't want to drip on your shirt or ruin some poor stranger's Keds.

6. Good work, you're now successfully chewing tobacco. If you're enjoying your chaw, then keep going until the flavor is gone—should take about an hour or so. Most likely you're already miserable—if you are, call it quits. Tobaccy isn't for you.

7. Once you've had enough, spit the gunk out, rinse your mouth with water—again, be careful not to swallow, you made it this far.

8. How was it? If you hated it—you're normal. If you liked it—there's only one more step:

9. Buy a spittoon. It's a classy addition to any living room.

Back in the day, tennis was played with bare hands.

BAD FISHING JOKES

Hook, line, and stinker

No(ah) Good

God: Did you do any fishing today?
Noah: Yes, I did.
God: How'd it go?
Noah: Not so well . . . I only fished for a few minutes.
God: How come?
Noah: I only had two worms!

Watch Out

Q. What did the fish say when it swam into the wall?
A. DAM!

Sexy Time

A man came home from work and was greeted by his wife, dressed in a supersexy nightie and holding a pair of handcuffs.

"Tie me up," she whispered, "and I'll let you do anything you want."

He tied her up and went fishing.

Expensive Hobby

Two fishermen heard about a great fishing spot hundreds of miles away. They traveled all the way there, bought their bait, a six-pack, and rented a boat. After a long day of unsuccessful fishing they returned to the dock with only a single fish.

"One fish?!" the first fisherman said. "Damn, this thing cost us about $100 bucks!"

"Well, it's a good thing we didn't catch anymore!" said the second fisherman.

Joe DiMaggio had 361 career home runs and only 369 strikeouts.

Wrong-Hole, Fool

A fisherman woke up early, excited for a great day of ice fishing. He headed out onto the ice with his tent, his pick, and his rod, and began picking at the ice. A moment later he heard a powerful, booming voice: "THERE ARE NO FISH UNDER THE ICE!"

The guy looked around, shrugged, and went back to picking at the ice again. Then, again, he heard the voice: "THERE ARE NO FISH UNDER THE ICE!"

Now the guy was getting a little nervous. He looks up, "God, is that you?"

There's no answer, so he goes back to picking at the ice. Then, again, "THERE ARE NO FISH UNDER THE ICE!!"

Now the guy's really scared. He looks up and yells, "God! Is that you?

"NO, IT'S THE MANAGER OF THE ICE RINK!!!"

Before Cell Phones

Q. How do you get in touch with fish?
A. Just drop them a line.

Holy Fish

A young student arrives for Sunday school halfway through the lesson. The boy is rarely late, so the teacher asks him if anything was wrong.

"No," the boy said, "I was going to go fishing but my dad said I needed to go to church instead."

The teacher was impressed and asked the boy if his father told him why it was so important to go to church rather than go fishing.

The boy replied, "Yes, ma'am, he sure did. My dad said that he didn't have enough bait for the both of us."

Volleyball players jump an average of 300 times a match.

1968 OLYMPICS BLACK POWER SALUTE

The story behind one of sports' most iconic moments: John Carlos and Tommie Smith's Power to the People salute at the 1968 Summer Olympics in Mexico City.

The Protest

U.S. track-and-field athlete Tommie Smith had just won the 200-meter race, setting a new record with a time of 19.83 seconds. In third place was his teammate John Carlos. As they went to collect their medals, they made history:

The two stood on the podium—both shoeless, but wearing black socks, to represent black poverty. Around his neck Smith wore a black scarf, representing black pride. Carlos wore beads around his neck, which he later said "were for those individuals that were lynched, or killed that no one said a prayer for, that were hung and tarred. It was for those thrown off the side of the boats in the Middle Passage." Most powerful (and controversial) of all, they had their fists raised high in the air, in the traditional black power salute.

Response

The Olympic Committee described the protest as a "a deliberate and violent breach of the fundamental principles of the Olympic spirit" and ordered Smith and Carlos suspended from the team and banned from the games. The U.S. track team refused—so the Olympic Committee had the two expelled from the Games altogether.

Following the protest, Smith said, "If I win, I am American, not a black American. But if I did something bad, then they would say I am a Negro. We are black and we are proud of being black. Black America will understand what we did tonight."

Smith was right. Black America understood—but the rest of the country didn't. *Time* magazine ran a story accompanied by the Olympic logo, with the words "Angrier, Nastier, Uglier" replacing "Faster, Higher, Stronger." The *Associated Press* described their protest as "a Nazi-like salute" while Chicago columnist Brent Musburger called them "black-skinned storm troopers."

The record for most consecutive NFL games without being shut out is 420 by the San Francisco 49ers from 1977 to 2004.

Smith and Carlos, Later

Both Smith and Carlos continued on in athletics. Smith played pro football for the Bengals before becoming a physical education professor at respected Oberlin College in Ohio. In 1999 he received the Sportsman of the Millennium award.

Carlos tied the 100-meter world record the next year—then moved on to football, getting drafted as a wide receiver for the Philadelphia Eagles before a knee injury put a halt to his career. The late '70s were extremely hard on him: The stress and negative attention resulting from the Olympic moment led to his wife committing suicide in 1977. Today, Carlos is a track-and-field coach at a California high school.

Peter Norman

Often forgotten in the story is Peter Norman, the silver medal winner from Australia who stood on the podium between Smith and Carlos. Norman was sympathetic to their cause and wore an Olympic Project for Human Rights (OPHR) badge as a show of support. It was Norman who suggested that Smith and Carlos share the famous black gloves used in the salute, as Carlos had forgotten his. Norman suffered for his support. He was reprimanded by the Australian Olympic Committee and painted as a villain by the Australian media. Despite finishing third in Australia's '72 Summer Olympic Trials, he was not sent to the Olympic Games in Munich. A 1985 accident left him unable to race—depression and a struggle with alcoholism followed. He died in 2006; Smith and Carlos were pallbearers at his funeral.

With Time

Years later, African-American sociologist Harry Edwards said, "History is funny. It's one of the few realities in life that is clarified and comes into greater detail and perspective with distance. Everything else you see more, the closer you get to it."

Today, their protest is recognized as courageous and one of the defining movements of the civil rights and black power movements. A statue honoring the two men stands on the campus of San José State University.

New York Islander Ken Morro was the first player to win both an Olympic gold medal and a Stanley Cup title in the same year.

TAKE ME OUT TO THE BALL GAME

America's national pastime gets the anthem it deserves.

Sign, Sign, Everywhere a Sign

It was 1908 when songwriter and vaudeville entertainer Jack Norworth was riding the subway into Manhattan and passed by a sign that read BASEBALL TODAY— POLO GROUNDS. That was all the inspiration Norworth needed—he began scribbling on a spare scrap of paper and by the time he reached the city, the lyrics for "Take Me Out to the Ball Game" were complete.

Music Needed

You need more than lyrics to make a classic (unless you're talking "Sympathy for the Devil"), so Norworth hooked up with composer Albert Von Tilzer. Von Tilzer penned the melody and by the end of the year the song was a hit. Ironically, neither Norworth or Von Tilzer had ever attended a baseball game—and didn't for decades to come.

Harry Caray Makes It Happen

Though the song was popular at ballparks for years, it wasn't until fans heard Harry Caray's rendition that it became baseball's one true anthem. While working as the announcer for the Chicago White Sox, Caray made a habit of leaning out of the booth during the seventh-inning stretch and belting out the song to the nearby fans. As Caray said, "It's the only song I knew the words to!"

In 1976 White Sox owner Bill Veeck asked Caray to sing the song over the loudspeaker. Caray refused. When Veeck told Caray he had already recorded him singing it and was going to play it either way, Caray begrudgingly agreed to do it live. The fans loved it, sang along, and the rest is baseball history.

Gaylord Perry's manager once remarked, "There'll be a man on the moon before he hits a home run." On July 20, 1969, Perry hit his first career home run, within an hour after the moon-landing.

Cracker Jack of a Deal

Cracker Jacks have been a staple of baseball games ever since Norworth name-checked them with the line, "Buy me some peanuts and Cracker Jack." NPR correspondent Mike Pesca once estimated that this unintentional product placement ended up being worth $25 million in free advertising!

The Original

There have been a few different versions of the song over the years. And these days, most people only know the chorus. But here's the true, original song as penned by Jack Norworth in 1908.

Take Me Out to the Ball Game

Katie Casey was baseball mad,
Had the fever and had it bad.
Just to root for the home town crew,
Ev'ry sou'
Katie blew.
On a Saturday her young beau
Called to see if she'd like to go
To see a show, but Miss Kate said "No,
I'll tell you what you can do:"

Take me out to the ball game,
Take me out with the crowds;
Buy me some peanuts and Cracker Jack,
I don't care if I never get back.
Let me root, root, root for the home team,
If they don't win, it's a shame.
For it's one, two, three strikes, you're out,
At the old ball game.

Katie Casey saw all the games,
Knew the players by their first names.
Told the umpire he was wrong,
All along,
Good and strong.

In 1989 Willie Anderson set the single-game NFL record for receiving yards with 336.

When the score was just two to two,
Katie Casey knew what to do,
Just to cheer up the boys she knew,
She made the gang sing this song:

Take me out to the ball game,
Take me out with the crowd;
Buy me some peanuts and Cracker Jack,
I don't care if I never get back.
Let me root, root, root for the home team,
If they don't win, it's a shame.
For it's one, two, three strikes, you're out,
At the old ball game.

Hank Aaron hit 20 or more home runs in 20 seasons.

SIX DEGREES OF BACON

Kevin Bacon's been around—he's sort of the Todd Zeile of Hollywood. So, how far removed are your favorite athletes-cum-actors from Kevin Bacon?

Yogi Berra: Bacon number—2

Yogi Berra was in *That Touch of Mink* (1962) with Yvonne Peattie.

Yvonne Peattie was in *The Big Picture* (1989) with Kevin Bacon.

Terry Bradshaw: Bacon number—2

Terry Bradshaw was in *Failure to Launch* (2006) with Jessica Stone.

Jessica Stone was in *Loverboy* (2005) with Kevin Bacon.

O. J. Simpson: Bacon number—2

O. J. Simpson was in *Firepower* (1979) with Eli Wallach.

Eli Wallach was in *Mystic River* (2003) with Kevin Bacon.

Shaquille O'Neal: Bacon number—2

Shaq was in *Blue Chips* (1994) with Alfre Woodard.

Alfre Woodard was in *Beauty Shop* (2005) with Kevin Bacon.

Babe Ruth: Bacon number—3

Babe Ruth was in *The Pride of the Yankees* (1942) with Don Brodie.

Don Brodie was in *Murphy's Law* (1986) with David Hayman.

David Hayman was in *Where the Truth Lies* (2005) with Kevin Bacon.

Moscow's Lenin Stadium can seat more than 100,000 people.

Jim Brown: Bacon number—2

Jim Brown was in *Small Soldiers* (1998) with Sarah Michelle Gellar.

Sarah Michelle Gellar was in *The Air I Breathe* (2007) with Kevin Bacon.

Dan Marino: Bacon number—2

Dan Marino was in *Bad Boys II* (2003) with Michael Shannon.

Michael Shannon was in *The Woodsman* (2004) with Kevin Bacon.

Don Drysdale: Bacon number—3

Don Drysdale was in *Experiment in Terror* (1962) with James T. Callahan.

James T. Callahan was in *Hero* (1992) with Maury Chaykin.

Maury Chaykin was in *Where the Truth Lies* (2005) with Kevin Bacon.

Mike Ditka: Bacon number—2

Mike Ditka was in *UP, Michigan!* (2001) with Erik Estrada.

Erik Estrada was in *We Married Margo* (2000) with Kevin Bacon.

Bacon, Billy Bob's pig in *Varsity Blues* has a Bacon number of 3 (it's Bacon to the third power!):

Bacon (portrayed by unnamed pig actor) was in *Varsity Blues* with John Voight.

Jon Voight was in *Transformers* (2007) with Jamie McBride.

Jamie McBride was in *Beauty Shop* (2005) with Kevin Bacon.

On December 8, 1989, Ron Hextall became the first goalie in NHL history to record a goal while in net.

Zany Minor League Promotions

It takes big-time creativity to promote a small-town team.

Nobody Night: Charleston RiverDogs

Hoping to set the record for professional baseball's lowest attendance, the Charleston RiverDogs organized Nobody Night. Fans weren't allowed into the stadium until the fifth inning.

Awful Night: Altoona Curve

Every year, the Altoona Curve organization does its best to be the worst. The 2003 edition featured music by William Shatner and Milli Vanilli, Bubble Wrap giveaways; batting averages displayed as failed averages (for example, a .250 hitter's would be displayed as .750, since batter is really failing three quarters of the time); concession stands selling Spam and Tang; autograph sessions with noncelebrities; the honoring of historically bad teams like the '62 Mets; and laughable between-innings contests such as "Bald Guys Race for the Toupee."

Pre-planned Funeral Night: Hagerstown Suns

Two thousand people entered this 2003 contest awarding one lucky (unlucky?) fan with a prepaid funeral package valued at $6,500, including embalming, casket, funeral-home use, and a death certificate.

Auctioned At-Bat: St. Paul Saints

In 2004, the St. Paul Saints auctioned off an in-game at-bat on eBay, pulling in a final bid of $5,601. The winner, Marc Turndorf, popped out in his at-bat; however, the Saints manager liked Turndorf so much that he let him start the next game too. Turndorf still couldn't muster a hit, going 0-4.

The longest golf hole is the 1,007-yard sixth hole at Chocolay Golf Course in Michigan.

Silent Night—Charleston RiverDogs

Going for the record for quietest game ever the RiverDogs forbade talking for the first five innings. Fans were given signs reading "YEAH!" BOO!" and "HEY BEER MAN!" Instead of ushers, the stadium employed librarians and golf marshals who held up "Quiet Please" signs.

Richard Nixon Bobblehead Night: National Pride

The Nashua Pride honored the 32nd anniversary of the Watergate break-in by handing out 1,000 Nixon bobbleheads. Folks named Woodward or Bernstein (journalists Bob Woodward and Carl Bernstein were the best-known reporters covering the Watergate story) got into the game for free. The stadium even observed 18½ minutes of silence in recognition of the mysterious gap in the secret tape-recording of Nixon's talking about Watergate.

Corky Night: Fort Myers Miracle

Following Sammy Sosa's corked-bat incident, the Fort Myers Miracle handed out free sheets of cork to the first 505 (Sosa's total number of home runs up to that point) fans to arrive at the stadium. Plus, anyone unlucky enough to be named Corky (or Sammy or Sosa) was admitted for free.

Who Wants to Be a Turkish Millionaire?: Nashua Pride

The Pride held this one a few times while the Regis show was still a big hit. The Pride gave away a million Turkish lira (worth about $1.16) to fans who answered trivia questions correctly.

Vasectomy Night: Charleston RiverDogs

Here's one so inane it was called off before it even started. Had it gone off as planned, one lucky fan would have received a free vasectomy in celebration of Father's Day. Sadly, the event was cancelled after the mayor and a local Catholic bishop complained.

**Ted Williams Popsicle Night:
Bisbee-Douglas Copper Kings**

For the one-year anniversary of Ted Williams' head being cryogenically frozen, the Bisbee-Douglas Copper Kings gave out free popsicles to fans as a way to "honor" him.

Frank Gifford is in the Pro Football Hall of Fame twice: once as a player and once as a broadcaster.

SUPER BOWL CHILI

Every big-time chili eater has their favorite recipe. Here's ours.

Chili is the classic football dish. There are a million different recipes and, for the most part, you really can't go wrong with any of them (unless it's vegan or something). If you don't yet have your own, try ours. It's a little unique because, unlike most chili recipes, this isn't made in a pot, it's made in a skillet.

(Makes 4–6 bowls)

Chili Ingredients

1 tablespoon vegetable oil
1½ pounds lean ground beef
½ pound Italian sausage
½ cup chopped regular yellow onion
1 envelope (1¾ ounces) chili seasoning mix. (Note: most people prefer to go this route and pick up chili seasoning at the store, as it saves a lot of time. But if you're particularly motivated, see our recipe for seasoning below.)
½ cup water
1 can (14.5 ounces) chopped tomatoes (don't drain)
½ can (2 ounces) green chili peppers, drained
2 red chili peppers, chopped
1 can (15 ounces) kidney beans (don't drain)
1½ tablespoon brown sugar
hot ground pepper, to taste

Chili Seasoning

1 tablespoon paprika
2½ teaspoons seasoning salt
1 teaspoon ground cayenne pepper
½ teaspoon dried oregano
1 teaspoon garlic powder
1 teaspoon onion powder

In the mid-1800s, the world record for the mile run was 4 minutes, 12¾ seconds. Today that would be considered an above-average time for a high school runner.

½ teaspoon dried thyme
1 teaspoon seasoned pepper

Preparation

1. Heat oil in a large, heavy skillet.

2. Cook ground beef, sausage, and onions over medium heat until meat is no longer pink. Don't overcook. An offensive line should be tough, your meat should not.

3. Stir in chili seasoning mix, then add remaining ingredients.

4. Bring to a boil.

5. Reduce heat, cover, and simmer for 10 minutes.

6. Enjoy!

Serve in a small bowl with shredded cheese and corn bread. If you're a drinker, serve with beer. If not, ginger ale goes well.

In 1910 football teams were penalized 15 yards for an incomplete forward pass.

DO YOU KNOW YOUR BASEBALL NUMBERS?

Statistics are important to every sport. But baseball cherishes its numbers like no other. The big ones are legendary to fans. So . . . do you know your numbers?

1. How many games did Joe DiMaggio's historic hit streak last?

a. 48
b. 56
c. 54
d. 62

2. How many no-hitters did Nolan Ryan throw in his career?

a. 5
b. 6
c. 7
d. 8

3. What was Ty Cobb's lifetime batting average?

a. .399
b. .378
c. .349
d. .367

4. How many career home runs did Hank Aaron hit?

a. 742
b. 766
c. 755
d. 718

5. How many career wins did Cy Young have?

a. 511
b. 611
c. 588
d. 612

The word "sport" comes from the old French word *desport* meaning "leisure."

6. How many feet are there between bases on a major league field?

a. 80
b. 85
c. 90
d. 95

7. How many consecutive games did Cal Ripken play in?

a. 2,632
b. 2,819
c. 2,448
d. 2,218

8. How many bases did Rickey Henderson steal during the course of his career?

a. 1,406
b. 1,218
c. 1,497
d. 1,512

9. How many hits did Pete Rose have in his career?

a. 4,371
b. 4,017
c. 4,189
d. 4,256

10. What was Ted Williams's batting average in 1941?

a. .401
b. .404
c. .406
d. .407

Turn to page 356 for answers.

127 people ran the first New York City Marathon in 1970.

KNUCKLEBALL QUOTES

Musings on the quirky pitch that's oh-so-hard to hit.

"THERE ARE TWO THEORIES ON CATCHING THE KNUCKLEBALL . . . UNFORTUNATELY, NEITHER OF THE THEORIES WORK."
—CHARLIE LAU

"IT'S NEVER RELAXING, THAT'S FOR SURE. IT'S LIKE SNOWFLAKES—NO TWO ARE EVER ALIKE."
—JASON VARITEK, ON CATCHING TIM WAKEFIELD'S KNUCKLEBALL

"I'D RATHER HAVE MY LEG CUT OFF THAN DO THAT ALL DAY. YOU JUST HOPE IT HITS YOUR BAT IN A GOOD SPOT."
—JOHN KRUK, ON HITTING THE KNUCKLEBALL

"I NEVER WORRY ABOUT IT. I JUST TAKE MY THREE SWINGS AND GO SIT ON THE BENCH. I'M AFRAID IF I EVER THINK ABOUT HITTING IT, I'LL MESS UP MY SWING FOR LIFE."
—DICK ALLEN

"YOU DON'T CATCH THE KNUCKLEBALL, YOU DEFEND AGAINST IT."
—JOE TORRE

"TRYING TO HIT [KNUCKLEBALLER] PHIL NIEKRO IS LIKE TRYING TO EAT JELL-O WITH CHOPSTICKS. SOMETIMES YOU GET A PIECE BUT MOST OF THE TIME YOU GET HUNGRY."
—BOBBY MURCER

"WHAT'S A KNUCKLEBALL? A CURVE BALL THAT DOESN'T GIVE A DAMN."
—JIMMY CANNON

Prior to each NFL game, the home team provides the referee with 24 footballs.

"[IT'S LIKE] A BUTTERFLY WITH HICCUPS."
—WILLIE STARGELL

"YOU LIVE AND DIE WITH IT, AND HOPEFULLY, YOU DON'T DIE TOO MUCH."
—DENNIS SPRINGER

"TRYING TO HIT THAT THING IS A MISERABLE WAY TO MAKE A LIVING."
—PETE ROSE

"YOU SEE THE BALL AND YOU JUST KNOW YOU'VE GOT A BEAD ON IT, THEN YOU SWING, AND POOF, IT'S NOT THERE ANYMORE."
—RANDY HUNDLEY

"HITTING THAT THING IS LIKE TRYING TO CATCH A BUTTERFLY WITH A PAIR OF TWEEZERS."
—TIM McCARVER

"WAIT'LL IT STOPS ROLLING, THEN GO PICK IT UP."
—BOB UECKER, ON THE BEST WAY TO CATCH THE KNUCKLEBALL

In 1923 Henry Sullivan became the first American to swim the English Channel.

ALL ABOUT THE IDITAROD

Everything you need to know about the "Last Great Race on Earth."

History of the Trail

Alaska's historic Iditarod trail originally functioned as a supply route in the 1880s, running the 1,150 miles from the eastern coastal town of Seward through the vast countryside, filled with gold mining camps, to the towns and villages that sat on the west coast. Supplies came in from the coast, gold went out—all transported by dog sled. But by the late 1920s, the mines began to dry up and, after a while, the trail became unused. Then, with the invention of snowmobiles in the 1960s, dog sledders and the trail they traveled became all but extinct.

Today

The first true Iditarod race was held in 1973 as a way of remembering that original trail and honoring the men that worked it. Today, it is one of the most grueling and competitive races in the world. Mushers and their 16-dog teams race from Willow to Nome, traveling from city through artic tundra, completing the 1,161 mile trail in anywhere from eight to 15 days.

The Mushers

Mushers are the people on back of the sleds, directing the dogs. Most mushers that run the Iditarod are professionals who make a living training and selling sled dogs, instructing, speaking about the Iditarod experience, and cashing in on advertising opportunities. And there are amateur mushers: lawyers, surgeons, CEOs, and others looking for a taste of adventure. Still, these "amateurs" must have some experience; per the rules, every musher must successfully run three smaller races to qualify.

The Los Angeles Rams were the first pro football team to feature emblems on their helmets.

The Dogs

Before the race begins all dogs are thoroughly examined by veterinarians who check their heart, make sure they aren't pregnant, and check for any signs of steroids. Along the trail, volunteer veterinarians examine the dogs at checkpoints, looking for injuries and signs of exhaustion. Sled dogs can never be administered drugs and, as of 2005, the Iditarod claims that no mushers have ever been banned as a result of this rule. In addition, all dogs are implanted with microchips so they can be tracked and monitored throughout the race.

The Things They Carry

For the most part, mushers can pack whatever they want. But there are a few things every musher brings with him.

Heavy-duty sleeping bag

Artic parka

Ax

Snowshoes

Snow boots for the dogs, to protect against injury

Food for themselves and for the dogs

Tortoise vs. Hare

All sled teams are required to make three stops: one 24-hour rest at any of the trail's 25 checkpoints, one eight-hour stop at any checkpoint along the Yukon river, and one eight-hour stop at the White Mountain checkpoint. These three stops aside, the mushers can choose to race and rest, sled and sleep, as they please.

Iditarod Facts

- ✓ The origin of the word *Iditarod* isn't quite clear, but most historians recognize it as meaning clear water, with the trail's name being taken from the Shageluk Indians' word for the Iditarod River.
- ✓ Martin Buser grabbed the record for quickest race time in 2002, traveling the trail in 8 days, 22 hours, 46 minutes, and 2 seconds; in contrast musher Carl Huntington holds the record for slowest time to have won the race: 20 days, 15 hours, 2 minutes, and 7 seconds.
- ✓ The last musher to finish the race is awarded the Red Lantern—a nod to the kerosene lamps that hung outside stations when the trail was in use, guiding mushers carrying supplies. John Schultz owns the record for longest Red Lantern time: 32 days, 15 hours, 9 minutes, and 1 second.
- ✓ The closest finish was in 1978, when musher Dick Mackey finished just 1 second ahead of Rick Swenson. Judges determined the winner by the nose of the first dog across the finish line.
- ✓ Seventy-seven mushers finished the race in 2004, the most in the competition's history.

THE WING BOWL

Everything you need to know about Philly's face-stuffing fest.

Started in 1993 by Philadelphia talk-radio hosts Al Morganti and Angelo Cataldi, the Wing Bowl is probably best described as the Super Bowl of gluttony: 50 contestants stuffing themselves full of all the fried chicken wings their bodies can handle. What started out as a distraction for depressed Philadelphia sports fans has since become a major Philly event.

Wingin' It

The goal is simple: Eat as many wings as possible in the time allotted. The contest is split into two 14-minute periods, each followed by a short break, and then a final 2-minute period. At the end of the first period, the 10 contestants who ate the most move on to round 2. In the event of a tie, all tied eaters compete in a two-minute "eat-off." Whoever's eaten the most total wings at the end is declared the winner and walks away with a monumental stomachache and the grand prize (usually an SUV).

Getting There

If you suddenly decide it's your life's goal to enter the Wing Bowl, you've got two options.

> Call into Philadelphia's 610 WIP's "Morning Show" and successfully perform a timed eating stunt on the air; eating the entire McDonald's $1 menu in less than 6 minutes or drinking a bottle of maple syrup in 7 seconds, for example. Even if you blow your stunt, you're not out of luck. A handful of failed callers are invited to a "Studio Wing Off," and the winner gains entry.

Leading up to the Wing Bowl, local wing-eating competitions called "Wing Offs" are held in bars throughout the tri-state area. Win one of those and you move on to the real thing.

It's All in the Name

If you do happen to make it, you should probably come up with a cool nickname for yourself. Past contestant nicknames have included Wing Tut, Obi-Wing-Kenobi, and Ted Bundy Serial Wing Killer.

Bowl Facts

✓ All Wing Bowl wings are supplied by local barbeque joint Rib Ranch. Each year they supply more than 7,000 wings for the contest. That's nearly 1,000 pounds of fried chicken.

✓ All contest wings are distributed by scantily clad gals known as Wingettes. At the end of the contest the best Wingette is crowned Miss Wingette.

✓ No napkins allowed—the messier the better.

✓ In 2004, 99-pound Sonya "The Black Widow" Thomas became the first female to win the contest, scarfing down 167 wings. She lost her title the following year—by a single wing!

✓ Disqualified! Wing eaters must eat all meat directly off the bone—pick at your food and you're out of there.

✓ No vomiting allowed. As they say, "You heave, you leave."

✓ Bill "El Wingador" Simmons was the first competitor to win the Wing Bowl three times. He practiced for the event by chewing on frozen tootsie rolls to strengthen his jaw. When Joey Chestnut won in 2008 with 241 total wings, he had consumed roughly 14,500 calories—that's seven times the recommended daily amount!—in an hour.

In 1993 Ping-Pong pros Jackie Bellinger and Lisa Lomas set a world record by hitting 173 balls back and forth in a single minute.

Host Your Own!

All you need for your own exciting, nauseating event.

Wings

Wing-loving friends

Beer (to wash down wings)

Wingettes (optional, but recommended)

The biggest mass bungee jump on record happened on September 6, 1998, when 25 people jumped 171 feet off the Deutsche Bank Headquarters in Germany.

THE ALL-AMERICAN GIRLS PROFESSIONAL BASEBALL LEAGUE

Remember A League of Their Own? Great movie. Here's the full story.

Background

It was 1942, World War II was in full swing, and as a result, Major League Baseball was suffering. Minor league teams were folding—too many players were being drafted away to the military. League owners, particularly chewing-gum mogul and Chicago Cubs owner Philip K. Wrigley, feared that the trend would continue and major league parks would be forced to shut down for the duration of the war, costing the owners loads of money. Wrigley assigned Ken Sells, assistant to the Cubs' GM, to head up a committee to come up with ideas. Their solution? Girls' baseball.

The Game

First, the owners had to come up with a set of rules. The United States and Canada already had semi-pro women's softball teams, so they played around with their rules. Because softball wasn't fast enough, they extended the base paths and pitching distance to speed up the game and make it more like men's baseball. Plus, they took a queue from the men's rules and allowed runners to lead off base and steal. They also went with nine players instead of softball's usual 10.

The Girls

So they had rules—now they just needed teams and players. Thirty-year veteran player, manager, and owner Jim Hamilton was hired as head of procurement and set upon the task of finding and signing women from all over the U.S. and Canada. Scouts were sent to dozens of major cities. Hundreds upon hundreds of women showed up to show off their skills—280 of which were

Bill Clinton played rugby while at Oxford, where it was said that he was "by no means athletic, in fact a bit lumpy, but made an excellent second-row forward."

invited to the final tryouts in Chicago. Finally, 60 were chosen as the first women to ever play professional baseball.

The ladies were expected to be ladies. Every day after practice the girls attended classes at Helena Rubenstein's Beauty Salon, where they were taught lessons in etiquette and hygiene. It was important that each girl be as attractive as possible. The uniforms sure didn't hurt: short skirts and one-piece flared tunics, complete with knee-high socks and a ball cap.

Four teams were put together: the Racine Belles (Wisconsin), the Kenosha Comets (Wisconsin), the Rockford Peaches (Illinois), and the South Bend Blue Sox (Indiana). Teams consisted of 15 players, a manager, a business manager, and a female chaperone (to keep the ladies acting like ladies). Team owners went out and hired notable men's sports figures as managers—specifically Johnny Gottselig, Bert Niehoff, Josh Billings, and Eddie Stumpf. Player salaries ranged from $45 to $85 a week—not too shabby for the time.

Play Ball!

League play officially kicked off on May 30, 1943, with the South Bend Blue Sox taking on the Rockford Peaches and the Kenosha Comets battling the Belles in Racine. The regular season was 108 games long—stretching from mid-May to September 1, culminating in a playoff series to determine a league champion.

Almost immediately, the league was a hit, with an unexpected surge of fans taking in the first season. Everyone was blown away by how well the girls played the game. The league capitalized on the wartime patriotism sweeping the country and relied heavily on selling the girls as classic "All-American Girls."

As the years went on, the league continued to expand—at the league's peak, ten teams competed. By 1944, however, it was readily apparent that Major League Baseball would not be forced to disband because of the war. Seeing this, Wrigley lost interest and sold the league to Chicago advertising exec Arthur Meyerhoff. Meyerhoff put together a league board of directors with representatives from each franchise, giving each club a say in the direction of the league.

In 1999 four members of the Arizona Airspeed Skydiving Team managed to arrange themselves in a record 39 different formations before finally landing.

Under Meyerhoff the league flourished, with teams attracting two to three thousand fans per game. An estimated 10,000 people attended a July 4, 1946, doubleheader. By 1948 the teams were attracting nearly a million paying fans per season.

The End

But it was all downhill after 1949. The team directors voted to purchase the league from Arthur Meyerhoff and operate each team independently. Without organized control of publicity, promotion, and player development, the league began to self-destruct. Televised major league games (real baseball, with real war heroes) in 1950 were another blow to the faltering league. When the 1954 season ended only five teams were left and the league was all but done.

In the end, the league not only provided more than 600 women with the opportunity to play baseball in the national spotlight but also inspired a great film 40 years later.

CRAZY MATT CHRISTOPHER PLOTS

As his official Web site says, "Matt Christopher is the writer young readers turn to when they're looking for fast-paced, action-packed sports novels." Here are a few of our favorite Christopher plots, taken from the publisher's official synopsis.

The Hockey Machine: Abducted by a "fan" and forced to become a member of a professional junior hockey team, 13-year-old star center Steve Crandall quickly realizes that he must play not only to win but also to survive.

The Dog That Stole Football Plays: Mike's football team is really put to the test when Harry, his telepathic dog, has to stay home. Can the team win without Harry's supernatural advice?

Skateboard Tough: When Brett's skateboarding abilities dramatically and inexplicably improve after using the Lizard, a skateboard that mysteriously unearthed in his front yard, his friends start to wonder if the skateboard is haunted.

Tough to Tackle: More than anything, Boots Raymond wants to be a quarterback for the Apollos. But because of his size, the coach assigns him to a tackle position. Boots rebels and almost quits the team, but his brother intercepts and teaches Boots the valuable lessons about commitment and teamwork that he learned from being a soldier in Vietnam.

Ice Magic: The twins' toy hockey game seems to be magic as it plays games identical to the real ones before they even happen.

Soccer Hero: Rob Lasher is just an ordinary soccer player, good at the game, but not great. Then one afternoon, he saves his coach's life in front of all his teammates. Suddenly, he's the team's hero.

Paintball was first played in 1980 in New Hampshire.

As some members of his team and the rest of the town continue to laud Rob's heroic act, Rob realizes he doesn't want the attention and any unearned accolades that come with it. Kids will learn that doing what is right should be the norm, not the exception.

Double Play at Short: Twelve-year-old Danny thinks that there is something very familiar about the girl who plays shortstop on the team he faces during the championship series, and his curiosity leads him to a surprising discovery about his own adoption.

Soccer Scoop: Who's Making a Fool of Mac?: Mac is the best goalie on the team—and he's not afraid to let everyone know it. Then someone on the school paper creates a new comic strip that caricatures Mac and his performance on and off the field, sending him on a chase for the artist before things get out of hand.

Mountain Bike Mania: Sixth-grader Will is looking for an afterschool activity, but when he joins the mountain-biking club, his old friendships and values are challenged.

On January 8, 1949, at Salisbury, Connecticut, the Salisbury Hill skiing record was broken 21 times—the most times any sports record has been broken in a single day.

"IT'S PRACTICALLY SCIENTIFIC 'SHINNEY' ON ICE SKATES."

Leading up to the 1896–1897 hockey season, the *New York Athletic Club Journal* published this review of the budding sport. The piece is a unique glimpse at the early days of the sport and a great look at the language used in turn-of-the-century sports-writing. By the way, shinney was an early, informal precursor to hockey, played on the street with wooden sticks.

Hockey

First published in the *New York Athletic Club Journal*, April 1896

> The *Journal* takes pleasure in announcing a new pastime for the wearers of the Mercury Foot in the game of hockey, adding another sport to the many fostered by the New York A. C. The game is practically scientific "shinney" on ice skates, and is vastly popular with our cousins across the border, where ice-skating is indulged in from the first of December until late in the spring.
>
> A number of games were played in this vicinity last winter, meeting with such pronounced approval as to insure hockey a prominent place among winter sports.
>
> Members of the New York A. C. were largely instrumental for the introduction of the game to the New York public, as among the members of the team which proved successful in every game which it played last season were A. R. Pope, A. L. Fry, Beverley Bogert, and E. M. Littell, conspicuous wearers of the Mercury Foot in aquatic and field sports.
>
> Recognizing the embryo talent in the club ranks, the Athletic Committee has decided to place a team in the field to represent the club, appreciating the fact that with the nucleus already developed in the club, a "seven" may be

formed that will prove second to none. Athletic Director Giannini, who has shown a keen interest in the game, has the matter in charge, and it is requested that all good skaters desiring to play will forward their names to him at once.

The game will be found interesting to the most exacting critic, his attention being fully occupied through every moment of play. From the time the referee blows his whistle signifying the start, the spectators' nerves are kept at a tension not relaxed until the call of time, there being very little or nothing of the element of "time calls," which have proved such a fruitful cause or criticism in football. Occasionally a skate will be broken, necessitating five or ten minutes' delay, which is fortunately, however, very rare; or a player insisting on continually being off-side will be sent from the ice, causing a momentary stoppage. Otherwise the time is employed in brilliant rushes, quick checking and clever passing.

Its requisites are few—a clear sheet of hard ice, invigorating atmosphere, and a number of quick and steady skaters, who, when aided and abetted by an enthusiastic audience, will furnish as interesting an evening's entertainment as any sport lover could desire.

The principles of the game are so simple as to be readily understood by even the most disinterested. Seven men compose a team—four forwards, or rushers, a cover-point (better understood, perhaps, by the term quarter-back), who backs up and feeds the forwards, a point whose main duty is to assist in goal defense, and a goal-keeper. Goal posts are erected at either end of a rink, placed six feet apart and not over four feet high, in which space the goalkeeper stands. Each player is equipped with a "stick," made preferably of second-growth ash, length to suit the holder, resembling in form, somewhat, a shepherd's crook, except it is less curved on the end, allowing for two or three inches' play on the ice. An ordinary pair of skates will suffice, although the regulation "hockey blade," its runner being almost straight, is better adapted for the quick turns and sudden stops necessary in the game. The "puck" is a circular disk of hard rubber nine inches in circumference and an inch thick, and it is the object of the game to place it through the opponent's goal posts.

Unlike shinney, a better result is obtained by shoving or scooping the puck than by striking it; in fact, the rules do not permit of the stick being lilted higher than the shoulder. The main object of an expert player, and difficult of accomplishment, is to "lift" the puck, making it travel over the heads of his opponents a distance of forty or fifty yards before striking the ice. Two halves of thirty minutes each constitute time of play, and the game is in charge of a referee and two umpires.

The formation of a league for the Metropolitan District is now in progress, and arrangements have been made for two or three nights a week practice for the New York A. C. team at the St. Nicholas Rink, Sixty-sixth Street and Columbus Avenue, when some excellent sport may be anticipated.

In baseball a forfeited game is recorded as a 9–0 score.

BIG BOYS AND HEAVY HITTERS

We've always had a special place in our hearts for overweight, out-of-shape pros (who or may may not remind us of ourselves).

John Daly

Daly is a prime example of professional athletes that don't look the least bit athletic . . . and that's why he love him. We don't see him losing the weight anytime soon—he wouldn't play the same without it! Daly went so far as to claim that his girth improves his golf game, once saying, "Actually it has helped because my right arm hugs this fat belly right here and it never gets out of place now."

Tony Stewart

Driver Helio Castroneves introduced fence-climbing as a post-race victory celebration after winning the 2000 Detroit Grand Prix. Soon, big boy Tony Stewart began duplicating the fence-climb celebration, prompting Castroneves to jokingly say, "The only thing I want is to get him on a diet, and get him in better shape. He doesn't look good when he climbs the fence with that big, unfit shape."

Just don't call Tony fat to his face though: He once threw a punch at driver Kurt Busch after he made a crack about the size of his belly.

Charles Barkley

They didn't call him the Round Mound of Rebound for nothing. And hey, at least he knows he's big: After Indiana Pacers' Jermaine O'Neal named himself the best forward in the NBA, Barkley said "Well, I think I am skinny, but that doesn't mean I am."

His size aside, that doesn't mean he loves all his fellow "round mounders." Witness this classic exchange with former pro Kenny Smith.

The Weissfluhjoch-Kublis Parsenn course in Switzerland is the longest downhill ski run in the world—9 miles.

Barkley: "I'm so sick of fat people."

Smith: "Why? You can't live with yourself?"

Barkley: "First of all, they killed Oreos. You know they can't make the Double Stuf Oreos anymore because fat people can't keep their mouths shut. Now they're killing the McDonald's Supersize. Can you believe that? Just because fat people are lazy and don't work out and can't keep their mouths shut, they have to ruin it for everybody. They'll probably kill ice cream next! Is that my fault they can't stop eating? I'm so sick of these fat people suing these companies. Stop eating!"

John Kruk

The country-music-loving, pick-up-truck-driving Kruk was never one to hold his tongue. Once, when criticized for his weight problems and the amount of drinking he did as an athlete, he responded "I ain't an athlete, lady. I'm a baseball player."

Chicago Sox fans once serenaded him with "Fee fi fo fum, John Kruk is a big fat bum."

Cecil Fielder

Fielder looked to be pushing 320 pounds by the end of his career. It took him 1,096 games to steal his first base—that's almost seven seasons (it's also a record). And when he did, he said, "The pressure is off now. [Manager Buddy Bell] might start moving me a little more now that he has seen me run. Hopefully he won't." Yeah . . . he didn't.

His son, first baseman Prince Fielder, appears to be following in his father's (rather large) footsteps.

William "The Refrigerator" Perry

The Fridge has the honor of owning the largest Super Bowl ring in history—size 25! To put that in perspective, the average ring size is 13, according to ring manufacturer Jostens. Rap group the Fat Boys even released a song about him titled "Chillin' with the Refrigerator." That's a lot of fat in one song.

Tennis player Ilie Nastase was the first pro athlete to sign with Nike.

Perry once said, "I take the food out of the fridge, put it in my rotisserie, and put it back in the Fridge."

Fat Facts

- ✓ First baseman Walter Young is the fattest professional baseball player ever—listed at 6-foot-2 and 322 pounds, that leaves him with a body mass index (BMI) of 38.2 (30 is considered "obese"). That's the highest BMI of any major leaguer in history.
- ✓ The lightest ever was 3-foot-7 Eddie Gaedel, the dwarf who made one famous at-bat for the St. Louis Browns in 1951. He was 65 pounds.

Bigisms

"A WAIST IS A TERRIBLE THING TO MIND."
—RELIEF PITCHER TERRY "FAT TUB OF GOO" FORSTER

"I ONLY EAT TWO MEALS A DAY, I JUST LIKE SNACKS."
—LEFTFIELDER WILLIE HORTON
(IN RESPONSE TO A QUESTION ABOUT HIS WEIGHT GAIN)

"MR. PRESIDENT [DWIGHT EISENHOWER], I WAS ON A DIET FOR 25 YEARS. NOW THAT I'M MAKIN' SOME MONEY, I'M MAKIN' SURE THAT I EAT ENOUGH TO MAKE UP FOR THE LEAN YEARS."
—PITCHER DIZZY DEAN
(TO THE PRESIDENT, WHEN ASKED WHY HE WEIGHED NEARLY 300 POUNDS)

GOOD EATS!

Competitive eating is one of the fastest growing sports in the world. Here are a few of the more bizarre eating records, and the eaters who hold them. Check out the official International Federation of Competitive Eating (yes, such a thing does exist!) Web site at www.ifoce.com for even more.

Vienna Sausage

Record: 8.31 pounds Armour Vienna Sausage—10 minutes
Eater: Sonya Thomas

Baked Beans

Record: 6 pounds—1 minute, 48 seconds
Eater: Don Lerman

Beef Tongue

Record: 3 pounds, 3 ounces pickled beef tongue—12 minutes
Eater: Dominic Cardo

Blueberry Pie (no hands)

Record: 9.17 pounds blueberry pie—8 minutes
Eater: Patrick Bertoletti

Buffet

Record: 5.5 pounds buffet food—12 minutes
Eater: Crazy Legs Conti

Burritos

Record: 15 BurritoVille burritos—8 minutes
Eater: Eric Booker

Polo can be played on horses, elephants, or bicycles.

Butter

Record: 7 quarter-pound sticks salted butter—5 minutes
Eater: Don Lerman

Cabbage

Record: 6 pounds, 9 ounces giant cabbage—9 minutes
Eater: Charles Hardy

Chili Cheese Fries

Record: 8 pounds, 2 ounces Wienerschnitzel Chili Cheese Fries—10 minutes
Eater: Sonya Thomas

Corned Beef and Cabbage

Record: 10.63 pounds corned beef and cabbage—10 Minutes
Eater: Patrick Bertoletti

Cow Brains

Record: 57 brains (17.7 pounds)—15 minutes
Eater: Takeru Kobayashi

Cranberry Sauce

Record: 13.23 pounds jellied cranberry sauce—8 Minutes
Eater: Juliet Lee

Crawfish

Record: 331 crawfish—12 minutes
Eater: Chris Hendrix

Deep-Fried Okra

Record: 9.75 pounds Deep Fried Okra—10 Minutes
Eater: Sonya Thomas

Toxophily is another word for the sport of archery.

RATTERMAN'S RADIO

The origin of the coach-to-quarterback radio helmet might surprise you.

Sneaky Frequency

The in-helmet coach-to-quarterback radio was the brainchild of two Ohio inventors, John Campbell and George Sarles. In 1956 they approached Browns coach Paul Brown with an idea for a wireless sideline-to-quarterback radio system. They theorized that with a receiver in the QB's helmet and a transmitter on the sidelines, Coach Brown could communicate directly with his QB, saving valuable time. Coach Brown, meticulous and disciplined, loved the idea because, as one player said, "Now you don't have to worry about your quarterback talking back to you. All he can do is listen."

Testing, Testing . . .

Brown ordered the two to test their device. Sarles went off to the woods with the helmet while Campbell stayed behind with the transmitter. Soon, the signal weakened and the communication broke off. Campbell set off to find his partner, only to discover that a local cop had intercepted the signal on his car's scanner! Luckily for Campbell and Sarles, the cop was a Browns fan and agreed to keep his mouth shut. The two inventors switched the frequency, presented it to Brown, and the plan was a go.

Ratterman's Head Gets the Lion's Share of the Damage

Brown unveiled the device in an exhibition game against the Detroit Lions. Unfortunately for Browns quarterback George Ratterman, the Lions had heard about the radio scheme and had come up with a solution: Get Ratterman to the ground and kick him in the head as hard as they could until the receiver broke. A frustrated Ratterman ended up calling over the Lions lineman, removing the helmet and slamming it against the ground, saying,

Lawn darts were banned in the U.S. in 1988 after being responsible for the deaths of three children.

"Look, you can't destroy the radio this way. It takes a lot of punishment." The Lions didn't care and the headhunting continued.

Giant Problems

Word of "Ratterman's Radio" had gotten around, and the Giants, who played the Browns in the third game of the season, headed into the match prepared. They scooped up former Cleveland halfback Gene Filipinksi off of waivers. Together with Giants staff member Bob Topp, who operated a radio receiver on the sidelines, they relayed the Browns calls to Giants coach Tom Landry. Landry then yelled the plays to his defensive players on the field. It worked—the Giants frustrated the Browns offensive all afternoon on the way to a 21–9 victory.

Transmission Interrupted

The experiment ended soon thereafter: By midseason NFL commissioner Bert Bell banned helmet radio devices throughout the league.

Signal Resurrected

In 1994, nearly 40 years after Ratterman's radio made its debut, the rules committee voted to allow coach-to-quarterback radio helmets in the game. Today, Ratterman's helmet sits on display at the Pro Football Hall of Fame in Canton.

BARKLEY BITES

Charles Barkley played forward for sixteen years in the NBA, first as a 76er and then as a Phoenix Sun and Houston Rocket. At 6-foot-6 and nearly 300 pounds, he was known as the Round Mound of Rebound. He also mused a lot. So here you go, musings from the Round Mound of Rebound.

"I DON'T THINK OF MYSELF AS GIVING INTERVIEWS. I JUST HAVE CONVERSATIONS. THAT GETS ME IN TROUBLE."

"I KNOW I'M NEVER AS GOOD OR BAD AS ONE SINGLE PERFORMANCE. I'VE NEVER BELIEVED IN MY CRITICS OR MY WORSHIPPERS, AND I'VE ALWAYS BEEN ABLE TO LEAVE THE GAME AT THE ARENA."

"SOMEBODY HITS ME, I'M GOING TO HIT HIM BACK. EVEN IF IT DOES LOOK LIKE HE HASN'T EATEN IN A WHILE."

"I DON'T KNOW WHAT THAT GAS IS MADE OF, BUT IT CAN'T SMELL ANY WORSE THAN ERNIE JOHNSON'S GYM BAG."

"I LOVE NEW YORK CITY; I'VE GOT A GUN."

"I THINK THAT THE TEAM THAT WINS GAME 5 WILL WIN THE SERIES. UNLESS WE LOSE GAME 5."

"I'M NOT A ROLE MODEL. JUST BECAUSE I DUNK A BASKETBALL DOESN'T MEAN I SHOULD RAISE YOUR KIDS."

"IF SOMEBODY HITS YOU WITH AN OBJECT, YOU SHOULD BEAT THE HELL OUT OF THEM."

In the year 2000, Canadians spent a grand total of 4,489,296 days ice fishing!

"Kids are great. That's one of the best things about our business, all the kids you get to meet. It's a shame they have to grow up to be regular people and come to the games and call you names."

"My family got all over me because they said Bush is only for the rich people. Then I reminded them, 'Hey, I'm rich.' "

"If I weren't earning $3 million a year to dunk a basketball, most people on the street would run in the other direction if they saw me coming."

"My initial response was to sue her for defamation of character, but then I realized that I had no character."

"Poor people cannot rely on the government to come to help you in times of need. You have to get your education. Then nobody can control your destiny."

"Sometimes that light at the end of the tunnel is a train."

"The only difference between a good shot and a bad shot is if it goes in or not."

"We don't need refs, but I guess white guys need something to do."

"You know [the world's] going to hell when the best rapper out there is white and the best golfer is black."

"These are my new shoes. They're good shoes. They won't make you rich like me, they won't make you rebound like me, they definitely won't make you handsome like me. They'll only make you have shoes like me. That's it."

"I don't care what people think. People are stupid."

San Francisco 49ers great Steve Young is the great-great-grandson of Mormon leader Brigham Young.

BEST OF THE BEST: *KINGPIN*

A look at the 10-pin comedy classic.

You know the deal. We pick the best flick for each sport. *Kingpin* was an easy choice. First of all, there aren't a whole lot of bowling movies. Second of all, there don't need to be, because *Kingpin* rules.

The Stats

Released: 1996
Director: Peter and Bobby Farrelly—the Farrelly brothers
Writer: Barry Fanaro and Mort Nathan
Starring: Woody Harrelson, Randy Quaid, Bill Murray, Vanessa Angel, Chris Elliot
Box Office Haul: $25 million

Tagline

"You wouldn't want to meet these pinheads in an alley."

The Basics

Woody Harrelson is Roy Munson, a once-promising bowler whose career (and life) came to a screeching halt in 1979 when he lost his hand after rival Ernie "Big Ern" McCracken (Bill Murray) left him high and dry during a hustle gone bad. Fifteen years later, Roy's a broken-down drunk, hawking bowling equipment and hustling for rent money. That is, until he meets Ishmael (Randy Quaid), an Amish bowler with an ace stroke. Roy convinces the naive Ishmael that he needs a manager, and together they hit the road, headed to Vegas for a shot at a $1 million championship tournament. Along the way they hook up with streetwise sexpot Claudia (Vanessa Angel), do their best to dodge an angry mobster, and tangle with Big Ern McCracken.

Hang gliders were used as the first spy planes.

Loyal Fans

Roger Ebert. Surprisingly, Ebert loves this movie. In his review he said, "Movies like this require a kind of daring. The Farrellys cut no corners and took no prisoners. *Kingpin* provides the release of many kinds of laughter, including the most rare: disbelieving."

Memorable Moment

Roy, forced to take over for Ishmael in the championship, bowls for the first time in years. He's forced to bowl with his rubber prosthetic hand and, of course, the hand gets stuck in the ball's holes, rips off, and rolls down the lane, attached to the ball.

Classic Quotes

Roy: How about a gross of fluorescent condoms for the novelty machine in the men's room? I mean, those are fun even when you're alone. We're talkin' the hula hoop of the '90s.
Lancaster Bowl Manager: Look, I've told you. We don't need nuthin'. We don't even have a novelty machine in the men's room anymore.
Roy: And you call yourselves a bowling alley?

Roy: Just because you spend most of your time in the missionary position . . . doesn't make you a missionary.

Claudia: Look, Mr. Munster, you're not exactly the smartest guy I ever ran across.
Roy: Oh yeah? And who are you, Alfred Einstein?

ESPN announcer: So, Roy, where have you been for the last 15 years?
Roy: Well, I uh, well, ya see, I uh . . . drinking. Lot a drinking.
ESPN announcer: I see. Well, are you still drinking?
Roy: No. I uh . . . I put . . . uh . . . why, you buying?

At one point Tokyo banned the hula hoop because it was causing so many traffic accidents.

Ernie McCracken: "It all comes down to this roll. Roy Munson, a man-child, with a dream to topple bowling giant Ernie McCracken. If he strikes, he's the 1979 Odor-Eaters Champion. He's got one foot in the frying pan and one in the pressure cooker. Believe me, as a bowler, I know that right about now, your bladder feels like an overstuffed vacuum-cleaner bag and your butt is kinda like an about-to-explode bratwurst."
Roy: "Hey! Do you mind? I wasn't talking when you were bowling."
Ernie McCracken: "Was I talking out loud? Was I? Sorry. Good luck."

Roy: "Are you sure this is legal?"
Ernie McCracken: "I don't know. It's fun though, isn't it?"

Ishmael: "You really should try to quit [smoking], Mr. Munson. They say it's bad for your heart, your lungs, it quickens the aging process."
Roy: "Is that right? Who's done more research than the good people at the American tobacco industry? They say it's harmless. Why would they lie? If you're dead, you can't smoke."

Roy: The world can really kick your ass. I only have a vague recollection of when it wasn't kickin' mine.

In the Know

Next time you're watching the movie with your buddies, look smart by tossing out these facts.

✓ Roger Clemens plays Skidmark, the local tough at the diner who loses his cool and picks a fight with Ishmael. Early signs of 'roid rage? We kid, we kid. . . .

- ✓ Several PBA bowlers appear in the film, including Parker Bohn III and Mark Roth.
- ✓ Bill Murray did all his own bowling for the film and really bowled three strikes in a row for the film's climax. The actors in the crowd were rooting for Murray and their cheers are genuine.

And Second Place Goes to . . .

Our choice for second-best bowling movie has to be *Sorority Babes in the Slimeball Bowl-O-Rama* (1988). In need of a laugh? Check out the box art.

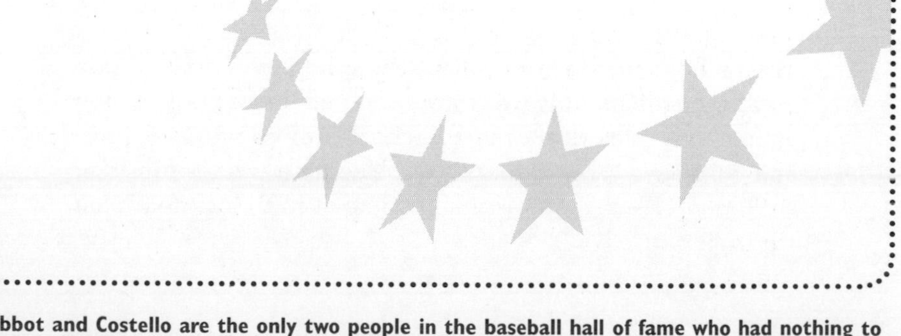

Abbot and Costello are the only two people in the baseball hall of fame who had nothing to do with the actual sport.

HOST YOUR SUPER BOWL OFFICE POOL, BOX STYLE

You don't even have to be a sports nut to enjoy the Super Bowl, you just have to like money. So get your friends, enemies, and coworkers involved and host a Super Bowl pool!

What Is It?

Never done a Super Bowl box? Don't worry, it's simple.

It's a pool in which people pay a certain fee (i.e., a bet) to buy a "box" in a 10-by-10 grid. The horizontal columns and vertical rows are assigned to one of the two teams in the Super Bowl.

Everyone pays for their boxes—commonly, anywhere from $1 to $100. Each person picks a box or boxes (as many as they want), writes in their name, and pays up. Once all 100 boxes are filled, numbers are drawn to go alongside each of the 10 columns and 10 rows. That's it.

Do It!

1. Create a 10-by-10 grid. Feel free to do this on your own, but if you're lazy, we've got one for you on the next page. Write the name of one Super Bowl team along the top and the other along the side. If the teams haven't been determined yet, just write AFC on the top and NFC on the side.

2. Find your bettors, have them pick squares by writing their names inside, and collect their money. A dollar a box or $5 a box is usually pretty good for an office pool. Which boxes they pick don't matter, the numbers will be determined once all the squares are filled, so it's all random. Still, people are superstitious, so be sure to let them pick on their own.

An All-Star Bonus

Your very own Super Bowl box.

AFC TEAM

NFC TEAM

3. If they're confused, explain the scoring system to them. In football pools, only the last number of a team's score is used to determine the winning square. Let's say Suzie from HR's box corresponds to Patriots 7 and Cowboys 9. So, if at the end of any quarter, the Patriots have a score ending in 7 (7, 17, 27, etc.) and the Cowboys have a score ending in 9 (9, 19, 29, etc.), Suzie wins that quarter.

   Let's say you charge $1 dollar a box. Your payout might work like this:

   $10 to whoever has the winning score at the end of the first quarter

   $20 for the second quarter

   $30 for the third quarter

   $40 for the final score

4. Once you've sold all your boxes, it's time to draw numbers for each row of squares. Draw 10 numbers going down and 10 numbers across, so that each square has two corresponding numbers. Pick the numbers from a hat, so it's totally random—and if you're buying boxes yourself, it's important to have a few other bettors around when you do this so no one's suspicious if you end up winning.

5. Once the grid is entirely filled out, make copies and hand one out to everyone who's in the pool so they can follow along during the big game.

6. That's it! Now the fun part. Sit back, watch the game, and pray no one kicks any last-minute field goals to blow your score.

In football a forfeited game is recorded as a 1–0 score.

BOOOO!!!

A history of hecklers.

The Olden Days

In sixth-century B.C., audiences would cheer and jeer playwrights as a way of judging which comedy or tragedy was best, applauding for what they liked and whistling and hollering for the bad stuff. Audience participation was seen as a civic duty.

In ancient Rome, heckling became a matter of life and death at the gladiatorial games. The response of the crowd would often determine whether a competitor lived or died—enough whistling and hissing, and a gladiator would end up tiger food. Random fact: Contrary to popular belief, in the gladiator days it was actually thumbs-up that meant kill the gladiator and thumbs-down that meant let him live, as in "swords down."

The actual English word *boo* first appeared in the 19th century to describe the low, mooing sound of a cow. Later, it took on its more modern use.

Nest of Death

Before its implosion in 2004, the 700 section at Philadelphia's Veteran's Stadium was the center of the heckling universe. Philly fans are infamously brutal. Some of their worst offenses:

Cheering as Dallas Cowboy Michael Irvin lay immobile on the field with a career-ending spinal injury

Pelting J. D. Drew with D batteries because he held out after the Phillies drafted him and ended up signing with the Cardinals

Pelting a halftime Santa Claus with snowballs

And worst of all is when Matthew Scott, receiver of the first successful hand transplant in America, was invited to throw out the first pitch at the Phillies home opener in 1999. The pitch, thrown from his new hand, just barely reached the plate—still quite remarkable. But of the course the Philly fans let him have it . . .

How To

Whether you're at the game or watching at home with your buddies, you have to be able to heckle with some authority. There are two groups who will be on the receiving end of your fury: the players and the refs. When dealing with umps, try these:

I thought only horses slept standing up!

I've gotten better calls from my ex-wife!

You couldn't call a cab!

When dealing with the players, give these general taunts a shot:

The steroids obviously ain't working!

What's a' matter? You trying to beat the spread?

Better grab a straw, buddy, you suck!

When all else fails, try starting a chant (note: use only at stadium—in your house, you'll look crazy):

Over Rated! (clap, clap, clap-clap-clap)

da da da da da HEY! YOU SUCK!

In 1957 the Milwaukee Braves became the first baseball team to win the World Series after being relocated.

THE SPORTS NUMERIST 41–60

The games. By the numbers. Forty-one through sixty.

41: Jersey number of fictional running back Billy Cole, who, in the violent opening to the Bruce Willis action movie the *Last Boy Scout,* is in the midst of the game of his life when he pulls out a gun on the field and kills himself because of gambling debts. One of the more absurd scenes in movie history.

In 19**42** the Chicago Cubs, who had already signed contracts to install lights at Wrigley Field, have to cancel their plans because of the military need for the material. It takes 46 more years for Wrigley to get lights.

With 1:**43** remaining in the 2001–2002 AFC divisional playoff game and the Patriots trailing 13–10, quarterback Tom Brady loses the football on a hit by Charles Woodson. Raiders linebacker Greg Biekert falls on the ball, essentially ending the game—until the tuck rule rears its head, and the play is ruled an incomplete pass. The Patriots go on to the win the game and the Super Bowl.

During the investigation into corrupt NBA referee Tim Donaghy, gambling expert P. J. Bell discovered that in games reffed by Donaghy, teams beat the Las Vegas "over" more than 57 percent of the time. During the two prior seasons, this occurred only **44** percent of the time.

Michael Jordan wore jersey No. **45** during his failed baseball experiment with the Chicago White Sox.

Former Arizona State student Benny Silman, alleged mastermind of Arizona State's 1994 basketball point-shaving scandal, was sentenced to **46** months in prison for his role in the scheme.

The highest bungee jump off a building was recorded on October 5, 1998, when A. J. Hackett jumped 590 feet off of the Sky Tower Casino in New Zealand.

Jesse Orosco, wearing jersey No. **47**, tossed the final pitch for the Mets' 1986 World Series victory over the Boston Red Sox. Sports fans across the country lose out as they are subjected to nearly two decades of Red Sox Nation moaning and groaning.

President Gerald Ford's No. **48** jersey is retired at the University of Michigan, where he played center and linebacker and helped lead the Wolverines to back-to-back undefeated seasons and national titles in the early 1930s.

On February 22, 2003, Mike Tyson, sporting an absurd new tattoo on his face, beat Clifford Etienne **49** seconds into Round 1.

Americans are outraged when Janet Jackson's breast pops out during the Super Bowl XXXVIII halftime show. Furious viewers flood the FCC with nearly 540,000 complaints. In contrast, the Canadian Broadcast Standards Council receives only **50** complaints from viewers.

In what USA Basketball calls "the most controversial game in international basketball history," 1972 Olympic men's basketball gold-medal game ended with the Soviet team (with a whole lot of help from the refs) defeating the USA basketball team **51**–50.

Retired NASCAR driver Jimmy Means drove car No. **52** for more than two decades.

In 1978, Islander Mike Bossy set the record for most goals scored by an NHL rookie with **53**.

54: Fewest points scored in an NBA playoff game: Chicago 96, Utah 54, June 7, 1998.

In the 2006 NASCAR flick *Talladega Nights: The Ballad of Ricky Bobby,* Sacha Baron Cohen's villainous Jean Girard drives the No. **55** Perrier.

The maximum weight for a golf ball is 1.62 oz.

In 1941 Joe DiMaggio famously hit in **56** consecutive games, still a record.

In 19**57**, two years after the Dodgers won their first World Series title, owner Walter O'Malley moved the team from Brooklyn to Los Angeles. Ebbets Field was demolished three years later.

On October 20, 1972, the Buffalo Braves scored **58** points in the fourth quarter against the Boston Celtics—the most ever in a fourth quarter.

Satchel Paige pitched for the Kansas City Athletics at age **59**, making him the oldest major league baseball player ever.

In the game of darts, **60** is the highest possible score a thrower can achieve with a single dart.

Dartboards are made from horse hair.

STRANGE SPORTS

Bizarre and unconventional games from around the world.

Cheese Chasing

Every May 22 in Gloucester, England, an 8-pound wheel of cheese is rolled down Cooper's Hill—and dozens of crazy contestants violently tumble after it. Blood, bruises, and broken limbs are standard. The real goal is to catch the cheese, but that's pretty rare, so whoever makes it down the hill first is declared winner. Their prize? The cheese.

Buzkashi

The national sport of Afghanistan and Kyrgyzstan, Buzkashi is similar to polo . . . only the mallet is replaced with bare hands and the ball with a headless goat. Two teams compete, with riders carrying the dead animal, passing it back and forth, and trying to score by throwing the carcass through a goal known as the "Circle of Justice." It's a violent and grueling game—players use whips and boots to battle while riding, and games can last for days.

To see the game in action, rent *Rambo III,* where (this is not a joke) Rambo is pulled into a pickup game of Buzkashi and proceeds to dominate with his natural skills . . . before being interrupted by flying gunships and machine-gun fire.

Bog Snorkeling

In this yearly event, competitors snorkel through two 60-yard lengths of Wales's filthy, foul Waen Rhydd peat bog. Standard swimming strokes are not allowed; instead, swimmers must rely solely on the strength of their flippers. The record time is 1 minute, 35 seconds. There's also a mountain-bike bog tournament, where competitors pedal their way through the muck.

Nike paid Michael Jordan $20 million a year for promoting Nike products.

Wife-Carrying World Championship

This Finnish sport is pretty simple: Grab hold of your significant other (man or woman, doesn't actually matter) and carry them to the finish line faster than anyone else. The minimum weight of the "wife" is 49 kilos—if she weighs less, a rucksack is attached to make up the weight. And, as if more proof was needed that this guy will do anything, Dennis Rodman competed in 2005's competition.

Chess Boxing

The ultimate combination of brains and brawn. Invented by Dutchman Iepe "the Joker" Rubingh, the sport consists of six rounds of chess intertwined with five rounds of boxing. Competitors can win in the ring or on the board; most contests end in a checkmate or knockout. In the event of a stalemate on the board, the contestant with the higher boxing score is declared winner. Too bad it's not more popular—we could have witnessed Mike Tyson versus Bobby Fischer!

Ba'

Played twice a year in Kirkwall, Scotland, Ba' is one of the most dangerous games on earth. The only piece of equipment is a 3-pound leather ball called ba' (when the game originated a thousand years ago, a severed head was used). There are two teams: the Uppies, from the north, and the Doonies, from the south. The Doonies have to get the ba' into the water of Kirkwall's harbor, while the Uppies have to touch the ba' to a wall at the far end of town. There are no referees and it's no-holds-barred: players race across rooftops, jump through windows, head-butt, eye gouge, and worse.

Q: What's the hardest part about skydiving? A: The ground!

THE END-ZONE CELEBRATION

A timeline

1965: The Spike
New York Giant Homer Jones started it all when he threw the ball to the field at his feet after catching a touchdown pass.

1974: The Funky Chicken
As a rookie with the Oilers in 1974, Billy "White Shoes" Johnson—who earned his nickname because he wore white shoes instead of the standard black—began celebrating touchdowns by doing the Funky Chicken. This is recognized as the first end-zone celebration.

1988: The Ickey Shuffle
Bengals rookie Ickey Woods came up with this classic during the 1988 season. Thanks to the Ickey Shuffle, the NFL began fining players whose celebration they deemed to be excessive. That's what caused fans to dub the NFL the No Fun League.

1991: Do the Heisman
The best of the NCAA celebrations. After returning a punt for a touchdown, Michigan's Desmond Howard mimicked the Heisman trophy pose. He won the Heisman that same year.

1992: The Slam Dunk
This classic, first performed by Alvin Harper as a Cowboy in the 1992 Super Bowl, has maintained its popularity and mystique because not just any old player is athletic enough to do it.

1993: The Lambeau Leap
Invented by Green Bay cornerback LeRoy Butler, the Lambeau Leap is a celebration where players jump into the end-zone stand and are grabbed by fans after a score. The celebration is now done by many different players in many different stadiums.

Carolyn Davidson of Orgeon University designed the world famous Nike "swoosh" logo. She was paid $35 dollars.

1998: The Dirty Bird
Popularized by Jamal Anderson and the 1998 Falcons, players shake and gyrate like a chicken.

2000: The Bob and Weave
This group celebration was made famous by the St. Louis Rams during their 2000 Super Bowl run. After a touchdown, the offense would gather in a circle, crouch down, and bob and weave, similar to shadowboxing. The No Fun League struck again, declaring all celebrations involving multiple players illegal and punishable by fine.

2003: Joe Horn Phone Home
After a big score against the Giants in 2003, Joe spiked the ball, went to the goal post, pulled a cell phone out of the yellow padding that surrounds the post, and called his kids. The NFL fined him $30,000—the most ever for an end-zone celebration.

2005: Minnesota Moon
In the playoffs against the Packers, Randy Moss pretended to pull down his pants and moon the Packer crowd. TV announcer Joe Buck had a mini-freak-out, yelling it's "a DISGUSTING act by Randy Moss, and it's unfortunate we had it on our air live!" Moss said he did it because Green Bay fans often moon the opposing team's bus as it pulls into the Lambeau Field parking lot. Makes sense to us.

1999–Present: Terrell Owens Touchdown Overload
T.O.'s first celebration was a doozy: Against the Falcons he imitated their Dirty Bird dance, then followed it up with a throat–slashing gesture. Twice while playing the Dallas Cowboys, T.O. enraged fans by celebrating on the Cowboys' midfield star. It was all forgotten, of course, when he signed with the Cowboys years later. After a score in a 2002 game versus the Seahawks, Owens pulled a sharpie out from his sock, signed the game ball, and handed it to his manager who was sitting in the end zone. A few games later he pulled a pair of pom-poms from the hands of a 49ers cheerleader and did a little dance. Once, while playing against the Ravens, he mocked Ray Lewis's patented "shake around a lot" dance.

In 1973 Steve Prefontaine became the first major track athlete to promote Nike.

2001–Present: The Chad Johnson Collection

Along with T.O., Chad Johnson is pretty much the king of the modern-day touchdown celebration. Against the Bears in 2005, Chad did his own little version of the *Riverdance* dance. Many of Chad's celebrations have drawn NFL fines, prompting him to celebrate one touchdown by holding up a sign that read "DEAR NFL, PLEASE DON'T FINE ME AGAIN!!!!" But they did. Another celebration saw him using the pylon as a mock golf club and "putting" the ball into an imaginary golf hole and then imitating Tiger Woods's trademark fist pump.

2002–Present: Steve Smith's End-Zone Wit

Carolina Panther Steve Smith's end zone shtick once included treating the football like a baby—wiping it down, rocking it to sleep, and in one case even changing its "diaper." He's been known to pose like a supermodel or lie on his back and make snow angels. Against the Tampa Bay Buccaneers, he mocked the Bucs mascot by using the football as a sword and swinging it around, swashbuckler style. (Buccaneers, swashbuckler . . . get it?)

BIATHLONS WE'D LIKE TO SEE

Shooting and skiing? At the same time? YES!!!

And This Makes Sense Because . . . ?

Technically a biathlon is any event that combines two sporting disciplines—but more often than not, when someone says biathlon, they're referring to the winter sport that combines cross-country skiing with riflery. Contestants ski around a cross country track, stopping either two or four times (half standing, half prone) at shooting stations to fire at targets. Depending on the racer's shooting performance, extra distance or time is added to their total. In the end, the racer with the shortest total time wins.

At each shooting station, the racer must hit five targets. If they miss a target, they're penalized in one of three different ways:

Having an extra minute added to their total time.

Skiing around a 490 ft. penalty loop.

Having to use an "extra cartridge"; only three are available per round, once you run out, it's a lap around the penalty loop.

While They're At It . . .

As Jerry Seinfeld said, combining skiing and shooting makes about as much sense as combining swimming and strangling a guy. We agree. So, while they're at it, we'd like to see some of these.

Pole Vaulting and Archery: Contestants must vault over the bar, then, while in mid-air, fire an arrow at a small target 50 yards away. Points deducted for maiming innocent spectators with stray arrows.

Fishing and Chess: The dullest, least exciting spectator sport in history.

Competitive Eating and Swimming: Your mom's least favorite sport. Eat, swim, eat, swim, eat, swim. No digesting, plenty of cramping.

Boxing and Watching *Rocky:* Competitors exchange blows, then at the end of each round, must answer one question about the scene they just watched. It doesn't matter how many right hooks you land, if you can't remember the name of Rocky's dog, you lose.

NASCAR and Polo: It's tough to hang onto those mallets at 200 mph, but it's fun to watch.

Cricket was first played by shepherds in 17th-century England.

MAKE YOUR OWN CRACKER JACKS!

Watch the game and eat Cracker Jacks in your underwear without going to jail.

Cracker Jacks and baseball go together like Babe Ruth and pinstripes. They're the classic ballpark snack, but there's no reason you should have to hike all the way to the stadium to enjoy them. Just make your own! Prizes not included.

Get Cooking!

What You Need

popcorn
peanuts
1 cup honey
½ stick butter

Directions

1. Pop your popcorn. We suggest you do it the old fashioned way, over the stove.
2. Mix the peanuts and the popcorn. Use as many peanuts as you like.
3. Heat honey and butter in a saucepan, stirring until the mixture is good and mixed.
4. Pour the honey and butter over popcorn and peanut mixture. Stir well.
5. Once the popcorn and peanuts are good and gooey, spread it all in a square pan.
6. Set your oven to 350 degrees. Cook 5 to 10 minutes, removing once or twice to stir.
7. Cook until crisp. Keep an eye on it, it'll burn if you're not careful.
8. Let cool for 10 minutes.
9. Flip on the game. Enjoy.

Q: What's the difference between a surfer and a savings account?
A: A savings account will mature and earn money!

Cracker Jack Facts

✓ Enough Cracker Jacks have been sold that if laid end-to-end they'd circle the Earth nearly 70 times.

✓ Since 1912, more than 23 billion Cracker Jack toys have been given out.

✓ July 5 is Cracker Jack Day.

Old-time bicycles were called "Penny Farthings."

YOGI BERRA DIDN'T SAY IT—BUT HE COULD HAVE!

Backwards wisdom in the style of the master.

"YANKEE PITCHERS HAVE HAD GREAT SUCCESS THIS YEAR AGAINST CABRERA WHEN THEY GET HIM OUT."
—TIM McCARVER

"DON'T SAY I DON'T GET ALONG WITH MY TEAMMATES. I JUST DON'T GET ALONG WITH SOME OF THE GUYS ON THE TEAM."
—TERRELL OWENS

"THE ONLY THING THAT KEEPS THIS ORGANIZATION FROM BEING RECOGNIZED AS ONE OF THE FINEST IN BASEBALL IS WINS AND LOSSES AT THE MAJOR LEAGUE LEVEL."
—FORMER DEVIL RAYS GENERAL MANAGER CHUCK LAMAR

"ALL I'M ASKING FOR IS WHAT I WANT."
—RICKEY HENDERSON

"THERAPY CAN BE A GOOD THING; IT CAN BE THERAPEUTIC."
—ALEX RODRIGUEZ

"ROY OSWALT IS A DROP-AND-DRIVE PITCHER. WHAT IS A DROP-AND-DRIVE PITCHER? HE IS A GUY WHO DROPS AND DRIVES. VERY SIMPLE."
—TIM McCARVER

Peter Rosendahl set a unicycle sprint record by going 100 meters in 12.11 seconds in 1994.

"I DON'T THINK ANYWHERE IS THERE A SYMBIOTIC RELATIONSHIP BETWEEN CADDIE AND PLAYER LIKE THERE IS IN GOLF."
—JOHNNY MILLER, TV ANALYST AND PRO GOLFER

"HE'S THE MAN OF THE HOUR AT THIS PARTICULAR MOMENT."
—DON KING

"MOST OF MY CLICHÉS AREN'T ORIGINAL."
—RAMS COACH CHUCK KNOX

"HE'S A GUY WHO GETS UP AT SIX O'CLOCK IN THE MORNING REGARDLESS OF WHAT TIME IT IS."
—BOXING TRAINER LOU DUVA, ON THE TRAINING REGIMEN OF HEAVYWEIGHT ANDREW GOLOTA

"SOMETIMES THEY WRITE WHAT I SAY AND NOT WHAT I MEAN."
—PEDRO GUERRERO, ON SPORTSWRITERS

"THE GAME WAS CLOSER THAN THE SCORE INDICATED."
—DIZZY DEAN, AFTER A 1–0 GAME

DO YOU KNOW YOUR FOOTBALL NUMBERS?

Let's see if you're on top of your football digits.

1. Bruce Smith holds the record for most QB sacks in a career. How many?
   a. 192
   b. 200
   c. 206
   d. 212

2. How many 1,000-yard receiving seasons did Jerry Rice record?
   a. 14
   b. 15
   c. 16
   d. 17

3. During which year did the Pittsburgh Steelers and the Philadelphia Eagles combine to become the Steagles?
   a. 1940
   b. 1941
   c. 1942
   d. 1943

4. The AFL and NFL merged together in what year?
   a. 1968
   b. 1970
   c. 1972
   d. 1974

5. Len Dawson holds the record for most fumbles in a game with how many?
   a. 5
   b. 6
   c. 7
   d. 8

Manfred Ruhmer holds the world record for longest distance traveled in a hang glider. He traveled 437 miles over Texas in 2001.

6. Ellis Hobbs set the record for longest kickoff return in 2007 when he was with the Patriots. How many yards did he return the kick for?

a. 99
b. 101
c. 108
d. 110

7. Paul Krause holds the record for most interceptions in a career. How many picks did he have?

a. 77
b. 81
c. 85
d. 89

8. Which number represents a perfect passing record in the NFL?

a. 99.9
b. 121.6
c. 158.3
d. 161.2

9. John Elway is the most-sacked quarterback in NFL history. During his 15-year career, how many times was he sacked?

a. 418
b. 516
c. 614
d. 712

10. Johnny Unitas holds the record for most consecutive games throwing a touchdown. In how many straight games did Unitas toss a TD?

a. 47
b. 49
c. 53
d. 59

Turn to page 356 for answers.

Between July 10 and August 22, 1992, Akira Matsushima, of Japan, rode his unicycle 3,261 miles from Newport, Oregon, to Washington DC.

THE PITTSBURGH DRUG TRIALS

More proof that '80s baseball was RIDICULOUS.

In 1985, 13 major league ballplayers, including big boppers like Keith Hernandez, Dave Parker, and Tim Raines, were subpoenaed and called before a Pittsburgh grand jury. In exchange for immunity from prosecution they offered up testimony on the cocaine problem that had invaded Major League Baseball. Their testimony led to the Pittsburgh drug trials.

The Testimony

Former Pirate John "The Hammer" Milner, already retired at this point, admitted to purchasing two grams of cocaine for $200 in a Three Rivers Stadium bathroom stall halfway through a Pirates-Astros game in 1980. Milner also confessed to receiving amphetamines, aka "greenies," from Hall of Famers Willie Mays and Willie Stargell. Similarly, Rod Scurry described a late-inning hunt for cocaine during a game at Three Rivers Stadium.

Keith Hernandez admitted to using cocaine for three years when he was a St. Louis Cardinal. He estimated that 40 percent of major leaguers used coke—then backtracked, saying he might have been "grossly wrong." "I consider cocaine the devil on this earth," said Keith Hernandez. "[It is] a demon in me."

Tim Raines's testimony was the most ridiculous. The four-time stolen-base champ admitted that his trademarked, headfirst slide was a result of not wanting to break the glass vile of coke that he stored in his back pocket on game days. He also confessed to snorting coke before, during, and after games.

Kevin Koch, the man in the Pittsburgh Parrot mascot suit, was even implicated in buying cocaine and introducing ballplayers to a local drug dealer who provided them with cocaine.

The Verdict

Eleven players were given suspensions—but none served. By donating a percentage of their 1986 salaries to a drug program and doing some community service work, every player got off. The 11 players were: Joaquín Andújar, Dale Berra, Enos Cabell, Keith Hernandez, Jeffrey Leonard, Dave Parker, Lonnie Smith, Al Holland, Lee Lacy, Lary Sorensen, and Claudell Washington.

Seven dealers, including ringleader Curtis Strong, were convicted and found guilty of 11 counts of distributing cocaine. Strong received a 12-year prison sentence but only served four. Pittsburgh local Dale Shiffman was indicted on 111 counts, pled guilty to 20, was sentenced to 12 years and served 24 months.

The Aftermath

Reputations were ruined. Dave Parker's shot at the Hall of Fame was destroyed by the scandal. Dale Berra's career ended prematurely. In 1992, at the age of 36, Rod Scurry died of a cocaine-induced heart attack. Some would argue that the event soured Pittsburgh Pirates fans from the organization altogether—and that the city and team still haven't recovered. The trials led to a greater awareness of the problem of the use of drugs in baseball, including amphetamines and marijuana. Kevin Koch flew the coop in Pittsburgh and hung up his Parrot outfit for good.

The modern ski jump technique of holding your arms behind you while leaning forwards was developed in the 1950s by Swiss jumper Andreas Daescher.

WHAT ARE THE ODDS?

We don't want to discourage any future athletes out there, but if you're set on making it big as a pro, you might want to take a look at these depressing odds.

Your chances of writing a *New York Times* best seller (1 in 220) are better than the odds of catching a ball at a Major League baseball game (1 in 563).

The odds of dying in a terrorist attack while on vacation in a foreign country (1 in 650,000) are better than the odds of winning an Olympic medal (1 in 662,000).

The odds of winning an Academy Award (1 in 11,500) are better than the odds of becoming a pro athlete (1 in 22,000).

The odds of dating a millionaire (1 in 215) are better than the odds of a fan catching two home runs at a baseball game (1 in 3,000).

Your chances of dying in an airplane accident (1 in 354,319) are better than the odds of getting a royal flush in poker on the first five cards dealt (1 in 649,740).

The odds of finding a four-leaf clover on first try (1 in 10,000) are better than the odds of bowling a 300 game (1 in 11,500).

Your chances of committing suicide (1 in 9,380) are better than the odds of getting a hole in one (1 in 12,500).

A fall from a wakeboard is called a durf.

THE BOOK WAS BETTER

Before running off to the video store, pick up these books. If you've already seen the movie, check the source material for the full story.

Friday Night Lights: A Town, a Team, and a Dream

H. G. "Buzz" Bissinger, 1990

> "*Friday Night Lights* offers a biting indictment of the sports craziness that grips . . . most of American society, while at the same time providing a moving evocation of its powerful allure."
>
> —*New York Times Book Review*

Bissinger spent much of 1988 in the declining, depressed, and football-obsessed town of Odessa, Texas, following the Permian High School Panthers football team as they worked toward the goal of a Texas state championship. The first sentence is a beaut: "In the beginning, on a dog-day Monday in the middle of August when the West Texas heat congealed in the sky, there were only the stirrings of dreams."

Seabiscuit: An American Legend

Laura Hillenbrand, 2001

> "Terrific . . . *Seabiscuit* brings alive the drama, the beauty, the louche charm, and the brutality of horseracing."
>
> —*USA Today*

Hillenbrand uses her one-of-a-kind way with words to tell the story of the underdog Seabiscuit, while simultaneously delving into the culture of 1930s and 1940s horseracing.

In 1968 a successful expedition to the North Pole was made on snowmobiles.

Heaven Is a Playground

Rick Telander, 1978

"Funny, sad, superbly written, and intensely involving."

—*New York Times Book Review*

Telander spent the summer of 1974 in Brooklyn, recording the lives and dreams of a number of inner-city basketball whiz kids. At once touching and depressing. If you enjoy it, check out Pete Axthelm's *The City Game*.

Eight Men Out: The Black Sox and the 1919 World Series

Eliot Asinof, 1963

"The most thorough investigation of the Black Sox scandal on record . . . A vividly, excitingly written book:"

—*Chicago Tribune*

A blow-by-blow, play-by-play, turn-by-turn account of the Black Sox and the throwing of the 1919 World Series.

A Season on the Brink

John Feinstein, 1986

"Nothing less than extraordinary."

—*Chicago Tribune*

Feinstein followed the outrageous and often out-of-control coach Bobby Knight and his Indiana University basketball team through a drama-filled 1985–86 season. Just read it, there's a reason it's the best-selling sports book of all time. The TV version, however, is memorable mostly because it was ESPN's first foray into the world of made-for-TV movies, and for its, ahem, "colorful" language.

GOOFY GOLF TERMS

Home run. Field goal. Double dribble. These are all sports terms that make relative sense. But golf is filled with terms like bogey, albatross, and mulligan. Here's the etymology behind some of the sport's stranger words.

Golf

Despite what a few old-timers might have you believe, the term *golf* is most definitely not an acronym for "gentlemen only, ladies forbidden." The Scots, the game's originators, picked up on the Dutch word *colf,* which means "bat" or "club." And from there it was just a short stop to golf.

Fore!

Fore!, the warning a golfer shouts when a wayward ball is headed toward an unaware person, comes from the Middle English *fore,* meaning ahead or front (as in foremost, forerunner, or forehead). In the case of a wild ball, it more literally means "too far forward." Don't forget, if you ever happen to whack a ball into a man's crotch, just go with Rodney Dangerfield *Caddyshack* line: "I should have yelled, 'Two!' "

Bogey

The term for one over par on a hole was inspired by the song, "The Bogey Man," a popular tune in late 1800s England. "The Bogey Man" was a sneaky, shadowy character who dared people to "catch me if you can." Turn-of-the-century golfers were said to chase the Bogey Man on the course, trying to catch a perfect score and soon, "bogey score" meant perfect game.

These days, however, bogey denotes a score of one over par: good, but not perfect. As the golf world split between professional and amateurs, par became term for an average pro score, and bogey became the term for a good score for amateurs.

You must be over 18 years old if you want to run with the bulls at Pamplona.

Dormie

A match is said to be "dormie" when one golfer has a lead that matches the number of holes remaining; for example, 4 holes up with 4 holes left to play. The word comes from the Latin word *dormir,* which means "to sleep." So basically, a golfer who is dormie can go to sleep, or relax, because he can't lose the match.

Sandbagger

In golf, a sandbagger is a hustler who lies about his skill so he can gain an advantage in tournaments or when gambling. In the old days, street toughs would fill bags with sand, then whip them around as a weapon. In golf terms, a sandbagger lures in his opponents, pulls out the "sand bag," and beats them.

Birdie

For some reason, golf is crazy about bird terminology. In 19th century American slang the word *bird* meant anything great. According to www.USGA.com, the first use of the term occurred at the Country Club in Atlantic City in 1898. Golfer Ab Smith was playing the par-4 second hole when his second shot landed inches from the hole. Smith exclaimed, "That was a bird of a shot!" and suggested he win double the cash if he won under par. He made his putt, won his money, and thereafter a score of one under par was a "birdie."

Eagle

See? More bird language. Eagle, a score of two under par on a hole, is simply the furthering of the term *birdie.* To Americans, an eagle is simply a bigger, better bird(ie).

Albatross

The birds keep coming. Albatross refers to a score of three under par on a hole, a feat that is quite rare. Fittingly, the albatross is quite the rare bird. A score of four under par, so rare it's damn near extinct, is known as a double-albatross, triple-eagle, or vulture.

Water skiing was invented in 1922 by 18-year-old Ralph Samuelson.

BASEBALL MYTHS . . . DEBUNKED!

Setting the record straight on some of baseball's strangest rumors

MYTH: The 1989 film *Back to the Future II* predicted that the Florida Marlins would win the 1997 World Series. After the Marlins' 1997 World Series win, a rumor spread that the character Biff, while looking at a 2000 sports almanac, says "Florida is going to win the World Series in 1997? Yeah, right." Weird huh?

TRUTH: Too bad there's simply nothing to this. The closest such thing in the movie is a news broadcast announcing that the Chicago Cubs beat an unnamed Miami baseball team in the 2015 World Series. There's no mention of the name Marlins, and, in fact, the unnamed team's logo is an alligator.

If you're looking for prophecy from '80s comedies, the closest thing you're going to get is *Coming to America*. In one scene Eddie Murphy says, "The Giants of New York took on the Packers of Green Bay. And in the end, the Giants triumphed by kicking an oblong ball made of pigskin through a big *H*." That's exactly how the 2007 NFC Championship Game ended.

MYTH: Fidel Castro tried out for the Washington Senators. It's fun to contemplate what might have happened had Castro played major league baseball: no political career, no Soviet-backed Cuban government, no Bay of Pigs, no Cuban Missile Crisis . . . all if some scout had thought a little more highly of Fidel's breaking ball.

TRUTH: Unfortunately, never happened. According to www.Snopes.com, the legend apparently started with an overzealous sports reporter and took off from there. Fidel did play a little baseball in college, but nothing more.

MYTH: Kevin Costner was caught in bed with Cal Ripken Jr.'s wife, causing the Orioles to cancel the day's game. This saucy rumor claims that Cal Ripken Jr. once walked in on Kevin Costner in bed with his wife and proceeded to pummel him. Ripken then

In 1994 Dave Phillips and Ralph Hildebrand water skied for 56 hours, 35 minutes around Indian Arm in British Columbia, Canada, using infrared binoculars when it was dark.

called the owner of the Orioles and said he would not be playing today. To preserve Ripken's streak, the Orioles owner made up a story about problems with the stadium's lighting and had the game cancelled.

TRUTH: This is all BS, of course. This tall tale can simply be attributed to the close friendship of Costner and Ripken, grumblings of marriage trouble between the Ripkens, and the odd cancellation of a game due to lightning.

MYTH: The Yankees adopted their famous pinstripes in an effort to hide Babe Ruth's huge gut. According to this story, Yankees owner Jake Ruppert had the pinstripes incorporated into the uniform because he thought it would make Ruth look slimmer.

TRUTH: Funny tale, but unfortunately the timeline doesn't add up. The Yankees first adorned the pinstripes in 1912, when Ruth was just a 17-year-old student at St. Mary's Industrial School for boys.

BASICS OF BETTING

Placing a few dollars on the occasional football or basketball game can be fun, but for the beginner it can also be confusing and overwhelming. We're here to break it down for you.

You, The Bettor

As the gambler, it's your job to beat the odds (and the casino or your bookie) and win some money. Of course, the first thing you have to do is place a bet. There are a few different ways to go about doing that. Following are the most basic ways of betting on baseball, basketball, football, or hockey (we're leaving the ponies out of this; that's a horse of a completely different color).

Futures

These are the most straightforward. You predict a future feat by a team or player and bet on it. For example, that the Redskins will win next year's Super Bowl or that Alex Rodriguez will be voted next year's AL MVP. Odds are expressed as a ratio of dollars paid to dollars wagered. For example, a futures bet on next year's World Series champion might be something like 11:1. Bet $1, win $11.

Point Spreads and Money Lines

There are point spreads and money lines (no spread). When there's a point spread, the favored team needs to win by more than that spread. For example, let's say Dallas is playing at Green Bay and Dallas is favored to win by 10 points. The line would look like this:

Dallas -10; GREEN BAY +10 (home team is always in caps)

If you bet on Dallas, you need them to win by 11 or more; if you bet on Green Bay, you want them to either win the game or lose by less than 10. If Dallas was to win by exactly 10, that's called a "push," and all money goes back to the bettors. Great, do-over, you get to try again. That's how you bet the spread.

Now, the money line. This is used for sports where there is no point spread—boxing, tennis, as well as games like baseball and hockey where the margins of victory are so small that it's not feasible to make point spreads for every single game.

In this example, we'll make the Pittsburgh Pirates the underdog (just like in real life!). Here's what an average money line between a subpar Pirates team and a good Red Sox team might look like:

Pittsburgh +130; BOSTON -120

If you want to bet on Pittsburgh to win, you place $100 down and you stand to win $130. If you bet on Boston, the favored team, you have to bet $120 just to win $100. The score doesn't matter here—all that matters is that your team wins. That's how you bet the money line.

Over/Under

You can also bet the over/under. Here, you're betting whether the combined total scores of both teams will be either over or under a set number. Let's say the over/under for a specific NBA game is 197.5 (bookmakers often use numbers ending in .5 so as to avoid a possible push). If you take the under, the total combined points scored by both teams must be 197 or less. If you take the over, the total points scored must be 198 or more. Simple as that.

Parlay

Now things start to get a bit complicated. A parlay is a single bet that links together multiple wagers—winning the parlay is dependent on all of those wagers winning. Obviously, the more teams involved in the bet, the more unlikely that'll you win—but if you do win, you'll take in a lot more money. So let's say you were placing separate, individual bets on four games with even spreads. You bet $10 per game; if you win all of them, you win $40. Now, if you were to parlay those same four bets and all four of your teams won, you would win $400 (given that a four-team parlay usually has odds of about 10:1). The downside is that if three of your teams win and one loses, you get nothing.

Now What?

So you understand the basics. What to do now? Your best bet (pardon the pun) is to head to Las Vegas, Atlantic City, Montreal, or some other place where gambling is legal (Indian casinos for example—they're popping up everywhere these days).

Unfortunately, most people don't live near a casino. That's why there are bookies (illegal, illegal, illegal!). Go into any sports bar and keep your ears open. You'll soon spot someone huffing and puffing about the spread of the game—that guy has a bookie. You can also use an online bookmaker, though the legality of these are up in the air and the laws vary from place to place. Bottom line, you're probably best off keeping a lid on your gambling jones until you get to Vegas or someplace similar.

Good Luck!

So there's your primer. As Paul Newman said in *The Color of Money,* "Money won is twice as sweet as money earned." Now this may be true, but you should never forget the Chinese Proverb, "If you must play, decide upon three things at the start: the rules of the game, the stakes, and the quitting time." Unless you're Charles Barkley, that is.

Seven-time Formula One World Champion Michael Schumacher began his career driving go-karts.

HISTORIC HOMERS

The 10 biggest and best, in order. Just our opinion, of course—but we're right!

1. Bobby Thomson wins 1951 playoffs (Giants)

Best known as the "Shot Heard Round the World," Thomson's ninth-inning walk-off homer won the 1951 National League pennant for the Giants. Heading into the inning the Dodgers were ahead 4–1, just three outs from winning the pennant. But pitcher Don Newcombe struggled, let up a run, and Ralph Branca was called in to face Thomson, clinging to a 4–2 lead with two runners on. Thomson took one pitch, a strike, and then swung—followed immediately by one major homer and the Russ Hodges screaming classic, "The Giants win the pennant! The Giants win the pennant!"

2. Bill Mazeroski wins Game 7, 1960 World Series (Pirates)

The underdog Pirates scored five in the eighth to take the lead, then the Yankees fought back and tied it in the top of the ninth. Mazeroski led off the bottom of the inning and promptly smacked Ralph Terry's second pitch over Forbes Field's ivy-covered left-field wall. Thirteen-year old Ted Szafranski caught the ball—and traded it to Mazeroski for two cases of beer. It was the first time a World Series had ever ended on a homer, and it's still the championship's only Game 7 walk-off.

3. Hank Aaron, No. 715, breaks Babe Ruth's record (Braves)

The other guys on our list of historic homers had to overcome the pressure and the tension of the moment to hit their dingers. Hank Aaron had to do all that—plus play through racism, hate mail, and death threats. In his first at-bat of the 1974 season, Aaron homered to tie the Babe at 714. Four days later he hit the record-breaking homer off of Al Downing in front of an ecstatic Atlanta crowd. On hand were 55,775 fans; commissioner Bowie Kuhn didn't show, as he was "busy" attending the Indians home opener.

Reported approximate cost of making one pair of Nike running shoes: $12. Retail cost of one pair of Nike Air Tuned Sirocco runners: $189.

4. Joe Carter wins 1993 World Series, Game 6 (Blue Jays)

Thirty-three years after Bill Mazeroski, Joe Carter hit only the second World Series–ending home run in baseball history—and the only one to be hit by a player whose team was trailing at the time. The Blue Jays were behind 6–5 with two men on when Carter smacked the three-run homer off of Phillies hurler Mitch Williams, ending the series.

Said Carter, "I dreamed of that moment when I was a little kid. I'd be sitting at my father's garage and daydreaming about that moment. I even wrote it down a few times: 'My dream is to hit a home run to win the World Series.' "

5. Roger Maris breaks single-season record with 61, 1961 (Yankees)

As the 1961 season progressed, it became clear that either Roger Maris or Mickey Mantle, or possibly both, might break Babe Ruth's 34-year-old single-season home run record. The press, ever protective of Babe Ruth, did their best to create controversy where there was none, inventing a rivalry between Maris and Mantle that never existed. A late-season leg injury knocked Mantle of the race—leaving only Maris with a shot at the record. In the final game of the season, Maris hit historic No. 61 off of Boston's Tracy Stallard. His record stood for 37 years.

6. Carlton Fisk, 1975 World Series, Game 6 (Red Sox)

The classic shot of Fisk waving fair his game 6, 12th-inning homer, jumping his way down the first base path, changed the way baseball was televised forever. Up until that point, cameramen simply followed the flight of the ball—after the drama of the Fisk scene, cameramen stuck with the batters. The shot was not the result of a stroke of dramatic genius by NBC cameraman Lou Gerard; rather, he had been distracted by a nearby rat, leaving him unable to follow the ball.

7. Kirk Gibson, 1988 World Series, Game 1 (Los Angeles Dodgers)

Gibson got only one at-bat in the 1988 World Series—but it was a doozy. Gibson spent much of the game in the clubhouse, suffering from a stomach bug and receiving physical therapy for a knee injury he suffered earlier in the playoffs. When a TV announcer noticed Gibson's absence from the dugout, Gibson forced himself out of the clubhouse and into the dugout, declaring himself available to manager Tommy Lasorda. Soon, Lasorda came calling.

Don Drysdale provided the call: "Well, the crowd on its feet and if there was ever a preface to "Casey at the Bat," it would have to be the ninth inning. Two out. The tying run aboard, the winning run at the plate, and Kirk Gibson, standing at the plate. Eckersley working out of the stretch, here's the 3-2 pitch . . . and a drive hit to rightfield WAY BACK! THIS BALL . . . IS GONE!!! I DO NOT BELIEVE WHAT I HAVE JUST SEEN!!! And this time, Mighty Casey did NOT strike out!"

8. Bucky Dent, 1978, one-game playoff for the AL East title (Yankees)

Out of all the guys on this list, Bucky Dent was probably the least likely to hit a big-time dinger. Dent had only hit 4 homers on the season when he hit his three-run, two-out shot over Fenway's Green Monster. The Yankees went on to win the game 5–4 and take the division title, the pennant, and the World Series. To Red Sox fans everywhere, he was no longer known as Bucky Dent, but as Bucky "FU*$%#G" Dent.

9. Reggie Jackson's third HR, Game 6, 1977 World Series (Yankees)

Reggie Jackson hit three home runs in Game 6 of the 1977 World Series, the final one coming in the eighth inning amid chants of "REG-GIE, REG-GIE, REG-GIE!" Howard Cosell's commentary said it all: "Oh, what a blow! What a way to top it off! Forget about who the most valuable player is in the World Series. How this man has responded to pressure! Oh, what a beam on his face. How can you blame him? He's answered the whole WORLD! After all the furor, after all the hassling, it comes down to this!"

10. Kirby Puckett, Game 6, 1991 World Series (Twins)

Puckett's Game 6 performance was about as good as it gets—three hits, two runs, three RBIs, one spectacular catch, and one legendary, game-winning 11th-inning home run.

Parkour, aka free running, was started in France and comes from the French word *parcour*, which means obstacle course.

ATHLETES SAY THE DUMBEST THINGS . . .

Professional athletes are often pegged as dumb jocks. Now, that isn't exactly true. But these guys aren't helping the cause.

"THE SUN HAS BEEN THERE FOR 500, 600 YEARS."
—MIKE CAMERON

"THEY SHOULD HAVE FOCUSED MORE ON ME."
—SEBASTIAN TELFAIR ON THE ESPN DOCUMENTARY *THROUGH THE FIRE*, ABOUT HIM

"THE BIBLE NEVER SAYS ANYTHING ABOUT DINOSAURS. YOU CAN'T SAY THERE WERE DINOSAURS WHEN YOU NEVER SAW THEM. SOMEBODY ACTUALLY SAW ADAM AND EVE. NO ONE EVER SAW A TYRANNOSAURUS REX."
—CARL EVERETT

"I'M TRAVELING TO ALL 51 STATES TO SEE WHO CAN STOP [NO.] 85."
—CHAD JOHNSON

"CANCER SURVIVOR."
—LANCE ARMSTRONG, ON WHAT HE WOULD LIKE HIS TOMBSTONE TO SAY

"EVERY TIME THAT I HAVE EVER TRIED TO HELP A WOMAN OUT, I HAVE BEEN INCARCERATED."
—JOSE CANSECO

"I AIN'T GONNA BE NO ESCAPE-GOAT!"
—KARL MALONE

In the late 19th century, German Otto Lilienthal designed the first hang glider out of wood and fabric.

"THE ONLY REASON I DON'T LIKE PLAYING IN THE WORLD SERIES IS I CAN'T WATCH MYSELF PLAY."
—REGGIE JACKSON

"THE REASON WE CALL THAT PITCH UP AND IN IS BECAUSE THE ARMS ARE ATTACHED TO THE SHOULDER."
—TIM McCARVER

"HE'S ONE OF THE BEST POWER FORWARDS OF ALL-TIME. I TAKE MY HANDS OFF TO HIM."
—SCOTTIE PIPPEN

"I'VE HAD TO OVERCOME A LOT OF DIVERSITY."
—DREW GOODEN

"HAVING A RECORD COMPANY AND PUTTING OUT MY OWN CD. THERE'S CLOTHES AND SHOES. THERE'S ALSO AN UPCOMING BOOK DEAL THAT I'M TRYING TO DO. I'M TRYING TO BE POSITIVE. I'M A BIG FAN OF THE NOBEL PEACE PRIZE."
—RON ARTEST, ON KEEPING BUSY

"HE TREATS US LIKE MEN. HE LETS US WEAR EARRINGS."
—TORRIN POLK, UNIVERSITY OF HOUSTON RECEIVER, ON HIS COACH, JOHN JENKINS

"NOBODY IN FOOTBALL SHOULD BE CALLED A GENIUS. A GENIUS IS A GUY LIKE NORMAN EINSTEIN."
—JOE THEISMANN

"LEFT HAND, RIGHT HAND, IT DOESN'T MATTER. I'M AMPHIBIOUS."
—CHARLES SHACKLEFORD

In 1947 Dick Pope Jr. became the first person to try barefoot water skiing.

NONTHREATENING, NOT-SO-INTIMIDATING TEAM NAMES

Really now, what opposing team is going to be scared of these guys?

Hiroshima Toyo Carp (Japanese Professional Baseball)
As described in Sir Izaak Walton's classic primer on fishing, *The Complete Angler,* "The carp is the queen of rivers; a stately, a good, and a very subtle fish." Uh-oh, watch out.

Teutopolis Wooden Shoes (High School)
Technically, a wooden shoe could be dangerous: Getting kicked in the head by one would sure hurt. But all we picture are little Dutch kids waiting for gifts from Father Christmas. FYI, the Teutopolis *Junior* High team is the Booties.

Brevard County Manatees (Minor League Baseball)
Manatees are often referred to as the cows of the sea because they're fat, slow, and lazy. They regularly get chewed up by propellers—doesn't exactly inspire confidence in your team.

Elon Fighting Christians (NCAA)
When it comes to full-contact sporting events, turning the other cheek doesn't always work out so well.

Scottsdale Community College Artichokes
Here's a hint—when naming your team, try to steer clear of words that have choke in them. Unless, of course, you're the . . .

Gray's Harbor College of Washington Chokers
In the olden days, *choker* was a term for the guy who attached the big metal cables around logs so they could be moved. Pretty

tough image, so we can see what they were going for. But today, choker just conjures up a big, fat image of failure.

Cairo Syrupmakers (High School)

Cairo, Georgia, is known as the syrup city because of the syrup plant located there—but that doesn't mean they had to go and name the local high school team after them! And yes, their mascot is, indeed, a giant syrup pitcher.

UC Santa Cruz Banana Slugs

When you think athletic talent, the first image that pops into your mind probably isn't a slug. Random fact: John Travolta's character in *Pulp Fiction* wore a USSC Banana Slugs shirt—skyrocketing T-shirt sales at the school bookstore.

New York University Violets

Yup, the Violets—the little purple plant also known as the pansy.

Toronto Maple Leafs

Uh oh, watch out, the Leafs are coming! Also, we're pretty sure the plural of "leaf" is "leaves." Your high school grammar teacher might find these guys threatening—but that's about it.

"Men own basketball teams. Every year cheerleaders' outfits get tighter and briefer, and players' shorts get baggier and longer." —Rita Rudner

"I'M GOING TO DISNEY WORLD!"

The story behind the iconic ad campaign.

Thanks, Hon

In his memoir, *Work in Progress,* former Disney CEO Michael Eisner credited his wife, Jane, with coming up with the campaign. Over dinner, Jane asked pilots Dick Rutan and Jeana Yeager, who had just finished piloting the first plane around the world without stopping or refueling, what they were going to do next, and they responded "Well, we're going to Disneyland." Jane thought the phrase would make a great advertising slogan. And it did . . .

Disney Dollars

New York Giants quarterback Phil Simms was the first athlete to utter the slogan. He was paid $75,000 by Disney to debut the phrase in 1987 after beating the Broncos in Super Bowl XXI. Today, athletes receive $30,000 to say the slogan and make an appearance at the park.

Quick Facts

✓ The Super Bowl has inspired the most "I'm going to Disney World" ads with 21.

✓ Since its inception, there have been 38 different "I'm going to Disney!" commercials.

✓ Only eight times have the post–Super Bowl spots featured non–Super Bowl MVPs.

✓ Joe Montana, Emmitt Smith, John Elway, and Tom Brady are the only players to utter those famous words more than once (and still get paid for it).

✓ Super Bowl XXV MVP Ottis Anderson was the first to stray from the script: When prompted, he replied, "I'm dedicating this one to our troops," referring to Operation Desert Storm, which had just begun.

Sorry, Ray

Traditionally, the Super Bowl MVP is given the job of reciting the line. In 2001, Baltimore Ravens linebacker Ray Lewis was chosen as the game's MVP, but Disney chose to go with quarterback Trent Dilfer instead. Apparently, Lewis, fresh off a murder indictment, didn't mix with the whole Disney image.

Break Time

In 2005 Disney took a break from the Super Bowl campaign. Some speculated Disney was nervous about another incident similar to Janet Jackson's breast-baring mess in 2004.

We're Back!

After a one-year hiatus, the slogan returned for Super Bowl XL. MVP Hines Ward said, "I'm going to Disney World . . . and I'm taking The Bus"—a nod to Jerome Bettis, aka The Bus, the 2005 Steeler's emotional leader.

During the post-game celebration, Steelers safety Mike Logan riffed on the slogan and referenced the Pittsburgh-area's biggest amusement park by saying, "Forget Disney World, I want them to open up Kennywood!" Random fact: Pittsburghers say "Kennywood's open!" to let someone know their fly is down.

And Here's One You'll Never Hear

"I'm going to Euro Disney!"

The NERF ball was invented in 1969.

THE CORKED BAT

How does it work, what does it do, and why do batters use it?

A corked bat is just what it sounds like—a modified bat filled with cork or any other substance that makes the bat lighter and gives it some pop.

Against the Rule

Major League baseball specifically prohibits the use of corked bats. Just check the rule book. Rule 6.06 (d) reads, in full:

> A batter is out for illegal action when:
>
> (d) He uses or attempts to use a bat that, in the umpire's judgment, has been altered or tampered with in such a way to improve the distance factor or cause an unusual reaction on the baseball. This includes, bats that are filled, flat-surfaced, nailed, hollowed, grooved or covered with a substance such as paraffin, wax, etc. No advancement on the bases will be allowed and any out or outs made during a play shall stand. In addition to being called out, the player shall be ejected from the game and may be subject to additional penalties as determined by his League President.

That's a pretty long-winded way of saying, "Use an altered bat, you're in trouble, and any hit you may have gotten on the play doesn't count."

Mod Squad

The process of corking a bat is pretty simple. First, a hole ½ inch in diameter and 6 inches deep is drilled down through the head of the bat. Then it's filled with cork or whatever the cheater prefers to use. It's a risky endeavor—messing with the bat makes it much more likely to break and get the batter busted. Since 1970, six players have been caught using corked bats. Our favorite corker is former Yankee Graig Nettles. Nettles was caught using a bat loaded with six SuperBalls. Yup—SuperBalls. Nettles claimed he received the bat from a fan in Chicago and had no idea it was loaded with bouncy balls.

Sosa

The most famous corked bat culprit is Sammy Sosa. Sosa wasn't just some run-of-the-mill hitter; at the time, he was one of the league's premier sluggers and had smacked 505 career home runs.

Sosa's bat cracked in 2003 while playing against the Tampa Bay Devil Rays. Umpires immediately noticed cork in the shards of the bat. The game was stopped, the bat was examined, and Sosa was tossed. Said Crew Chief Tim McClelland, "I turned it over and there was a small, probably half-dollar-size piece of cork in the bat right about halfway down the barrel head, I guess. It was notched in there. I felt it, and it obviously was cork."

Sosa had driven in a run with the hit that shattered the bat. The runners were sent back to second and third.

Major League Baseball tested 81 of Sosa's bats, including five he had sent to the Hall of Fame—all were clean. Sosa claimed to have accidentally used one of his batting-practice bats—somewhat suspicious considering how careful he'd admitted to being with his bats in an earlier *Sports Illustrated* article:

> "I'm very, very protective of my bats. Look, I keep them at my locker. I don't like anybody to touch them. I care for my bats like I would care for my baby—with love and protection.
>
> "When I was playing in the Dominican Republic, I used to sleep with my bat. A bat is something you can trust and love. I don't have a problem if someone asks to borrow a bat. But if you grab it without my knowledge—that's a bad idea. A very bad idea."

Albert Belle, Bat Burglar?

In 1994, White Sox manager Gene Lamont, acting on a tip, had the umps check out Cleveland Indian Albert Belle's bat. The umps didn't notice anything unusual, but they confiscated the bat and locked it away in the ump's office/dressing room at Comiskey to be sent to the league office for further examination.

Then it was Jason Grimsley to the rescue! Almost. The Indians reliever crawled through the locker-room ventilation system, *Die Hard*–style, and broke through an escape hatch in the umpire's office, where he stole back Belle's bat and left a replacement. The plan might have worked had he not swapped it with a bat engraved with Paul Sorrento's name! Belle was suspended for seven games.

But does a corked bat really work?

On August 8, 2007, the Discovery Channel TV show *MythBusters* did a piece on corked bats. They determined that a corked bat, in reality, doesn't do much at all. The cork inside the bat acts like a sponge, absorbing energy. A ball hit by a corked bat actually only travels half the speed, and thus half the distance, of a ball hit by a regulation bat. They concluded that corked bats offer few, if any, advantages over a regulation bat.

Former first baseman Norm Cash disagrees with that assessment. He claims to have used a corked bat during the 1961 season—his only great season. He led the AL in batting, recording a .361 average, smacking 193 hits, hitting 41 homers, and driving in 132 runs.

BEST OF THE BEST: *SLAP SHOT*

The G.O.A.T. hockey movie, bar none.

The Stats

Released: 1977
Director: George Roy Hill
Starring: Paul Newman, Strother Martin, Jeff Carlson, Steve Carlson, David Hanson, Brad Sullivan
Box Office: $28,000,000

Tagline

"You'll see Paul Newman doing things you'd never expect him to do, saying things you'd never expect him to say!"

The Basics

Reggie Dunlop (Paul Newman) is player-coach of the Charlestown Chiefs, a small, western Pennsylvania professional hockey team in financial trouble due to the local mill being shut down. A trio of hockey goons, the Hanson brothers (Jeff Carlson, Steve Carlson, David Hanson), are brought on board—and as the Chiefs start playing rough and dirty, the fans come flocking. It's a funny, foul-mouthed, and fantastic look at small-time professional hockey. The hockey action isn't so bad either.

Loyal Fans

Vincent Camby, *New York Times:* "*Slap Shot* has a kind of vitality to it that overwhelms most of the questions relating to consistency of character and point of view. You know that it's an original and that it's alive, whether you like it or not."

Memorable Moment

The Hanson brothers' Chiefs debut is a helluva thing to watch. The nutcase trio storm the ice, tripping, punching, whacking, and

There are over 1,000,000 swimming pools in Florida.

generally beating the hell out of the other team. And the fans love it.

The Chiefs announcer describes the action with confused glee: "There goes Jeff Hanson into the corner. No, it's Jack. 17. I'll have to check that later. A crushing check on the boards! Things are really going on out there now! Now Steve is in front of the net. I think that's Steve. Yes. No. Yeah, it is Steve. And I think that was Jack. It was Jeff or Jack. These brothers are stomping all over . . . "

In the Know

Next time you're watching the movie with your buddies, look smart by tossing out these facts.

✓ The Charlestown Chiefs were based on minor-pro team the Johnstown Jets, and a number of real Jets players were used for the film's game scenes.

✓ All three Hanson brothers played professional hockey. They refused an offer by Universal Pictures to do a spin-off film so that they could return to their hockey careers.

✓ Al Pacino was considered for the lead role, but things fell apart after director George Roy Hill asked Pacino if he knew how to skate. Pacino thought the question was "facetious." He later admitted that he regretted not taking the role.

✓ *Slap Shot* is often referred to as the ultimate "guy" movie. But, believe it or not, it was written by a woman: Nancy Dowd.

And Second Place Goes to . . .

Sudden Death. Sure, *Miracle* would be a good choice—after all, it does faithfully document one of the greatest moments in American sports history. But *Sudden Death* has Jean-Claude Van Damme launching roundhouse kicks at the Pittsburgh Penguins' mascot. Easy choice, no?

ORIGIN OF THE TERM

The etymology behind some of the most common terms and phrases in sports.

Doubleheader

Originally a railroad term, referring to a single train with two engines. In baseball, a doubleheader is a single day packed with two games played by two teams.

Touchdown

American football borrowed a number of things from rugby—the term *touchdown* being one of them. In rugby, the ball must actually "touch down" on the ground when a player crosses the end zone line for the score to count.

Bases Juiced

Back in the day, when players were heavy into chewing tobacco, the spit would often get on the bases. When the bases were loaded, every base was "juiced."

Alley-oop

This term comes from the French *allez-oup,* which is the scream a circus acrobat lets out as he leaps. For a while, alley-oop described a Hail Mary in football, but it eventually made its way over to basketball.

Southpaw

Early ballparks were often arranged so that the pitcher's mound faced west, leaving a left-handed pitcher's "paw" hanging south.

Bullpen

The actual origins of this one aren't quite clear. There are a few theories, the most obvious being that a bullpen looks and pretty much acts just like a bull's pen at a bullfight. But what's the fun in the obvious? Hall of Fame manager Casey Stengel claims the term came from relief pitchers getting their own pen away from the other players because managers were sick of listening to them "shootin' the bull." Another theory suggests that back in the olden days, fans who showed up late to the games were rounded up like cattle and stuffed into a standing-room-only section later dubbed the bullpen. Pitchers soon took over the spot, but the name stayed.

Sudden Death

The term was first used by gamblers to describe the sudden twist of fate that could accompany a throw of the dice or a turn of the cards.

Seed

The term *seed,* as used in reference to positions in brackets, comes from the selection committee "planting" the teams within the bracket.

RIDDLE ME THIS

Can you solve these brain teasers?

Q: In major league baseball, there are seven different ways a player can legally get to first base without getting a hit. What are they?

Q: What is the minimum number of pitches that could be thrown in a major league baseball game?

Q: There's one professional sport in which neither the participants nor the spectators know the winner or the score until the contest ends. What sport is it?

Q: In which sport is the ball always in possession of the defense, and the offense can score without even touching the ball?

Q: What is harder to catch the faster you run?

Q: My buddy Charlie can guess the score of a basketball game before the game begins. How can that be?

Q: A man left home one day, made three left turns, and was greeted by a man with a mask on. What was the first man's profession?

Turn to page 353 for answers.

Nolan Ryan was the first major league baseball player to sign for a salary of $1 million as a free agent.

THE TRAGIC TALE OF TED'S HEAD

The Splendid Splinter becomes the "most famous decapitated person of the modern era."

What Happened

When Ted Williams died on July 5, 2002, so began one of the stranger and sadder tales in recent sports memory. His son, John Henry Williams, announced there would be no funeral—instead, the body was flown to the Alcor Life Extension Foundation in Scottsdale, Arizona. Alcor is a cryonics center, where recently deceased humans are preserved in liquid nitrogen, with the hopes of one day restoring them to full health.

As reported by *Sports Illustrated,* Ted's head is now stored in a steel can filled with liquid nitrogen (that's after it was shaved, drilled with holes, and cracked 10 times). In case you've got similar plans for the afterlife, the grand total for something like this is $136,000.

Controversy

Ted's daughter Barbara Joyce Ferrell claimed that Ted had wanted to be cremated, but son John Henry had (questionable) legal proof that Ted wanted to be preserved. That legal proof is an oil-stained scrap of paper, signed by Ted Williams and dated November 2, 2000, which reads: "JHW, Claudia, and Dad all agree to be put into biostasis after we die. This is what we want, to be able to be together in the future, even if it is only a chance."

The authenticity of this legal "document" has been called into question. The slugger typically signed legal documents with the signature "Theodore S. Williams." The scrap of paper only has written Ted Williams on it—leading some to speculate that Williams was only practicing his autograph on the paper scrap and the rest of the "contract" was written around it.

Making the case more suspicious, Williams's seven-page consent for cryonic suspension was submitted to Alcor upon his death with the line for his signature blank.

Pittsburgh's Forbes Field was the world's first baseball stadium. It opened in 1909.

Pay Up . . . or Else!

After the procedure took place, John Henry was billed $136,000 for the procedure and the cost of transporting Ted. He cut a $25,000 check to Alcor, but for a long time, the balance remained unpaid, which Alcor was less than pleased about.

Alcor's former COO Larry Johnson, who resigned from his position and took a stand against the company's "horrific" and "unethical" practices, revealed taped conversations between employees joking about how to deal with the outstanding payment, including posting Ted Williams's frozen body and head on eBay and sending it to John Henry C.O.D. in a "frosted cardboard box."

Johnson was also one of the few people to see the head, and he said, "It's been in there for a year, and it's ghastly." He then went on to claim that samples of Williams's DNA were missing, possibly stolen.

Apparently, sometime before John Henry's death in 2004, the bill was paid, because Alcor promptly accepted his body into cryostasis.

Is It Even Possible to Bring a Frozen Body Back to Life?

According to most scientists, no.

"BELIEVING CRYONICS COULD REANIMATE SOMEBODY WHO HAS BEEN FROZEN IS LIKE BELIEVING YOU CAN TURN HAMBURGER BACK INTO A COW."
—DR. ARTHUR ROWE, CRYOBIOLOGIST

"TO SEE THE FLAW IN THIS SYSTEM, THAW OUT A CAN OF FROZEN STRAWBERRIES. DURING FREEZING, THE WATER WITHIN EACH CELL EXPANDS, CRYSTALLIZES, AND RUPTURES THE CELL MEMBRANES. WHEN DEFROSTED, ALL THE INTRACELLULAR GOO OOZES OUT, TURNING YOUR STRAWBERRIES INTO RUNNY MUSH. THIS IS YOUR BRAIN ON CRYONICS."
—DR. MICHAEL SHERMER, HISTORIAN AND FOUNDER OF *SKEPTIC* MAGAZINE

WHAT'S IN AN (NFL) NAME?

Delving a little deeper into the names behind the franchises.

Pittsburgh Steelers

Up until 1940, the franchise was known as the Pirates, after the city's major league baseball team. Team owner Art Rooney Sr. changed the team name to Steelers as a nod to the city's premier industry. The Steelers logo is actually based on the logo used by the American Iron and Steel Institute.

New Orleans Saints

The name Saints was the winner of a fan contest. The contest results were kismet—the franchise was awarded to New Orleans on All Saints Day, November 1, 1966, and the city is famous for the jazz and gospel favorite, "When the Saints Go Marching In."

Detroit Lions

Owner George A. Richards chose the name Lions after he bought the Portsmouth Spartans and moved the team to Detroit in 1934. Said a team spokesperson: "The lion is the monarch of the jungle and we hope to be the monarch of the league." That didn't work out so well—although the Lions were dominant in the pre–Super Bowl era, they've struggled since, failing to reach a single Super Bowl and winning only one playoff game.

Green Bay Packers

The Packers took their name from their first sponsor, the Indian Packing Company. The company eventually went out of business, but the team prospered.

On October 31, 1950, Earl Lloyd became the first African-American to play in the NBA.

New York Giants

The Giants took a cue from the city's MLB franchise of the same name, a common practice in the early days of pro football. At one point there were football franchises known as the Pittsburgh Pirates, Brooklyn Dodgers, Cleveland Indians, Detroit Tigers, and Cincinnati Reds.

Cleveland Browns

When the Browns were founded in 1945 as a charter member of the All-America Football Conference, the as-yet-unnamed franchise held a fan contest to name the team. Browns, a nod to the team's first coach and GM Paul Brown, was the most popular entry. Paul Brown didn't like the idea, however, so the team tried to go with another entry—the Panthers. But a local businessman already owned the rights to the name Cleveland Panthers from an earlier, failed football enterprise. Brown relented.

Baltimore Ravens

In 1996 Art Modell moved his franchise from Cleveland to Baltimore. The city of Cleveland was allowed to keep the name Browns for a future franchise, so Modell's Baltimore team needed a new name. The *Baltimore Sun* held a poll and fans chose Ravens in honor of writer Edgar Allen Poe, who authored the famous poem "The Raven" while a Baltimore resident.

Chicago Bears

As a charter member of the American Professional Football Association in 1920, the team was sponsored by the Staley Starch Company and went by the name the Chicago Staleys. George Halas purchased the team in 1922 and changed the name to the Bears, reasoning that the city's baseball team was the Cubs and that football players are by and large bigger than baseball players, so they should be the Bears.

Buffalo Bills

As a member of the All-America Football Conference, Buffalo's football team was known as the Bisons. Buffalo's minor league baseball and hockey teams also went by the name Bisons, so, in an effort to set the football team apart, a contest was held to pick a new name. Bills, a reference to Western hero William "Buffalo Bill" Cody, won out over Nickels, Bullets, and Blue Devils. The winning contestant compared the trailblazer William Cody's path through the American frontier to the Frontier Oil–backed Buffalo football team, which was said to be opening a new frontier in New York sports.

On November 1, 1946, New York Knick, Ossie Schectman scored the NBA's first points.

GOOD ATHLETES, BAD TUNES

Why can't athletes just stick to what they do best?

Barry Zito

The 2002 Cy Young winner gets his musical kicks playing with his sister's band, The Sally Zito Project. Barry played guitar and also handled singing duties on the track "Boy Next Door." Y'know, because that's what Barry is—just your average, run-of-the-mill, $126-million-contract-signing, boy next door.

Allen Iverson

Thankfully, A.I.'s gangster-inspired, massively misogynistic track "40 bars" was so trashed upon release that we were saved from a full album. AI was so heavily criticized that the onetime 76er point guard was forced to release this statement: "If individuals of the gay community and women of the world are offended by any of the material in my upcoming album, let the record show that I wish to extend a profound apology. If a kid thinks that I promote violence by the lyrics of my songs, I beg them not to buy it or listen to it. I want kids to dream and to develop new dreams."

John McEnroe

McEnroe became musically inspired after getting together with rock singer Patty Smyth—so he formed the Johnny Smyth Band and did small gigs between competitions. Said the owner of one Manhattan bar where McEnroe often performed: "We loved having him, but he couldn't sing to save his life." Apparently the crowd agreed—they hurled tennis balls at him.

Oscar De La Hoya

Oscar De La Hoya's 2000 self-titled CD was actually nominated for a Grammy (despite being co-written by the Bee-Gees!). Still,

NERF stands for "Non-Expanding Recreational Foam."

it's just a little weird listening to a professional puncher belt out Latin love tunes.

Deion Sanders

Deion released a full album stuffed with tracks like "Time For Prime," "Prime Time Keeps on Ticking," "Y U NV Me?," and of course "Time for Prime (Reprise)"—and then if that wasn't enough, he released a remix album, with new versions of every song from his first album!

Shaq

Shaq released five full albums, as well as jumping on a whole bunch of other tracks. His 1993 debut *Shaq Diesel* even went platinum. But he's still a modest guy—he's got a track called "I Hate 2 Brag"! Sure you do, Shaq.

Kobe Bryant

Kobe had a full album of tunes ready for us, but it never made it to the stores. Reported the Daily Standard's Matthew Continetti, "The album was supposed to be out in March, but then they (Columbia) listened to it again, and it was so bad they put the kibosh on it." Consider us thankful, Columbia.

Macho Man Randy Savage

The Macho Man unleashed his lyrical fury in the form of a hip-hop diss track aimed at Hulk Hogan.

Manon Rheaume, a goaltender from Canada, was signed as a free agent by the Tampa Bay Lightning and in a preseason game on September 23, 1992, became the first female to play in the NHL.

SCOUTING AIN'T SCIENCE

Professional sports scouts make a decent living evaluating talent. But as you can see, they're not always right. Take a look at these high school and college scouting reports that were way, way off base.

Joe Montana

Three-time Super Bowl winner, four-time MVP, started a lot

"He can thread the needle, but usually goes with his primary receiver and forces the ball to him even when he's in a crowd. He's a gutty, gambling, cocky type. Doesn't have great tools, but could eventually start."

Greg Maddux

Hall of Famer, 400 game winner, threw a lot of strikes

"Lacks overall control on all pitches."

Clinton Portis

Four 1,000-yard seasons, has taken a lot of pounding

"Does not translate his stopwatch speed onto the football field; cannot bounce it to the outside, run to daylight, nor does he show a burst. Best between the tackles but may not have the size to take an every down pounding."

Randy Johnson

Three-time Cy Young winner, claims his four no-hitters involved pitching mechanics

"Timid due to awkwardness and plenty of room to fill out. No concept yet, just a thrower. Johnson is like a box of Cracker Jacks, there's a surprise inside. Our only problem is whether or not we

The first *Sports Illustrated* swimsuit edition was published in 1964. Babette March was the cover girl.

will like the surprise. He's a boom or bust. Long way to go yet. Has no pitching mechanics. . . ."

Orel Hershiser

Pitched most consecutive scoreless innings ever; only things empty were the bases

"No command or control. Fastball lacking velocity for big man. Doesn't throw curveball properly but has possibilities. Didn't like arm action as he labors through the throwing zone. . . . Delivery inconsistent, threw several wild pitches. Looks like he rattles easily. Questionable makeup with physical question marks in a 21-year-old leaves me with an empty feeling about him."

Tom Brady

Three-time Super Bowl winner and 2007's league MVP, and one of the world's most beautiful models gets a kick out of his build

"Poor build, very skinny and narrow, will get pushed down more easily than you'd like. Lacks mobility and the ability to avoid the rush, lacks a really strong arm."

BILL "SPACEMAN" LEE QUOTES

The Red Sox pitcher known as Spaceman made for a heck of a quote.

Bill "Spaceman" Lee was a finesse pitcher known more for his outer-space personality than his skills on the mound. Not that he wasn't a decent ballplayer—he retired with 119 wins and a 3.92 ERA. He was a starter for much of his 13-year career before being released by the Expos in 1982.

In 1998, he ran for president of the United States as a member of the Canadian Political Rhinoceros Party ticket. His slogan? "No guns. No butter. Both can kill."

The Quotable Spaceman

"If I can't smoke it, I don't want to play on it."

"That was real baseball. We weren't playing for money. They gave us Mickey Mouse watches that ran backwards."

"I think about the cosmic snowball theory. A few million years from now, the sun will burn out and lose its gravitational pull. The earth will turn into a giant snowball and be hurled through space. When that happens it won't matter if I get this guy out."

"You have two hemispheres in your brain—a left and a right side. The left side controls the right side of your body and right controls the left half. It's a fact. Therefore, left-handers are the only people in their right minds."

"I'm mad at Hank Aaron for deciding to play one more season. I threw him his last home run and

thought I'd be remembered forever. Now, I'll have to throw him another."

"Most of the managers are lifetime .220 hitters. For years pitchers have been getting these managers out 75 percent of the time and that's why they don't like us."

"The only way I'm coming to Washington is if I am elected. And if I do, I will paint the White House pink and turn it into a Mexican restaurant."

"People are too hung up on winning. I can get off on a really good helmet throw."

"The more self-centered and egotistical a guy is, the better ballplayer he's going to be."

"The only rule I got is if you slide, get up."

"The other day they asked me about mandatory drug testing. I said I believed in drug testing a long time ago. All through the '60s I tested everything."

"When cerebral processes enter into sports, you start screwing up. It's like the Constitution, which says separate church and state. You have to separate mind and body."

"You should enter a ballpark the way you enter a church."

"I would change policy, bring back natural grass and nickel beer. Baseball is the belly button of our society. Straighten out baseball, and you straighten out the rest of the world."

WHAT THEY MAKE, WHAT WE MAKE

The sporting life versus the real life, salary-wise.

What They Make	**Versus**	**What We Make**
Pedro Martinez: $2,800,447 per game started (2007)		*Boston-area nurse's assistant:* $108 per day worked
Roger Clemens: $191,919 dollars per inning pitched (2008)		*New York City elementary school teacher:* $34 dollars per period taught
Allen Houston: $876,563 per game played (2005)		*Chicago garbage man:* $208 per day worked
Mike Hampton: $9,503,543 for the season (2002)		*Pediatrician:* $140,000 a year
Mo Vaughn: $5,722,222 per home run hit (2003)		*Short-order cook:* $.81 per burger flipped
Larry Brown: $848,000 per Knicks victory coached (2006)		*Obstetrician:* $9,000 per baby delivered
Average first-year salary for NFL first-round draft pick: $10.86 million		*Private first class (Army):* $19,746 per year

The longest undefeated streak in football is held by Washington University. In 63 games from 1907 to 1917 their record was 59 wins and 4 ties.

GOLF HUSTLERS

In the early days of professional golf, many of the game's greatest talents never turned pro because they could make more money hustling the country-club crowd. Here are some of the most infamous.

Titanic Thompson

In the early 1900s Alvin Clarence Thomas (1892–1974) assumed the secret identity of "Titanic Thompson." Thomas was an extraordinary athlete and could easily have gone pro, but during those days, professional golfers were lucky if they pulled in $30,000 or $40,000 a year. Titanic could rake in that much in a single day hustling wealthy country-club players.

Titanic worked a few hustles, including betting that he could drive a ball 500 yards—then taking his unfortunate victim to a frozen lake and easily driving the ball that length and further on the ice. In another hustle, he would beat a player right-handed, then offer to play them again, double or nothing, with his left hand—but he was actually left-handed all along!

Informants fingered Titanic as the man who murdered mob boss Arnold Rothstein, the suspected money and muscle behind the Black Sox scandal—but he was never charged.

Amarillo Slim

Gambling legend Amarillo Slim (1928–Present) is in the *Guinness World Records* for being in five halls of fame: poker, gambling, seniors, legends of Nevada, and legends of Texas. He taught himself to drive a golf ball with a regular old hammer, then made a small fortune on the Las Vegas greens, even getting it over on daredevil Evel Knievel. Slim was a natural athlete and a born hustler—: He once beat pool great Minnesota Fats using a broomstick as a cue and even defeated tennis star Bobby Riggs at Ping-Pong with a frying pan.

He was once kidnapped by Pablo Escobar's thugs but was released. Apparently, it was just a big misunderstanding.

Bobby Riggs

Riggs (1918–1995) may have been on the losing end of Amarillo Slim's frying pan, but that doesn't mean he didn't have a trick or two of his own up his sleeve. Riggs often hustled on the golf course—with the stakes so high that it wasn't uncommon to see bookies following Riggs and his latest sucker in a golf cart, making side bets along the way. As Riggs once said, "The second worst thing in the world is betting on a golf game and losing. The worst is not betting at all."

Jeanne Carmen

Carmen (1930–2007) wasn't just a great golf hustler—she was a trick-shot artist, a model, a prolific B-movie actress, and a pin-up girl. The ambidextrous Carmen studied under golf legend Jimmy Demaret before taking her show on the road, hustling country-club players across the country. In her most famous trick, she would stack three balls on top of each other and drive the middle ball 200 yards without ever touching the bottom ball. And, in a feat straight out of the movies, the talented femme would drive a ball off a tee in the lips of a male volunteer.

CELEBRITY AT-BATS

One of the stranger customs in baseball is the practice of letting celebrities play an inning or two in spring-training games. Here are a few Hollywood honchos who got the opportunity to test their stuff against big-league competition and how they fared.

Billy Crystal

Crystal's known almost as much for being a Yankee fan as he is for his comedy. In 2008 he got a chance to live the dream in a spring-training game against Pittsburgh. He struck out in his only at-bat, though he did manage to foul one off. He dubbed himself the Designated Hebrew.

Tom Selleck

Mr. Baseball didn't quite live up to his name. He made one appearance at the plate with the Detroit Tigers in spring training. He fouled away six pitches before finally striking out.

Garth Brooks

Garth must have friends in high places, because teams just kept letting him hang around. He attended spring training with the New York Mets, San Diego Padres, and Kansas City Royals. In 47 at-bats he squeaked out just two hits.

Kevin Costner

Costner got his shot in the minors—fitting, for the *Bull Durham* star. He played in one game with the Inland Empire 66ers, a minor-league affiliate of the Dodgers. Costner started the game at shortstop then moved to pitcher. He threw to coaching legend Lou Piniella—18 years removed from his playing days—and walked him on four pitches.

In Wales there is a sport called "purring" in which two men face each other with their hands on each other's shoulders and kick each other in the shins with the reinforced toes of heavy shoes.

Bruce Hornsby

Grammy Award–winning singer-songwriter Bruce Hornsby got his turn in the big leagues with the Angels in 1997, when he was inserted as a pinch runner for Kevin Bass. Hornsby didn't get the chance to show off his base-running skills though, as he was left stranded on base when third baseman George Arias popped out to end the inning.

Kurt Russell

Unlike the other guys on this list, Kurt Russell played some serious ball for a time. He played second base for the California Angels' Double-A affiliate the El Paso Sun Kings during the early '70s. He led the Texas League with a .563 average before tearing his rotator cuff, forcing his return to acting (to the joy of Snake Plissken fans everywhere).

In 1900 Johann Huslinger walked from Vienna to Paris, 871 miles, on his hands. It took him 55 days.

AWFUL REFEREE JOKES

Dumb laughs at the expense of the zebras.

Q: What do you call a good umpire?
A: Rare.

The umpire had called strikes on two low, outside-corner pitches, giving the batter a tough time.

"Hey," asked the batter, 'how do you spell your name?'

"Rollins,' said the umpire, "R-o-l-l-i-n-s."

"That's what I figured," murmured the batter, "only one *i* . . ."

Q: How many umps does it take to change a light bulb?
A: No answer—the ability to see clearly has no application in their lives.

The referee of a high school baseball game was being heckled unmercifully by the crowd. He finally got fed up, walked over to the bleachers, and took a seat next to his chief critic.

"What the hell are you doing?" asked the fan.

"Well," the umpire said, "apparently you get the best view from here."

It was the day of the high school basketball state championships and the local team was a serious underdog. The coach brought one

Mini-golf holes were originally 50 to 100 yards long.

of his players aside and said, "Hey, here's 20 bucks. Go out and buy a new ball or something. Anything that might give us a shot at winning."

The game began and the coach noticed they were using the same old ball. He called his player over. "Hey, what's the deal? What did you do with the 20 bucks I gave you?

"Well, you said anything to help us win."

"Yeah?"

"So I gave it to the ref."

Q: How'd the umpire injure his hand?
A: His guide dog bit him.

Husband: "Man, I love that Matt McArdle."
Wife: "Who's Matt McArdle?"
Husband: "He saved us from losing last week."
Wife: "Oh. Is he a pitcher or a fielder?"
Husband: "Neither. He's the umpire."

The devil challenged Saint Peter to a baseball game.

"Sure," said Saint Peter. "But how can you win? All the famous ballplayers are up here."

"How can I lose?" replied Satan. "All the umpires are down here."

In 1894 the first major auto race was held on a course between Paris and Rouen, France. The winning car had a top speed of about 11 mph.

SUPER BOWL SMACK

The two weeks leading up to the Super Bowl are full of trash talk, promises, and guarantees. Some smart, some not-so-smart.

Fred "The Hammer" Williamson vs. Packers Receivers, 1967 AFL–NFL Championship

The Trash

Defensive back Fred Williamson earned the nickname "The Hammer" because of his habit of using his forearm to hammer opposing wideouts across the head. Prior to the big game, Williamson taunted Packers receivers Boyd Dowler and Carroll Dale through the media, saying, "Two hammers to Dowler and one to Dale ought to be enough" to put them out of the game.

Did It Work?

Nope, the Hammer's trash talk was most definitely not effective. He was knocked out of the game and the Packers cakewalked to a 35–10 victory.

Joe Namath vs. the Colts, the Doubters, and Everyone Else

The Trash

Joe Namath and his underdog Jets were preparing for Super Bowl III. They were going against what many considered the greatest football team in history. Then Namath made his legendary promise, "We'll win the game. I guarantee you."

Did It Work?

Yup. Namath's guarantee came true and the Jets won and Namath was the game's MVP.

At the 1971 Indy 500, A. J. Foyt's 9-second fuel stop on the 14th lap set a standing record for the fastest pit stop ever.

Cliff Harris (Cowboys) vs. Lynn Swann (Steelers), Super Bowl X

The Trash

Steelers receiver Lynn Swann, hurting from a concussion suffered during the AFC Championship game, was described as "soft" by Cowboys safety Cliff Harris, who warned Swann that he'd pay if we went across the middle.

Did It Work?

Harris's harsh words weren't effective in the least. Swann had four catches for 161 yards and a touchdown. To make matters worse, when Harris taunted Steelers kicker Roy Gerela for missing a 36-yard field-goal try, toothless Steelers enforcer Jack Lambert body-slammed Harris to the turf.

Thomas "Hollywood" Henderson (Cowboys) vs. Terry Bradshaw (Steelers), Super Bowl XIII

The Trash

In the week leading up to Super Bowl XIII, Cowboys linebacker Hollywood Henderson famously berated Bradshaw's intelligence, saying "Bradshaw is so dumb, he couldn't spell 'cat' if you spotted him the *c* and the *a*."

Did It Work?

If anything, Hollywood Henderson's insult motivated Bradshaw, who tossed 4 TDs and was voted Super Bowl MVP. Also, it was later revealed that Henderson was high on cocaine during the interview.

Dexter Manley (Redskins) vs. Marcus Allen (Raiders), Super Bowl XVIII

The Trash

Redskins defensive end Dexter Manley went after Raiders running back Marcus Allen, saying, "We're gonna find out about

Ann Butz is the only archer to win the Las Vegas, Detroit, and National championships; that's archery's Triple Crown.

Marcus's manhood," implying that he was soft and didn't like to run inside.

Did It Work?

It was the Redskins who came off looking less than "manl(e)y" as Allen rushed for a then–Super Bowl record 191 yards and 2 touchdowns.

Joey Porter (Steelers) vs. Jeremy Stevens (Seahawks), Super Bowl XL

The Trash

When asked about Jerome Bettis playing his first Super Bowl in his hometown of Detroit, Stevens said, "The story of Jerome Bettis returning to his hometown [Detroit] is heartwarming, but it's going be a sad day when he doesn't walk away with that trophy." Steelers linebacker Joey Porter was less than pleased with that comment and responded as such, "A guy running in and out on special teams shouldn't be sayin' things like that." Porter added, "We're going to try to tap out as many people as we can, I'm going to put it like that. We're going to try to send as many people to the sideline as we can."

Did It Work?

Yep. When game time started, Porter was on the winning end. Though the Steelers linebacker was invisible most of the game, Stevens appeared rattled and dropped three big passes in the Seahawks 21–10 loss.

Ray Buchanan (Falcons) vs. Shannon Sharpe (Broncos), Super Bowl XXXIII

The Trash

In probably the most famous pre–Super Bowl taunting session ever, cornerback Ray Buchanan and tight end Shannon Sharpe exchanged insults. Just check the transcript.

Catcher Duke Farrell once threw out 8 men trying to steal during the course of a single game.

Buchanan: "Shannon looks like a horse. I'll tell you, that's an ugly dude. You can't tell me he doesn't look like Mr. Ed."

Sharpe: "Ray said that? Well, I think he's ugly, but did I ever call him that? No. Tell Ray to put the eyeliner, the lipstick, and the high heels away. I'm not saying he's a cross-dresser, but that's just what I heard. If I see Ray in a snowstorm and his truck is broken down and mine is running perfect, would I pick him up? No."

Buchanan: "Shannon just runs his mouth saying anything, so we don't need to pay attention to him. He'd better watch out for himself, because he might get knocked out like he did that last game. We're not a team that's going to go out on the field and pull up our skirts and show our panties. I'm not saying we wear panties, but I'm saying we can't go out there and play like females and win the game."

Sharpe: "I'm not hard to find. I'm No. 84, and I've got the biggest mouth on the field. Tell Ray I'll be looking for him also."

Did It Work?

Depends whose side you're on. The Broncos beat the Falcons, 34–19.

NFL REFEREE SIGNALS

The funny moves behind the call.

Loss of Down

Pass Juggled Inbounds and Caught Out of Bounds

Tripping

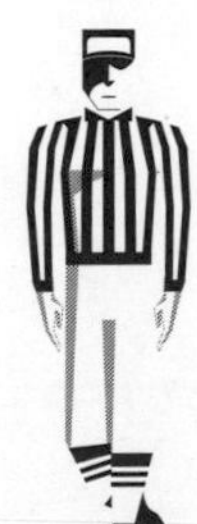

In 1951 a basketball attendance record was set in Olympic Stadium, West Berlin, when 75,000 fans showed up to watch the Harlem Globetrotters.

Reset Play Clock

Touching a Forward Pass or Scrimmage Kick

Illegal Block

THE STORY BEHIND THE TRADITION

Brush up on the history of a few of sports' more interesting traditions.

The Gatorade Bath

The origin of this one is up in the air. Some sources claim that New York Giant Jim Burt originated the Gatorade bath when he soaked Bill Parcells out of anger. But former Chicago Bears tackle Dan Hampton claims he was the one that started the trend when he soaked Mike Ditka after clinching the NFC Central in 1984.

The true inventor may remain a mystery, but there's no question about when the tradition took off—after Bill Parcells was showered by his players on national TV after winning Super Bowl XXI in 1986.

Once considered a strictly football thing, the tradition jumped to the NBA in 2008 when Paul Pierce showered coach Doc Rivers as the clock wound down on the Celtics' first NBA title in 22 years. Most likely, the NBA version won't stick around—the stadium's hardwood floors were stained and the drink left the court dangerously slick.

The Rally Cap

The rally cap made its debut in 1942 when Detroit Tigers fans began wearing their Tigers caps inside out in hopes of generating a little late-inning luck for the home team.

The theory behind the rally cap is that by turning your hat inside out and making yourself look a little ridiculous, you trade a bit of your own dignity for a bit of luck for your team.

Soon, the tradition spread to the Tigers players themselves, who adopted the hopeful habit. It entered the general consciousness during the 1945 World Series between the Tigers and the Cubs. In the sixth inning of Game 5, the Tigers radio announcer mentioned that players in the dugout were wearing their caps inside out. That same inning, the Tigers scored 4 runs thanks to a

The first *Sports Illustrated* was published on August 16, 1954.

bit of rally-cup luck—a ball rolled between the legs of White Sox first baseman Phil Cavarretta. The Tigers won the game 8–4 and went on to win the series in seven. The rally cap was born.

The rally cap made a particularly memorable appearance in 1986 when the Mets donned them in their edge-of-defeat, come-from-behind World Series win over the Red Sox.

Most recently, the tradition made the jump to hockey. Onetime Atlanta Thrasher Marc Savard started the tradition, whereby players place their helmets on their heads backwards. Said Savard, "We'd lost, like, seven in a row. We won, like, our next seven in a row."

Cutting the Net

North Carolina State head coach Everett Case started the practice of cutting the net in 1947, after leading the Wolfpack to the Southern Conference tournament in his first year as head coach.

He was forced to retire during the 1964–1965 season because of cancer. Wheelchair-bound when his team won the 1965 ACC tournament, they wheeled him onto the court and allowed him the honor of cutting the last strand of the net.

Victory Cigar

Whether or not Red Auerbach actually invented the victory cigar is up for debate, but there's no question that he's the man who popularized it. Red drew the ire of other coaches for his habit of lighting up a stogie as soon as he felt the game was over, whether or not there was time left on the clock. And he was never wrong. The cigars became a phenomenon in Boston during the '60s, with a number of Boston restaurants displaying signs that read NO CIGAR OR PIPE SMOKING, EXCEPT FOR RED AUERBACH.

Funny enough, for a man famous for his cigars, Red didn't smoke the good ones. Said former Celtics coach Rick Pitino, "I'd try to never smoke with Red, though. He would always smoke the cheapest, foulest-smelling cigars you could buy. I swear, he'd never spend more than three bucks for one."

Pool legend George Henry Sutton had no hands but still won a national billiard championship, and once made a consecutive run of 3,000 balls.

Indy Milk

Olden days Indy great Louis Meyer regularly drank buttermilk on hot days (*Anchorman,* anyone?). So, just out of habit, he chugged a bottle in Victory Lane after winning the 1936 Indy 500. A board member of the Milk Foundation thought the moment made for some great advertising, and it's been an Indy staple ever since (with a brief hiatus from 1947 to 1955).

Tokyo World Lanes Bowling Center has 252 lanes, making it the largest bowling alley in the world.

SIGNS OF THE TIMES

Sporting signage at its best.

No Bonds Allowed

Major League Baseball cracked down on anti-Bonds signs as he made his way toward Aaron's record, and one fan had his sign taken away at Chase Park in Phoenix. Team officials stated, "As Mr. Bonds approaches the home run record, we have been asked by Major League Baseball to carefully screen the signs that are brought into the ballpark by our fans."

John 3:16

His name's Rollin Frederick Stewart (born May 20, 1944), but you probably know him better by the names Rainbow Man, Rock 'n' Rollin, or simply the JOHN 3:16 Guy. During the '70s and '80s, Stewart was a common sight at sporting events, sporting his rainbow-afro wig and carrying his big old JOHN 3:16 sign.

His constant appearances turned Stewart into something of a celebrity—he got a gig in a Budweiser ad and Christopher Walken famously portrayed him in a *Saturday Night Live* skit.

Nice story. But then things get weird. In the late '80s, Rainbow Man began a series of stink-bomb attacks, culminating with an assault at the American Music Awards in an effort to show the public that "God thinks this stinks."

The text of John 3:16 reads: "For God so loved the world, that he gave his only begotten son, that whosoever believeth in him should not perish, but have everlasting life."

Stewart should have listened to that "God loves the world" message: He's currently in jail, serving three consecutive life sentences on kidnapping charges. In 1992, believing the Rapture was days away, Stewart attempted to kidnap two men and, in the process, ended up taking a chambermaid hostage, leading to a police standoff at a California hotel. He plastered the hotel room windows with JOHN 3:16 signs and threatened to shoot at airplanes coming and going from nearby LAX.

In a 1902 boxing match at Hot Spring, South Dakota, Oscar Nelson and Christy Williams knocked each other down a record 47 times.

For more on the Rainbow Man, check out the documentary of the same name by acclaimed filmmaker Sam Green.

BE SEEN

Interested in making your own sign and getting some attention at a ball game? Try these tricks.

Use thick letters and dark colors. Black's the best.

Sit with friends and make one big, long sign.

Shell out for the good seats. The closer you are to the field, the better chance that you'll make it to prime time. No matter how lame your sign is, if you're right behind home plate, someone's going to see it.

Networks loves free advertising, so let your sign appeal to their pocket. For a game on ESPN, for example, we suggest:

Everyone
Should
Purchase *The All-Star Sports Fan's Bathroom Reader*
Now!!!

Signs We Love

MLS soccer fans were ecstatic when David Beckham signed with the L.A. Galaxy, but when a knee injury caused him to miss 22 of the season's 30 games, fans grew restless. Visible on TV was a huge sign, directly behind the goal, reading BENCH IT LIKE BECKHAM, playing off the title of the hit movie *Bend it Like Beckham.*

Caught on camera, this sign was positioned perfectly to appear as a thought bubble coming out of an NHL ref's head, with him "thinking" I'M THE BIGGEST IDIOT EVER!!!

The longest bareknuckle fight on record occurred in Melbourne, Australia, in 1856 when James Kelly and Jack Smith fought for 6 hours, 15 minutes.

Ugh, college signs are the meanest—but often, the funniest. This classic has two fans holding up a pair of huge, gigantic, oversize underwear (the words WORLD'S LARGEST are printed along the elastic) with MANGINO, ARE THESE YOURS? written across them. If you didn't know, Kansas State's football coach Mark Mangino's a pretty hefty guy.

In order to make the required weight for a race, jockey Alfred Johnson once lost 14 pounds in a single day.

THE BASEBALL MOVIE QUOTE QUIZ

Can you match the quote with the movie?

Quote	Movie
"Quit trying to strike everybody out. Strikeouts are boring and besides that, they're fascist. Throw some ground balls. They're more democratic."	*A League of Their Own*
"I love baseball. You know it doesn't have to mean anything, it's just beautiful to watch."	*The Sandlot*
"Those Yankees are real turds."	*Eight Men Out*
"When the bat meets that ball and you feel that ball just give, you know it's going to go a long way. Damn if you don't feel like you're going to live forever."	*Bad News Bears*
"Man, this is baseball, you gotta stop thinking! Just have fun."	*Zelig*
"There's no crying in baseball!"	*Major League*
"Remember, fans, Tuesday is Die Hard Night. Free admission for anyone who was actually alive the last time the Indians won the pennant."	*The Natural*

"The one constant through all the years, Ray, has been baseball. America has rolled by like an army of steamrollers. It has been erased like a blackboard, rebuilt, and erased again. But baseball has marked the time. This field, this game—it's a part of our past, Ray. It reminds us of all that once was good and could be good again."	*Bull Durham*
"Tonight, he will make the fateful walk to the loneliest spot in the world, the pitching mound at Yankee Stadium, to push the sun back into the sky and give us one more day of summer."	*Field of Dreams*
"God, I just love baseball."	*For the Love of the Game*

Turn to page 354 for answers.

POKER SLANG

Here are some of our favorites and the meanings behind them.

Anna Kournikova (Ace, King)

Looks great, but rarely wins. Ouch.

Assault Rifle (Ace, King, 4, 7)

Get it, AK-47?

Beer Hand (7, 2)

The worst starting hand in Texas hold 'em. If you win with 7-2, you should probably buy everyone at the table a beer. Plus, you'd probably have to be drunk to play this hand in the first place.

Broderick Crawford (10, 4)

Named for actor Broderick Crawford who played Chief Dan Mathews on the '50s cop show *Highway Patrol*, where he spent a heckuva lot of time driving around yelling "10-4, 10-4" into his radio.

Canine (King, 9)

K9

Computer Hand (Queen, 7)

The history behind this one is up in the air. One story says that an old computer simulation picked this as the best hand to compete against two aces ("pocket rockets"). But this isn't very likely, not unless there was some pretty poor programming involved. The

The Yale golf course is laid out so that someone playing 18 holes covers one city and three towns: New Haven, Woodbridge, Orange, and West Haven.

best hand to play against a pair of aces is one that contains two suited connectors, like 7 of hearts and 8 of hearts.

The other theory is that a computer simulation picked Q-7 off-suit as the median starting hand. That is, when Q-7 off-suit is played against a random starting hand, it wins very close to 50 percent of the time. This story seems more likely.

Curse of Scotland (9 of Diamonds)

During Queen Mary's 16th-century reign, nine diamonds were stolen from the crown of Scotland and the people of Scotland were forced to pay a tax to compensate for the missing stones. The tax was known as the Curse of Scotland. Soon, the card was too.

Dames (Queen, Queen)

An important lady in English society is known as a Dame. Queens are pretty important ladies, so a pair of them are Dames.

Dead Man's Hand (Ace, 8)

Known as Dead Man's Hand because Wild Bill Hickok was holding this hand when he was fatally shot in the back.

Dirty Harry (4, 4)

C'mon, you know the line: "'Did he fire six shots or only five?' Now, to tell you the truth, in all this excitement I kind of lost track myself. But being as this is the .44 Magnum, the most powerful handgun in the world and could blow your head clean off, you've got to ask yourself a question: 'Do I feel lucky?' Well, do ya, punk?"

Dolly Parton (9, 5)

Dolly starred in the comedy *9 to 5.*

Doyle Brunson (10, 2)

Brunson won back-to-back Texas hold 'em world championships on the final hand with these cards.

Five and Dime (5, 10)

A nickle's worth 5 cents, a dime 10.

Flat Tire (Jack, 4)

If you have a flat tire, that's what you use the jack "four."

Golf Bag (Club Flush—as in all cards suited clubs)

A whole lot of clubs in one place.

Heinz (5, 7)

The Heinz company in Pittsburgh is famous for its 57 varieties of condiments, the most famous being ketchup. Random fact: The 57 is a little outdated—Heinz now has more than 1,100 products.

Jack Benny: (3, 9)

Benny would never admit to being a day over 39.

Jeffrey Dahmer (8, Jack)

Get it, Jeffrey Dahmer ate Jack?

Jesse James (4, 5)

The legendary outlaw carried a Colt .45.

Kuwait (Queen, 8)

Q8 sounds like the country

Marriage (King, Queen)

A King's wife is the Queen.

Art Wall Jr. holds the record for most holes-in-one during a career—he had 37.

Maverick (Jack, Queen)

Taken from the lyrics to the TV show *Maverick*'s theme song, "Livin' on jacks and queens, Maverick is a legend of the west."

Meat Hooks (9, 9)

This one's not too complex—nines look like meat hooks.

Motown (Jack, 5)

Because of the Jackson Five.

Oedipus Rex (Queen, Jack)

We'll let you figure this one out on your own.

Orwell (8, 4)

George Orwell wrote the sci-fi classic *1984*.

Speed Limit (5, 5)

55 is a pretty common speed limit on US highways.

T. J. Cloutier (Jack of Clubs, 9 of Clubs)

Texas hold 'em great T. J. Cloutier managed to flop three flushes in one year with these cards, hence the name.

Walking Back to Houston (Ace, King)

Poker legend T. J. Cloutier is responsible for this one as well, once saying, "I can see you learned to play in Houston. Those Houston players would come to Dallas and play that ace-king, but they'd always end up against a pair of aces. That's why we call that hand 'Walking back to Houston.' "

Walking Sticks (7, 7)

Two sevens resemble a pair of canes.

Wrestler Stanley Pinto once entangled himself in the ropes and lost after he forced his own shoulders to the mat for 3 seconds.

GET MOTIVATED, PAUL "BEAR" BRYANT STYLE

Ultramotivational, ultratough guy, ultra-ass-kicking words of wisdom from one of college pigskin's great leaders

"Losing doesn't make me want to quit. It makes me want to fight that much harder."

"I'm no miracle man. I guarantee nothing but hard work."

"Be aware of yes-men. Generally, they are losers. Surround yourself with winners. Never forget—people win."

"Sacrifice. Work. Self-discipline. I teach these things, and my boys don't forget them when they leave."

"The fun never goes out, but it changes with the years, with winning and losing."

"Never quit. It is the easiest cop-out in the world. Set a goal and don't quit until you attain it. When you do attain it, set another goal, and don't quit until you reach it. Never quit."

"I'll put you through hell, but at the end of it all we'll be champions."

"I plan on staying at Alabama for the rest of my career. I guarantee that I'll be here for you through it all, regardless of what happens."

Tap dancer Bill Robinson holds the backward running record in the 50-yard, 75-yard, and 100-yard races at 6 seconds, 8.2 seconds, and 13.2 seconds, respectively.

"It's not the will to win that matters—everyone has that. It's the will to prepare to win that matters."

"Mama wanted me to be a preacher. I told her coachin' and preachin' were a lot alike."

"If anything goes bad, I did it. If anything goes semi-good, we did it. If anything goes really good, then you did it. That's all it takes to get people to win football games for you."

"If wanting to win is a fault, as some of my critics seem to insist, then I plead guilty. I like to win. I know no other way. It's in my blood."

"I'll never give up on a player regardless of his ability as long as he never gives up on himself. In time he will develop."

"What matters . . . is not the size of the dog in the fight, but of the fight in the dog."

"I ain't never been nothing but a winner."

"If you believe in yourself and have dedication and pride—and never quit, you'll be a winner. The price of victory is high but so are the rewards."

"Tough times don't last, but tough people do."

Jack Dempsey's 8-to-10-inch punches moved at an estimated 135 mph.

CASEY'S REVENGE

In Grantland Rice's follow-up to the Ernest Thayer classic, Casey gets another shot against his least favorite pitcher.

Casey's Revenge
Grantland Rice (writing as James Wilson)
First published in *The Speaker* (June 1907)

There were saddened hearts in Mudville for a week or even more;
There were muttered oaths and curses—every fan in town was sore.
"Just think," said one, "how soft it looked with Casey at the bat,
And then to think he'd go and spring a bush league trick like that!"

All his past fame was forgotten—he was now a hopeless "shine."
They called him "Strike-Out Casey," from the mayor down the line;
And as he came to bat each day his bosom heaved a sigh,
While a look of hopeless fury shone in mighty Casey's eye.

He pondered in the days gone by that he had been their king,
That when he strolled up to the plate they made the welkin ring;
But now his nerve had vanished, for when he heard them hoot
He "fanned" or "popped out" daily, like some minor league recruit.

He soon began to sulk and loaf, his batting eye went lame;
No home runs on the scorecard now were chalked against his name;
The fans without exception gave the manager no peace,
For one and all kept clamoring for Casey's quick release.

The Mudville squad began to slump, the team was in the air;
Their playing went from bad to worse—nobody seemed to care.
"Back to the woods with Casey!" was the cry from Rooters' Row.
"Get some one who can hit the ball, and let that big dub go!"

The 2nd Marquess of Ripon (1867–1923) holds the record for the most birds shot by one man in a lifetime. He killed 556,000 birds.

The lane is long, someone has said, that never turns again,
And Fate, though fickle, often gives another chance to men;
And Casey smiled; his rugged face no longer wore a frown—
The pitcher who had started all the trouble came to town.

All Mudville had assembled—ten thousand fans had come
To see the twirler who had put big Casey on the bum;
And when he stepped into the box, the multitude went wild;
He doffed his cap in proud disdain, but Casey only smiled.

"Play ball!" the umpire's voice rang out, and then the game began.
But in that throng of thousands there was not a single fan
Who thought that Mudville had a chance, and with the setting sun
Their hopes sank low—the rival team was leading "four to one."

The last half of the ninth came round, with no change in the score;
But when the first man up hit safe, the crowd began to roar;
The din increased, the echo of ten thousand shouts was heard
When the pitcher hit the second and gave "four balls" to the third.

Three men on base—nobody out—three runs to tie the game!
A triple meant the highest niche in Mudville's hall of fame;
But here the rally ended and the gloom was deep as night,
When the fourth one "fouled to catcher" and the fifth "flew out to right."

A dismal groan in chorus came; a scowl was on each face
When Casey walked up, bat in hand, and slowly took his place;
His bloodshot eyes in fury gleamed, his teeth were clenched in hate;
He gave his cap a vicious hook and pounded on the plate.

But fame is fleeting as the wind and glory fades away;
There were no wild and woolly cheers, no glad acclaim this day;
They hissed and groaned and hooted as they clamored: "Strike him out!"
But Casey gave no outward sign that he had heard this shout.

The pitcher smiled and cut one loose—across the plate it sped;
Another hiss, another groan. "Strike one!" the umpire said.
Zip! Like a shot the second curve broke just below the knee.
"Strike two!" the umpire roared aloud; but Casey made no plea.

Q: What's the difference between a basketball player and a dog? A: One drools, the other dribbles.

No roasting for the umpire now—his was an easy lot;
But here the pitcher whirled again—was that a rifle shot?
A whack, a crack, and out through the space the leather pellet flew,
A blot against the distant sky, a speck against the blue.

Above the fence in centerfield in rapid whirling flight
The sphere sailed on—the blot grew dim and then was lost to sight.
Ten thousand hats were thrown in air, ten thousand threw a fit,
But no one ever found the ball that mighty Casey hit.

O, somewhere in this favored land dark clouds may hide the sun,
And somewhere bands no longer play and children have no fun!
And somewhere over blighted lives there hangs a heavy pall,
But Mudville hearts are happy now, for Casey hit the ball.

Alaskan Allen Dale Murphy killed two 2,000 pound buffalo in a single day using only two bullets. He was eight years old.

THROW THE ULTIMATE SUPER BOWL PARTY

Everything you need to know to make sure your big game bash isn't a bust.

Guest List

OK, right off the bat, you've got some choices to make. You might not want to invite any die-hard fans of the teams playing: If you invite your nutso Packer-fan friend to a Packers/any-other-team Super Bowl, well, things will probably get interesting. Now, this could either be really uncomfortable and awkward or really entertaining. You know your buddies better than we do, so we'll leave it up to you.

Do be sure to invite at least one friend who doesn't give a damn about football but loves the commercials. That way they'll keep you posted on the good ones and you won't be out of the loop at work on Monday.

Invite your friends at least a month in advance. Super Bowl parties are a dime a dozen. Sure, yours is going to the best, but no one knows that yet. So get the word out early.

Decorate

Want to get seriously festive? Decorate. Sure, your buddies might rag on you a bit, but it will go a long way to making your Super Bowl party feel like an event. And it's easy. Just print out a few images and hang them up around your pad, behind the TV, by the food line. Pictures of the team's cheerleaders are always a hit (or pictures of Jon Gruden for the ladies).

The TV

These days, a top-of-the-line HDTV is a necessity. Maybe you already own one—if you do, well, good for you, fancy-pants. If you don't, here's our suggestion: Go to the store. Buy one. Enjoy the game. Return it. It takes some legwork, sure, but it's worth it for a great party. HOWEVER, make sure you check the store's return policy before you swipe your plastic! We're not taking the blame for your $3,000 credit-card bill come February. If this little scheme isn't quite up your alley, there are plenty of places to rent one these days. You might even be able to convince your friends to chip in.

Beverages

Drinks are key—specifically, having enough drinks are key. Keep a few six-packs cold in the fridge. If the party's big enough for it, get a keg. Everyone loves a keg. A little soda too. If you're low on cash, make it BYOB. Your friends will deal with it. Plus, that way your friend who refuses to drink anything but some stupid specific Belgium lager can't complain when you don't have his Reitzengarden.

Food

Snacks, snacks, and more snacks. Get a variety; the more the better. Give people stuff to pick at—chips, dip, cheese thingies, pretzels, even throw a few vegetables in there. When it comes to the main course, if you can cook, by all means, go for it. Check out our recipe for our ultimate Super Bowl Chili elsewhere in this book.

If you can't cook, don't risk it. Just order. Get a few pizzas, some subs, some wings. Everyone will be happy. Just don't forget to place your order at least a day ahead of time—you don't want to spend the whole game waiting for the food to get there.

A Little Action?

Some friendly action never hurt anyone (except for the 1919 Chicago Black Sox, Pete Rose, Tim Donaghy, and our uncle Vic). If people are into it, you can organize a pool or set up boxes ahead of time. Check elsewhere in the book for a premade set of boxes and directions to run a great pool. If you don't want to do that, tell your friends to bring a bunch of one-dollar bills, then place small wagers throughout the game. For example:

"Pistole" Pete Sampras earned $41,994,440 from the time he turned tennis pro in 1988 to August 2001.

The next receiver with a catch will be . . .

The next team to recover a fumble will be . . .

The next player to do a ridiculous little dance move after a tackle will be . . .

Halftime

It's more than likely that you'll have zero interest in the halftime show, so provide entertainment. Videogames are a good way to pass the time—fire up a game of Madden and everyone will be happy.

How Not to Get Killed by Your Girlfriend

Clean up afterward! Simple as that. Keep trash cans at arm's reach throughout the game and the postgame mess shouldn't be too bad.

Air fresheners galore. Important no matter what, but essential if you'll be smoking stogies.

Before anyone arrives, go out and buy some flowers. When they leave, whip them out. No lady can resist.

10 DOCUMENTARIES WORTH SEEING

In the mood for a little reality? Add these to your Netflix queue.

One Day in September
2000, directed by Kevin Macdonald
The 2000 Academy Award winner for Best Documentary examines the September 5, 1972, murder of 11 Israeli athletes at the 1972 Summer Olympics in Munich. Michael Douglas provides narration. Watch alongside Steven Spielberg's factually questionable but nonetheless intriguing *Munich*.

Baseball: A Film by Ken Burns
1994, directed by Ken Burns
Ken Burns's ode to America's pastime should be required viewing for just about everyone. Divided into nine parts ("innings"), *Baseball* is 23 hours of history, insight, and that always-great Ken Burns moving-photograph trick.

The Endless Summer II
1994, directed by Bruce Brown
The original is a classic in its own right and highly recommended; but the camera work in the sequel is just so damn amazing that we're going to suggest you check that out first.

Unforgivable Blackness: The Rise and Fall of Jack Johnson
2004, directed by Ken Burns
Based on the equally excellent book of the same name by Geoffrey C. Ward, Ken Burns's Emmy Award–winning PBS documentary tells the story of the first African-American heavyweight champion of the world while exploring the inequalities of the Jim Crow era. As the movie's tagline says, "They couldn't knock him out, so they tried to tear him down."

Murderball

2005, directed by Henry Alex Rubin and Dana Adam Shapiro

This moving but still entertaining film documents the rough-and-tumble sport known as Murderball, in which quadriplegics of varying degrees of severity play full-contact rugby. As Roger Ebert said in his review, "To consider the bleak months and sleepless nights when these men first confronted the reality of their injuries, and now to see them in the full force of athletic exuberance, is to learn something valuable about the human will."

Hoop Dreams

1994, directed by Steve James

Filmmaker Steve James followed Chicago teens Arthur Agee and William Gates for five years, documenting their struggles for basketball success. Simultaneously powerful, depressing, and sweet. Plus, it features our favorite quote from any movie, any genre, ever: "People always say to me, 'When you get to the NBA, don't forget about me.' Well, I should've said back, 'If I don't make it to the NBA, don't you forget about me.' "

Pumping Iron

1977, directed by George Butler and Robert Fiore

Worth seeing just to watch Governor Schwarzenegger, dressed in a shirt reading ARNOLD IS NUMERO UNO, leading a crowd in singing the happy birthday song while puffing on a joint.

On the Ropes

1999, directed by Nanette Burstein and Brett Morgen

This Academy Award–nominated documentary follows three struggling young boxers and their coach as they use the sport to attempt to escape from the slums of New York. Powerful.

When We Were Kings

1997, directed by Leon Gast

In 1974 Muhammad Ali is 32 and possibly past his prime; George Forman is a decade younger and the heavyweight champion of the world. Don King offers the fighters $5 million to do battle in the ring, and the Rumble in the Jungle is on. Academy Award winner for Best Documentary Feature.

Dogtown and Z-Boys
2001, directed by Stacy Peralta
The 2001 Independent Spirit Award for Best Documentary tells the story of a group of California teen surfers and skateboarders and, through them, the history of skateboarding.

Dan Reeves, Tony Dungy, and Mike Ditka have all appeared in the Super Bowl as a player, assistant coach, and head coach.

THE SPORTS NUMERIST 61–80

The games. By the numbers. Sixty-one through eighty.

Roger Maris. **61** home runs in '61. Zero steroids.

Brett Hull scored **62** goals in playoff games.

Michael Jordan scored an NBA playoff record **63** points in a double-overtime loss to the Celtics on April 20, 1986.

There are a total of **64** squares on a chessboard.

Each year, **65** teams compete in the NCAA Men's Basketball Tournament.

In 19**66**, the Houston Cougars beat the Washington State Cougars at the Astrodome. It was the first-ever football game played on Astroturf.

On June 24, 2006, amateur golfer Sanjay Kuttemperoor made two holes-in-one in a five-hole span at Michigan's Treetops Resort golf course. Lloyds of London estimated the odds of such an accomplishment at **67** million to 1. That means she would have to shoot one round of golf 365 days a year for 183,561 years to accomplish it again.

Jaromir Jagr wore jersey No. **68** as a tribute to his grandfather, who died in prison during the Soviet Union's 1968 invasion of Czechoslovakia.

Mel Angelstad was the first NHL player to wear jersey No. **69**—and he played just two games in his career! The NHL was in existence for more than 80 years before a player wore No. 69.

On March 12, 1988, a hailstorm resulted in a stampede at Nepal's national soccer stadium, killing **70** fans.

In 1996 Sylvain Lefebvre of the Colorado Avalanche had his first child baptized in the Stanley Cup.

New York City launched its first OTB on April 8, 19**71**; it would eventually ruin horse racing in New York.

In 2008, Latrell Sprewell reportedly owed more than $**72**,000 in unpaid taxes.

Barry Bonds set the single-season home run record in 2001 with **73** dingers.

To combat the '**74** gas crisis, NASCAR reduced the number of races by 10 percent.

Southern Airways Flight 932 crashed on November 14, 1970, killing all **75** people on board including 37 members of the Marshall University football team, eight members of the coaching staff, 25 team boosters, four members of the flight crew, and one employee of the charter company.

Gas released from a nearby chemical plant sent **76** fans to the hospital during a game between Niagara University and Siena College.

Kenesaw Mountain Landis, Major League Baseball's first commissioner, ruled over the sport like a dictator for 24 years until his death at age **77** in 1944.

Hall of Fame basketball coach Don Haskins helped smash through college sports' color barriers when he used five black starters to win a national basketball title for Texas Western. He died at age **78**.

Thurman Munson's No. 15 was retired by the New York Yankees after his death in a plane crash in 19**79**.

At the 19**80** Olympic Winter Games, U.S. Men's Olympic Hockey coach Herb Brooks led a team of amateur and collegiate players past the Soviet Union in the "Miracle on Ice."

The Little League World Series has a 10 run "Mercy Rule."

"GREENIES"

The story behind baseball's obsession with amphetamines.

Long before Jose Canseco, Barry Bonds, HGH, or the "cream" and the "clear," baseball was overrun with another performance enhancer: amphetamines. Dubbed "greenies" because Dexedrine, one popular brand, came as small green tablets, these pills gave players the get-up-and-go they needed.

Let's face it, baseball's a fairly grueling sport. 162 games in 183 days. Double headers. Wind sprints. Red-eye flights. Said one veteran ballplayer, "Players use amphetamines to be the player they can't be when they're tired."

WWII

Baseball's obsession with amphetamines began during World War II. Soldiers were given amphetamines, aka "go pills," to help them stay alert and aware. British troops alone consumed 72 million of these go pills during the war. The Royal Air Force relied so heavily on them that one report claimed, "Methedrine won the Battle of Britain."

Back to the States

At the time, greenies were completely legal and could be found over-the-counter at any old drugstore. So when the war ended and ballplayers called into service returned home, they brought their greenies with them.

When Hall of Famer Ralph Kiner, who flew for the Navy during the war, returned to the game he found amphetamines in the training room waiting for him.

"You needed to perform your best and you were going to use everything that's legal to help you do it," Kiner said. "You worked to get that job and you wanted to stay in the lineup. If you got out of the lineup, you might never get back in."

During the '50s and '60s, team trainers freely dispensed them and players grew to rely on them. Their common use became something of a clubhouse joke. When a player would get thrown out trying to stretch a single into a double, his teammates would often joke, "The greenies must have lied to him."

First Deaths

By the end of the '60s, amphetamines were being used and abused by people all over the world, and they continued to be particularly popular in the high-pressure, high-stress world of professional athletics—not just baseball.

Danish cyclist Knud Jensen collapsed during a race at the 1960 Olympic games and fractured his skull. Autopsies showed a high level of amphetamines in his system, making his death the first documented death from performance-enhancing drugs.

In 1967, English cyclist Tommy Simpson, severely dehydrated and with amphetamines in his system, died from heart failure during Stage 13 of the Tour de France. Wrote British reporter J. L. Manning: "Tommy Simpson rode to his death in the Tour de France so doped that he did not know he had reached the limit of his endurance. He died in the saddle, slowly asphyxiated by intense effort in a heat wave after taking methylamphetamine drugs and alcoholic stimulants forbidden by French law. Police reports were that three glass tubes were found in his racing jersey satchel at Avignon, where he was taken after his death. Two were empty. The third contained tablets."

Congress Steps In

Congress passed the Comprehensive Drug Abuse Prevention and Control Act of 1970 and labeled amphetamines a Schedule II drug, which limited their availability. Among regular folks, amphetamine prescriptions dropped 88 percent within two years. But baseball didn't stop—the players kept taking go pills and baseball kept looking the other way.

Banned

Even though they've been illegal without a prescription since the '70s, they were never officially on baseball's list of banned substances. In 2005, after months of negotiations, MLB commissioner Bud Selig got approval from the players union and amphetamines were added to the list of banned substances.

Jai Alai is also as known as "the fastest game in the world" —the ball moves at speeds of up to 188 mph.

Said Selig, "Amphetamines have been around for a long, long time, but I was startled by some of the things I heard—the severity, the significance, the deep abiding concern. I could see it, not only with what they were saying, but by the looks on [the doctors' and trainers'] faces."

How Widespread?

Once they were banned from baseball, the question was, how prevalent had they been? And how prevalent would they continue to be after the ban?

Estimates varied. Ten-year-pro Chad Curtis said on an episode of *Costas Now* that he guessed 85 percent of big leaguers had at least tried greenies.

Texas Rangers trainer Dan Wheat once told investigators the drugs were "prevalent" in baseball. He asked a player, "Of the nine players on the field, how many took greenies today?" The answer was eight.

A *USA Today* survey stated that 35 percent of players suspected at least half were using them.

Heck, even Willie Mays was using. Outfielder John Milner testified during the Pittsburgh drug trials that Willie Mays kept a bottle of "red juice," basically liquid greenies, in his locker.

Leaded Coffee—The Breakfast of Champions

After being busted for accepting a $3,200 shipment of steroids from an undercover postal inspector, pitcher Jason Grimsley cooperated with federal investigators. In an affidavit, he said, "Everybody had greenies. [They're] like aspirin," and described how clubhouses kept separate pots of coffee on hand, one labeled LEADED—which meant it was laced with amphetamines—and one labeled UNLEADED.

Today

Espresso, soda, tea, Red Bull, and other energy drinks are now a clubhouse staple. Said Mets pitcher Tom Glavine, "I guarantee guys are trying to find something simply because it's a grind going out there every single night. Someone needs to put a Starbucks or a Dunkin' Donuts, or both, right by Shea."

BEST OF THE BEST: *HOOSIERS*

Here's the deal. We pick the best flick for each sport. Basketball was a pretty easy choice, considering Hoosiers is the absolute definition of a classic. Moving, entertaining, timeless. The ultimate sports drama.

The Stats

Released: 1986
Director: David Anspaugh
Writer: Angelo Pizzo
Starring: Gene Hackman, Dennis Hopper, Barbara Hershey, Sheb Wooley
Box Office: $29 million

Tagline

"They needed a second chance to finish first."

The Basics

This iconic, Academy Award–nominated film tells the (somewhat) true tale of a small-town Indiana high school basketball team that went all the way to the 1951 state championship. Gene Hackman is Norman Dale, the newly hired coach who's made to feel less than welcome by the locals. Dennis Hopper was nominated for an Academy Award for his performance as Wilbur "Shooter" Flatch, a walking basketball encyclopedia with a serious drinking problem.

Die-Hard Fans

Roger Ebert: "The climax of the movie will come as no great surprise to anyone who has seen other sports movies. *Hoosiers* works a magic, however, in getting us to really care about the fate of the team and the people depending on it. It's a movie that is all heart."

Memorable Moment

Just about every scene is a classic. But the slow-motion, grand-finale image of star player Jimmy Chitwood draining the game winner in the championship is just spine-tingling.

Classic Quotes

Myra Fleener: You know, a basketball hero around here is treated like a god . . . how can he ever find out what he can really do? I don't want this to be the high point of his life. I've seen them, the real sad ones. They sit around the rest of their lives talking about the glory days when they were 17 years old.
Coach Norman Dale: You know, most people would kill to be treated like a god, just for a few moments.

Myra Fleener: Leave him alone, all right? He's a real special kid and, and I have high hopes for him and . . . I think if he works really hard, he can get an academic scholarship to Wabash College and can get out of this place.
Coach Norman Dale: Why, do you have something against this place?

Merle Webb: Let's win this game for all the small schools that never had a chance to get here.

Coach Norman Dale to star player Jimmy Chitwood: You know, in the 10 years that I coached, I never met anybody who wanted to win as badly as I did. I'd do anything I had to do to increase my advantage. Anybody who tried to block the pursuit of that advantage, I'd just push 'em out of the way. Didn't matter who they were, or what they were doing. But that was then. You have special talent, a gift. Not the school's, not the townspeople, not the team's, not Myra Fleener's, not mine. It's yours, to do with what you choose. Because that's what I believe, I can tell you this: I don't care if you play on the team or not.

Wilbur "Shooter" Flatch: I know everything there is to know about the greatest game ever invented.

Coach Norman Dale: Five players on the floor functioning as one single unit: team, team, team—no one more important than the other.

Coach Norman Dale: If you put your effort and concentration into playing to your potential, to be the best that you can be, I don't care what the scoreboard says at the end of the game, in my book we're gonna be winners.

In the Know

Next time you're watching the movie with your buddies, look smart by tossing out these facts.

- ✓ Before the final game, the locker-room blackboard displays the names of the players on the opposing Hickory team. These are the real names of the young actors who made up the team.
- ✓ The movie was released in Europe with the title *Best Shot* because Europeans had no idea what a Hoosier was.

And Second Place Goes to . . .

Hoop Dreams. This 1994 inner-city hoops documentary is must-see stuff.

MASCOT MADNESS, PART II

More stories of costumed disaster.

November 1996: Wisconsin's Bucky the Badger is hauled into the hoosegow and issued a $141.50 fine for crowd-surfing. When asked by police to spell his name, the student states, "Badger. B-A-D-G . . . "

May 1997: Miami Heat's Burnie soaks the Orlando Magic's cheering section with a water gun. NBA Hall of Famer Dolph Schayes, 69, is none too pleased and responds with a right hook to Burnie's head.

May 1999: A Philadelphia electrician pushes the Baltimore Orioles' Oriole Bird off the rightfield wall at Camden Yards, breaking his left ankle. The mascot sues and is awarded $59,000.

July 2000: The Florida Marlins' Billy the Marlin hits an elderly man in the eye with a T-shirt fired from a T-shirt gun, knocking him out cold. The man sues.

January 2001: During the Sugar Bowl, the Miami Hurricanes' Sebastian the Ibis runs onto the field after a touchdown and taunts the Gators. The refs hit the Hurricanes with a 15-yard penalty.

January 2003: Edmonton Oilers coach Craig MacTavish grows tired of Calgary mascot Harvey the Hound hovering over his team's bench. MacTavish yanks out the dog's fabric tongue and throws it into the stands.

March 2003: The University of Utah's Swoop and the Oregon Duck get into a scuffle during halftime of a first-round NCAA tournament game—and the Oregon Duck's head gets ripped off! The mascots hug and make up at center court to a standing ovation.

There are more than 2,200 different names engraved on the Stanley Cup.

December 2006: New Orleans Saints backup QB Adrian McPherson sues the Tennessee Titans for $20 million after Titans mascot T-Rac plows into McPherson with a golf cart during a preseason game.

February 2006: The Stanford Tree gets tossed from a basketball game after blowing a .157 on a Breathalyzer. Stanford, unhappy with the Tree's behavior, gets a new student to play the mascot. A month later, the new Tree is suspended for dancing in an undesignated spot at an NCAA woman's basketball game.

July 2006: Chicago's Benny the Bull is performing at a local festival when he begins driving a miniature motorcycle through the crowd. When a local policeman tries to stop him, Benny flees, then punches the cop in the face, breaking the officer's watch and knocking off his glasses. Benny claimed he was performing in "character" and avoided assault charges. He did, however, have to shell out for some new glasses for the cop.

September 2007: The Oregon Duck is suspended after getting into a brawl with the Houston Cougar. The Duck took offense to the Cougar imitating one of the Duck's moves—push-ups for the team's total points scored after a touchdown.

April 2008: The Boston Celtics are understandably ticked off when Chicago's Benny the Bull blasts Kevin Garnett and James Posey in the back with T-shirts fired from a T-shirt cannon. The Bulls protest, claiming it was just an accident. Said Posey, "I felt threatened. Two T-shirts were thrown at me and KG. I don't feel safe. The T-shirts were fired out of that gun or whatever. I feel a little sore in one spot. I might have to get treatment."

Jack Dempsey fought only 138 minutes as world champion—but he made $2,137,000.

BOFFO BASEBALL INJURIES

You don't necessarily have to be dumb to injure yourself, but it doesn't hurt. Bear witness.

Vince Coleman, St. Louis Cardinals

Coleman holds the distinct honor of being the only person in the 138-year history of baseball to be eaten by a tarp machine. True story. Coleman was stretching on the field before the 1985 NLCS. Unfortunately for Coleman, he didn't notice the automatic tarp machine starting up. It rolled over his leg, trapping him, bruising his leg, and chipping a bone in his knee. He missed the entire postseason.

Glenallen Hill, Toronto Blue Jays

Hill is a serious arachnophobe. One night he had a nightmare that he was being chased by a spider. Half-awake and in the process of escaping, Hill tumbled out of his bed, sliced his foot open on a glass table, and fell down a flight of stairs. Opposing fans stuck him with the nickname Spiderman.

Sammy Sosa, Chicago Cubs

Sosa was hanging out in the clubhouse when he violently sneezed twice, bringing on back spasms. His back landed him on the 15-day DL. Obviously a bad back is nothing to sneeze at.

John Smoltz, Atlanta Braves

This is our favorite. Smoltz, no doubt a brilliant pitcher, might not be the brightest guy. He once burned his chest trying to iron his shirt while he was wearing it.

Adam Eaton, Texas Rangers

Adam Eaton was having trouble opening a new DVD and decided to use a paring knife. You see where this is going? The knife slipped and Eaton proceeded to stab himself in the stomach, sending him on a brief road trip to the hospital for stitches.

Jeff Kent, San Francisco Giants

The 2000 National League MVP broke a bone in his wrist cleaning his pickup truck at an Arizona self-service car wash. He claimed he slipped and snapped the wrist trying to break his fall. But reports later surfaced that Kent may have injured his wrist while doing motorcycle tricks in a parking lot—an act that his contract specifically forbade. Kent insists it was his commitment to car cleanliness that did the damage.

Steve Sparks, Milwaukee Brewers

Sparks attended a motivational speaking seminar hosted by the Brewers. As part of the seminar, the group ripped phone books in half. Sparks, amped up and looking to get motivated, attempted the phone book trick on his own. Didn't work. He dislocated his shoulder and went to the DL.

Clint Barmes, Colorado Rockies

Clint Barmes broke his collarbone in a fall after he got sick of waiting for the elevator in his apartment building and decided to lug a huge slab of deer meat given to him by Todd Helton up the stairs. Barmes originally lied about the incident because he didn't want to embarrass Helton and said he was carrying regular old groceries. There was also a rumor floating around that the entire carrying-something-up-the-stairs story was a big fib and that he messed up the shoulder while out riding ATVs with Todd Helton.

Wade Boggs, Boston Red Sox

Boggs had the sinewy, tough-guy act down perfect. From his stance in the batter's box to his dugout grimace to his . . . shoes? Yep. Boggs regularly wore cowboy boots. He once missed seven games after he strained his back trying to put on a pair.

After the New Jersey Devils won the Stanley Cup in 2003, goaltender Martin Brodeur took the Cup to a movie theater and ate popcorn out of it.

GREAT RACEHORSE NAMES

Possible ideas for your kids?

Why the Weirdness?

Ever wonder why racehorses have such bizarre names? It's simple. To keep racing records clear, all monikers must be registered with the Jockey Club, a 100-plus-year-old organization that signs off on all racehorse names. No duplicate names are allowed, so creativity is a must. However, you can't just go giving your horse any crazy name you want. See the rules below.

The Rules

Names can't be more than 18 characters (one owner actually named their horse Eighteencharacters).

No initials such as C.O.D., S.O.B., etc.

No names of persons without written permission.

No names of "famous" deceased people unless approved by the JC.

No names of "notorious" people.

No names with a clear commercial significance, such as trade names. Saves us from seeing Willie Wal-Mart at the Preakness.

No copyrighted material. Sorry, you can't name your horse Optimus Prime.

No names with a vulgar/obscene meaning or that are deemed offensive.

Super Bowl XXXI was built around promoting the film *Blues Brothers 2000.* The movie lost $14 million at the box office.

Easy Money

If, by chance, you actually own a horse and can't come up with a half-decent name, have no fear. There's a company called Thoroughbred Naming Specialists that will come up with a great name for your equine for just $27.

Marvelous Monikers

The names of racehorses can range from the touching to the outrageous, from the obvious to the illogical. If you poke around on the Internet, you can find various lists and discussions regarding horse naming. But as poking around on the Internet is not necessarily a good thing to be doing while on the john, here you go. . . .

Obviously Named by Men

No Fat Chicks

Ohbeegeewhyen

Short Skirt Flirt

Oliver Klozov

Shefoggedmyglasses

Bodacious Tatas

Sexual Harassment

Chicks Dig Me

For the Drunks

Sotally Tober

Anita Cocktail

Sheikh'nnotstirred

Plastered

The 1989 World Series between the San Francisco Giants and the Oakland A's had to be postponed for 10 days after an earthquake hit Northern California.

All-Around Great Names

Forty Dollar Bra

Hello Newman

No Stinking Badges

But Your Honor

Don't Choke the Cat

Reduced Sentence

Owner Hated His Horse

Badly Bred

Government Mule

Spineless Jellyfish

Lags Behind

Jai Alai originated in Spain and was originally played against church walls.

ON THE SWEET SCIENCE

A few of our favorite quotes on the brutal beauty of boxing.

"Boxing is smoky halls and kidneys battered until they bleed."

—ROGER KAHN

"The bell that tolls for all in boxing belongs to a cash register."

—BOB VERDI

"A boxing match is like a cowboy movie. There's got to be good guys and there's got to be bad guys. And that's what people pay for—to see the bad guys get beat."

—SONNY LISTON

"I especially like boxing, because you're really on your own: If you lose the fight, there's no one to blame but yourself."

—OLIVER NORTH

"Boxing is the magic of men in combat, the magic of will, and skill, and pain, and the risking of everything so you can respect yourself for the rest of your life."

—F. X. TOOLE

There's no stealing in the Little League World Series.

"Boxing is a sport at its most brutal, most primitive, and most natural. Two men defending their honor and courage, in a ring surrounded by observers, whose love for the sport is essentially spiritual. Boxing is the last refuge of the modern-day warrior."

—THOMAS DONELSON

"Boxing is drama on its grandest scale."

—HOWARD COSELL

OATES QUOTES

It's a little odd (and a little great, we think) that three-time Nobel Prize–nominee Joyce Carol Oates, whose novels tended to focus on themes like mutilation, incest, murder, and suicide, would also pen the classic *On Boxing,* one of literature's premier books on the sport. But she did. Here are a few quotes.

"[The] third man in the ring makes boxing possible."

"Boxing has become America's tragic theater."

"Boxing is a celebration of the lost religion of masculinity all the more trenchant for its being lost."

"To be knocked out doesn't mean what it seems. A boxer does not have to get up."

"Boxing is about being hit rather more than it is about hitting, just as it is about feeling pain, if not devastating psychological paralysis, more than it is about winning."

The Jai Alai ball, known as the "pelota," is the hardest ball used in any sporting event.

EDDIE GUARDADO PRANKS

His die-hard arm earned him the nickname Everyday Eddie. His devotion to devious pranks earned him the reputation of clubhouse clown. Here are a few of the relief pitcher's best gags.

Screwed

One unlucky Guardado teammate walked into the locker room to find everything he owned bolted down: glove, toothbrush, shower shoes, spikes, everything. It took him 20 minutes to get it all back up.

Itching and Scratching

For four days Christian Guzman could not stop scratching at what he was pretty sure was the worst itch in the history of itches. Guzman finally confronted clubhouse attendants to ask what type of soap they used. His Minnesota teammates, who overheard, burst out laughing. Guardado (and some itching powder) had struck again.

Dude, Where's My Car? No, Seriously, Eddie. Where Is It . . .

This one, an Eddie classic, had the prankster stealing a teammate's car and hiding it down the street.

Frozen Distraction

When David Ortiz couldn't find his shorts, Guardado fessed up: "Look in the freezer. They're nice and folded—and hard as a rock." Frozen shorts . . . that's a heckuva prank on its own. But it was only the distraction; while Ortiz fiddled with his frozen shorts, Guardado lined the inside of his jeans with peanut butter. Ortiz didn't realize until he suited up and found himself covered in Jif.

By 1989 improvements in javelin technology had resulted in throws so long that the event was almost forced out of stadiums. Ultimately, they were redesigned.

Immigration Troubles

Guardado capitalized on the country's immigrant boycott to lead his Mariner teammates on a prank on manager Mike Hargrove. Led by Dominican third baseman Adrian Beltre, a number of the team's Hispanic players went to speak to Hargrove, saying they refused to play.

Said Beltre, "He [Hargrove] bought it. He said three times, 'Are you serious?' "

Asked if they had fooled him or not, Hargrove said, "Yes and no. For the longest time, I didn't believe it. Then for about 15 seconds, I did. Then I thought they weren't [going to boycott]. Then, finally, Eddie gave it away."

Hargrove's thought process during those 15 seconds? "Which one could I reach out and rip their throat out? Who was closest?"

In the early days of bowling, 200 was considered a perfect score.

WONDERING ABOUT THE WONDERLIC

Want to know a little more about that test they're always talking about on NFL draft day?

Testing 1, 2, 3 . . .

The Wonderlic is a 12-minute, 50-question intelligence test best known for its use as a predraft assessment of the intelligence of prospective NFL players. A person's score is simply the number of correct answers given in the allotted time. A 20 indicates average intelligence; a 50 is perfect.

Score!

In Paul Zimmerman's book *The New Thinking Man's Guide to Pro Football,* he lists the average scores of NFL players by position as:

Offensive tackles: 26

Centers: 25

Quarterbacks: 24

Guards: 23

Tight Ends: 22

Safeties: 19

Middle linebackers: 19

Cornerbacks: 18

Wide receivers: 17

Fullbacks: 17

Halfbacks: 16

While the average scores for other common professions look like this:

Chemist: 31

Programmer: 29

Newswriter: 26

Sales: 24

Bank teller: 22

Clerical Worker: 21

Security Guard: 17

Warehouse: 15

Vince Young

The Wonderlic gained national media attention after it was reported that Texas QB Vince Young scored only a 6 and it was causing his draft stock to drop. Charlie Wonderlic Jr., president of Wonderlic, Inc., wouldn't compare a Wonderlic score to an IQ score, but he did say, "A score of 10 is literacy, that's about all we can say." So if 10 is literate, and Vince Young got a 6—well, that's not good.

The NFL soon reported that the reported 6 was inaccurate. Vince retook the test and got a 16—much more respectable.

Highs and Lows

Notable High Scores

Drew Henson: 42

Eli Manning: 39

Drew Bledsoe: 36

Matt Leinart: 35

Kellen Clemens: 35

Tom Brady: 33

Notable Low Scores

Dan Marino: 15

Terry Bradshaw: 15

David Garrard: 14

Kordell Stewart: 13

Marcus Vick: 11

Jeff George: 10

Does It Even Work and Does Anyone Even Care?

The big question is this: Does the Wonderlic even matter? According to a study done by Arthur J. Adams and Frank E. Kuzmits of the University of Louisville, no. They determined that an NFL player's Wonderlic score is unrelated to that player's draft order, salary, and on-field success.

And even if it did matter, would NFL teams pay attention? Yes and no. One former NFL scout said that a low score "raises a huge red flag."

But a member of the Oakland Raiders' personnel department said the opposite, stating, "All I need to know about Vince Young is that he came up with one of the greatest performances ever in the Rose Bowl. In the fourth quarter, I saw [USC coach] Pete Carroll throw every kind of blitz at Vince. I saw Vince read the blitz and beat the blitz. I don't care what his Wonderlic score is. The only score I care about is 41–38."

Wonderlicious

Harvard grad and former Bengals punter Pat McInally is the only NFL player to score a perfect 50 on the test. (Continued on page 304.)

SAMPLE QUESTIONS
(JUST AN EXAMPLE, DON'T SUE US!)

1. Pencils are $1.22 per box. What will four boxes cost? ___________

2. The seventh month of the year is:
a. October
b. March
c. January
d. July

3. DECEIVE/DESERVE Do these words:
a. have similar meanings?
b. have contradictory meanings?
c. mean neither the same nor the opposite?

4. Assume the first two statements are true:
1. Laurie met Jess
2. Jess met Ruby
3. Laurie did not meet Ruby

Is the final one:
a. True
b. False
c. Not Certain

5. Which number in the following group is the smallest?
a. 9
b. .6
c. 42
d. .43
e. 2

On Super Bowl Sunday, it's estimated that 14,500 tons of potato chips are devoured by fans.

In 1997 the Bengals drafted the "dumbest" player in NFL history, judging by Wonderlic scores. Florida State University defensive end Reinard Wilson scored a 4 out of a possible 50 on the test. Drafted with the 14th pick in the first round, Reinard was out of the league by 2003.

More than a few people accused Akili Smith of actually cheating on the test—he got a 15 his first go-round and a 37 the second time.

Today pro tennis uses a computerized tracking system that shows whether a ball is in or out. That means no more John McEnroe style fits.

MORE GOOD EATS!

More strange competitive eating records.

Dumplings

Record: 91 Chinese dumplings—8 minutes
Eater: Cookie Jarvis

Fruitcake

Record: 4 pounds, 14¼ ounces Wegmans Fruitcake—10 minutes
Eater: Sonya Thomas

Grits

Record: 21 pounds of grits at Harrah's Louisiana Downs—10 minutes
Eater: Patrick Bertoletti

Pickled Jalapeños

Record: 177 Pickled Jalapeño Peppers—15 Minutes
Eater: Patrick Bertoletti

Jambalaya

Record: 9 Pounds Crawfish Jambalaya—10 Minutes
Eater: Sonya Thomas

Mayonnaise

Record: 4 32-ounce bowls mayonnaise—8 minutes
Eater: Oleg Zhornitskiy

Mince Pies

Record: 46 Mince Pies—10 minutes
Eater: Sonya Thomas

Pickles in Vinegar

Record: 2.7 pounds Kosher Dills—6 minutes
Eater: Brian Seiken

Pigs' Feet and Knuckles

Record: 2.89 pounds pigs' feet meat—10 minutes
Eater: Arturo Rios Jr.

Shoo-Fly Pie

Record: 11.1 pounds shoofly pie—8 minutes
Eater: Patrick Bertoletti

SPAM

Record: 6 pounds of SPAM from the can—12 minutes
Eater: Richard LeFevre

Tamales

Record: 71 tamales—12 minutes
Eater: Timothy Janus

Turducken

Record: 7¾ pounds www.Turducken.com Thanksgiving Dinner—12 minutes
Eater: Sonya Thomas

A bowling pin's height and circumference is the same—15 inches high and 15 inches around at the widest spot.

WHAT'S IN AN (NHL) NAME?

The history behind a few of hockey's team names.

Boston Bruins

Usually, when a city is granted a franchise, they pick a name for their team first and then figure out the color scheme second. Not the Bruins. Charles Adams, the team's original owner, was the president of Brookside Stores and demanded that his hockey team's color be the same as Brookside's yellow and brown. It was the GM's secretary who came up with the Bruins name.

Detroit Red Wings

Team owner James Norris used to play for a Montreal amateur team known as the Winged Wheelers. He had fond memories of the team, so he dubbed his new unit the Red Wings. The winged wheel logo made perfect sense for Detroit, the car capital of the world.

Tampa Bay Lightning

Tampa Bay GM Phil Esposito was sitting on a deck with some friends when a lightning bolt struck. His friend thought that Lightning would be a pretty fine name for a hockey team, especially a Florida hockey team, since the Sunshine State claims to be the lightning capital of the world.

Philadelphia Flyers

There's no real good reason for this one. Philadelphia got a team in 1967, and owner Ed Snider and general manager Bud Poile held a contest to pick the name. Someone submitted Flyers and they just liked the way it sounded coming after Philadelphia. Sometimes it's as simple as that.

Q: What's the difference between Yankee fans and dentists?
A: One roots for the Yanks, the other yanks for the roots.

New York Rangers

New York and Texas are about as different as they get—but that didn't matter to Madison Square Garden president Tex Rickard. After Tex watched New York's first hockey team, the Americans, become a smashing success, he decided to start a team of his own. Taking a cue from the owner's name, fans started calling the team "Tex's Rangers," and the rest is history.

New Jersey Devils

The franchise bounced around for a while, beginning as the Kansas City Scouts and then the Colorado Rockies. When they landed in New Jersey in 1982, a naming contest was held. Nearly a quarter of the team's new fans suggested Devils—inspired by the monstrous creature known as the New Jersey Devil, which has supposedly roamed South Jersey since the 1700s.

Calgary Flames

The name Flames began with the franchise's start in Atlanta as a reference to the city being burned down during the Civil War. When the team moved to Calgary, the name stayed, supposedly because they had so little time to relocate that they simply switched the flaming *A* to a flaming *C*.

Fred Flintstone and Barney Rubble were members of The Bedrock Bowl-O-Rama.

JOHN "TURK" WENDELL

The teeth-brushing, beast-hunting Wild Thing . . .

John "Turk" Wendell worked as a reliever, spending the majority of his career with the Cubs and Mets during the '90s. Turk became a fan favorite for his superstrange behavior on the mound. Simply put, he was one of the oddest ducks to ever play the game.

Idiosyncrasies

Wendell insisted that the umpire roll the ball to the mound instead of throwing it; if the ump refused, Wendell would let the ball sail past him or, sometimes, let it bounce off his chest.

Instead of chewing tobacco, Wendell chewed black licorice.

Wendell brushed his teeth between innings (between every single inning, according to some people).

Between outs he slammed the rosin bag to the ground.

Wendell wore jersey No. 99 in honor of Rick "Wild Thing" Vaughn from the film *Major League,* the out-of-control pitcher played by Charlie Sheen.

While on the mound he wore a necklace made from the teeth and claws of animals he'd hunted and killed.

Whenever leaving the field Wendell would make a dramatic leap over the baseline.

In 2000 he signed a contract worth $9,999,999.99.

Just plain wrong! Q: Who was the last person to box Rocky Marciano? A: His undertaker.

While in the minor leagues, he drank only orange juice on days he pitched. No food, no water, nothing else—just OJ.

Whenever his catcher stood up, Wendell would crouch down; when the catcher crouched back down, Wendell would stand up.

Before every inning, Wendell turned and waved to the centerfielder. He wouldn't pitch until the centerfielder waved back.

The Turk's Big Mouth

After being tossed from a game for throwing behind St. Louis Cardinal Mike Matheny, Wendell asked, when control-challenged pitcher "[Rick] Ankiel is out there and he throws balls everywhere, why don't they throw him out of the game?"

When asked about Barry Bonds and steroids, Wendell said he was "obviously" on steroids. Bonds responded, "You got something to say, you come to my face and say it and we'll deal with each other. Don't talk through the media like you're some tough guy."

In 2001, after Vlad Guerrero made it clear he was unhappy about being beaned by Wendell, Wendell replied, "If he doesn't like it, he can freakin' go back to the Dominican and find another line of work."

Most recently, in 2007, Wendell was in the news for proclaiming that former teammate Sammy Sosa was "of course" on steroids.

MORE BAD FISHING JOKES

We probably should have thrown these ones back.

Cats and Dogs

A man comes home late one day, and his annoyed wife demands he explain.

"Well," he says, "I was doing a little fishing. As soon as my line hit the water I had a bite. I pulled in a big ol' catfish . . . then realized I forgot my fish basket! So I put the catfish under a tree behind me and went back to fishing. Next thing you know, I caught a great big dogfish. I didn't want to throw it back, so I threw that under the tree too.

Next thing I hear a huge ruckus, turn around, and see that the catfish and the dogfish got into a huge fight and the dogfish chased the catfish up a tree! So I had to bait back up and sit there all damn day until I caught a swordfish so I could cut the three down and get my catfish.

Clueless Catholic

A priest was walking along the shore when he passed two men pulling another man ashore on the end of a rope.

"That's what I like to see," said the priest. "A man helping his fellow man."

As the priest walked away, one man turned to the other and said, "Boy, that guy doesn't know the first thing about shark fishing."

Just Bad

Q: What do you call a fish with no eye?
A: Fsh

The Baltimore Ravens have three mascots—Edgar, Allan, and Poe.

An Affair to Forget

"You don't honestly believe your husband when he tells you he goes fishing every weekend, do you?" asked Judy's best friend.

"Why shouldn't I?" asked Judy.

"He could be having an affair?"

"No way, he returns every time without any fish."

Respect

Two men are fishing on a boat beneath a bridge when a funeral procession starts across the bridge. One man stands up, takes off his cap, and bows his head. As the procession passes he puts his cap back on, sits back down, and continues fishing.

"Wow, that was really touching," the other man said. "I'm impressed."

The first man responds, "Well, it was the least I could do. After all, I was married to her for 30 years."

River Bank

Q: Where do fish keep their money?
A: In the riverbank.

More Than One Way

Every Sunday afternoon all the fisherman in a small town gather at the country store and compare their weekend catches. The towns-folk all have an average haul, but one old farmer shows up every week with a huge collection of fish.

Pretty soon, the local game warden gets wind of this and demands the farmer show him his fishing spot. The farmer said sure and told the warden to come out to his farm the next morning.

The warden shows up bright and early with his fishing gear, expecting to head out to a large lake. Instead, the fisherman just takes the warden to a small pond and they shove out on a rusty little skiff. Before the warden can say anything, the farmer reaches into a box, pulls out a stick of dynamite, lights it, and throws it into the pond. There's a huge explosion, and then, a moment later, dozens of dead fish float to the surface. The farmer paddles around, collecting the fish.

The warden goes nuts, ranting and raving about all the regulations the farmer is breaking. Calmly, the farmer reaches into his box, pulls out another stick of dynamite, hands it to the warden, and says, "Are you gonna talk all day or are you gonna fish?"

A Jai Alai ball once shattered a pane of bullet-proof glass.

KICKOFF WEEKEND DRINKS: NFC

Kick off the NFL season right. If you're an NFC fan, we've got the perfect opening day drink for you. AFC fan? *See page 56.*

Spiced Arizona Iced Tea
Arizona Cardinals

5 ounces Arizona lemon iced tea
1¼ ounces spiced rum

1. Combine Arizona lemon iced tea and spiced rum.
2. Serve over ice in a highball glass.

Dirty (Bird) Martini
Atlanta Falcons

2 ounces gin
1 tablespoon dry vermouth
2 tablespoons olive juice
2 olives

1. Place an ice cube and a small amount of water in a cocktail glass. Place in freezer for 2 to 3 minutes.
2. Fill mixer with all ingredients. Cover and shake hard a half-dozen times.
3. Remove cocktail glass from freezer, and empty. Strain martini into cocktail glasses.
4. Tell your friends that, while no one is quite sure who invented the Dirty Martini, it was O. J. Santiago and Jamal Anderson who invented the Falcons Dirty Bird dance.

The draft class of 1983 produced quarterback greats John Elway, Jim Kelly, and Dan Marino.

Berry (Sanders) Blue Kool-Aid Slammer
Detroit Lions

½ ounce Berry Blue Kool-Aid
½ ounce vodka

1. Fill a shot glass halfway with Berry Blue Kool-Aid.
2. Place a paper towel over the top of the shot glass and slowly pour in the vodka.
3. Done correctly, the liquids will remain separated, with the vodka on top. Remove the paper towel.
4. Picture a Matt Millen draft day. As images of Joey Harrington, Charles Rodgers, and Mike Williams float past your eyes—
5. Slam it! The last thing you'll taste is the Kool-Aid. And for those true Lions fans out there, those who manage to stay positive, you'll need to keep on drinking the Kool-Aid. And we salute you.

New Orleans Hurricane
New Orleans Saints

1 ounce white rum
1 ounce Jamaican dark rum
2 ounces orange juice
2 ounces grape fruit juice
2 ounces pineapple juice
½ ounce grenadine syrup
crushed ice
1 ounce Bacardi 151 rum

1. Combine all ingredients except Bacardi 151 and ice.
2. Pour over crushed ice in hurricane glass.
3. Float the Bacardi 151 on top of the drink.
4. Hang on to your hat.

Ray Lewis' favorite song is "In the Air Tonight" by Phil Collins.

Captain Gruden's Rum and Coke

Tampa Bay Buccaneers

1½ ounces spiced rum
4½ ounces Coca-Cola

1. Pour rum and Coca-Cola into a highball glass over ice.
2. Mix. Serve.
3. Argue about whether it was Tony Dungy's players or Jon Gruden's coaching that got you that Super Bowl.

Whiskey

Dallas Cowboys

1 shot whiskey

1. Just like the real Cowboys drank. Take shot. Repeat until you're drunk enough to try to rope a bronco.

Mead

Minnesota Vikings

This fermented alcoholic beverage made of honey, water, malt, and yeast was what the true Vikings drank. It's not the most common alcoholic beverage these days, but poke around online and you'll find a dozen places you can order it from. Serve in a gigantic chalice.

Irish Coffee

Seattle Seahawks

1½ ounces Irish whiskey
1 teaspoon brown sugar
6 ounces Starbucks coffee
half-and-half

1. Combine whiskey, sugar, and coffee in a mug and stir to dissolve.

Richard Nixon was a huge poker player and, according to some, financed part of his campaigns with his winnings.

2. Float half-and-half on top. Do not mix.
3. Serve in a coffee mug.

Favre's Green Fizz
Green Bay Packers

2 ounces dry gin
1 teaspoon green crème de menthe
1 ounce lemon juice
1 egg white
1 teaspoon superfine sugar
club soda

1. Mix all ingredients (except club soda), shake, and strain into a highball glass over ice.
2. Fill with club soda and serve.

Yuengling
Philadelphia Eagles

Yuengling Lager

1. Grab a cold one. Philadelphia boys love their Yuengling.

Snyder's Cider
Washington Redskins

Head online to find your favorite brand of hard cider. If you want to get the true Snyder effect, make sure you way overpay.

Blue Manhattan
New York Giants

2 ounces blended whiskey
½ ounce sweet vermouth
½ ounce dry vermouth
splash blue Curaçao

An estimated 8 million pounds of guacamole is consumed each year on Super Bowl Sunday.

1. Mix all ingredients; shake with ice to chill.
2. Serve in a cocktail glass and garnish with a maraschino cherry.

Goldschläger
San Francisco 49ers

1 shot Goldschläger liqueur

In honor of the gold-crazy fortune hunters that flooded San Francisco (and gave the 49ers their name), we suggest you throw down a few shots of Goldschläger, the only liquor with visible flakes of gold leaf floating in it.

Be careful, those gold flakes have been known to slice up the throat and stomach once swallowed, allowing the alcohol to directly enter your bloodstream and get you blotto real fast (kidding, kidding, that's just an urban legend—but still, the stuff will get you wasted, so go slow).

Mike Ditka Wine: Kick Ass Red
Chicago Bears

Yep, Mike Ditka has his own line of wines. He partnered with Mendocino Wine Company to create his own lines of high-quality, Ditka-fied wines. As his Web site boasts, they're all about Attitude, Character, and Enthusiasm. We're recommending the Kick Ass Red, which is Mike's personal favorite.

The *Chicago Sun-Times* held a wine tasting where one Ditka wine fan described it as "round . . . well-balanced in fruit tannins and body." If you're in the Chicago area, you should be able to find these at most well-stocked wine stores; otherwise, just head online to, what else, www.MikeDitkaWines.com.

Sex Panther Ice Ale
Carolina Panthers

Panther Ice Ale

Sixty percent of the time it gets you drunk every time. And it's made with real bits of Steve Smith, so you know it's good.

Greatest Show on Turf Cocktail
St. Louis Rams

1 part gin
1 part French vermouth
3 dashes of absinthe (it's legal now, enjoy!)
1 orange peel

1. Mix all your ingredients (except orange peel) in a cocktail shaker with ice.
2. Strain into a cocktail glass. Garnish with a twist of orange peel.

Curling is known as "The Roaring Game" because of the sound the stones make moving over the ice.

CORPORATE SPONSORSHIP GONE WILD

Longing for the days of Ebbets Field, Three Rivers Stadium, and the Boston Garden.

Worst Offenders

PacBell/SBC/ATT Park: Home to the San Francisco Giants. Could they come up with anything more impersonal? Really?

U.S. Cellular Field: Home to the Chicago White Sox. Sorry, but we can't help but think you might get cancer if you stayed in here too long.

INVESCO Field at Mile High Stadium: Home to the Denver Broncos. Wacky Denver columnist Woody Paige revealed that even INVESCO officials refuse to call it by that lumbering name—they just refer to it as the Diaphragm (because it look likes a—you guessed it). We really prefer that name.

Quicken Loans Arena: Home to the Cleveland Cavaliers. A quick loan—so you can afford a beer and a dog at a ball game these days.

PETCO Park: Home to the San Diego Padres. No pets allowed.

The BankAtlantic Center (previously known as Broward County Civic Arena, National Car Rental Center, and Office Depot Center): Home to the Florida Panthers. That's just an awful little name history there—no town's fans should be subjected to something like that. The National Car Rental . . . really? Really?!?

EnergySolutions Arena: Home to the Utah Jazz. EnergySolutions is a nuclear waste disposal company—doesn't make you want to spend much time in their stadium. And why does a nuclear waste disposal company need to advertise anyway?

The Colts were the first NFL team to have cheerleaders.

Good Ones

Believe it or not, not all corporate naming right situations are awful. Here are two we actually kind of like:

Great American Ballpark: Home to the Cincinnati Reds. The Great American Insurance Company bought the naming rights for the Reds stadium—and thankfully Great American Ballpark just sounds right.

Minute Maid Park: Home to the Houston Astros. Was once Enron Stadium, which is about as bad as it gets. But Minute Maid Park just makes us think of orange soda, which is about as good as it gets.

Sorry, We're Done With You

In 1986, Villanova University named its new basketball arena Du Pont Pavilion after influential majority donor John du Pont. In 1996 he was convicted in the murder of Olympic wrestling gold medalist Dave Schultz. Villanova dropped the Du Pont but kept the Pavilion, the basketball team's current home.

The Astros were put in a tough situation in 2002 when Enron went under in one of the biggest business scandals in American history. The team bought out Enron's naming rights contract and got rid of everything Enron-related in the stadium. The home of the 'Stros now goes by Minute Maid Park.

When CoreStates Bank merged with First Union Bank in 1995, the home of the Philadelphia Flyers and 76ers became the First Union Center. Perpetually pissed-off Philly fans dubbed it the F.U. Center. First Union sidestepped the PR disaster by switching the name to the First Union National Bank Center ("F.U.N. Center . . . get it?).

Emmitt Smith had the same number of rushing yards in his first season as he did in his last: 937.

3K to Stick It to the Sox? Sure!

The TD BankNorth Garden in Boston, home to the Celtics and Bruins, has carried 34 different names since its construction was announced in 1993, including the Shawmut Center, Fleet Center, YourGarden, and TD BankNorth Garden. In the midst of the hunt, the naming rights were auctioned off on eBay, with one day's naming rights averaging $3,000. A New York lawyer/Yankees fan won the rights and attempted to name it the Derek Jeter Center. It was rejected.

AS BAD AS IT SOUNDS

In 2004, a new species of monkey was discovered in western Bolivia's Madidi National Park. Naming rights were auctioned off and online casino the Golden Palace had the top bid with $650,000. So there is indeed a species of animal officially recognized as TheGoldenPalace.com monkey.

BASEBALL GAVE US THAT!?

The number of baseball words and phrases that ended up in the general English lexicon is astonishing. Some are obvious, like ballpark figure or batting a thousand, but others might surprise you.

Bleachers, as in rows of seats from which fans can watch the game

A reference to fans sitting in the stands, watching the game, and bleaching their skin in the sun.

Boner, as in "mistake" (get your mind out of the gutter)

Derives from bonehead; probably some boneheaded ump.

The Breaks, as in luck

Stems from the way a curveball breaks—if it breaks in your favor, that's some good luck.

Charley horse, as in a pulled muscle

The term definitely originated with baseball, though who this Charley fella was isn't clear. Most likely some player who bet on a horse with a bad limp.

Heads up, as in wide awake, alert

In reference to players keeping their heads in the game, particularly the first baseman, who better be alert with his head up lest he take a ball to the family jewels.

Ladies night, as in reduced price or free admission for women

The concept of "ladies day" or "ladies night" began in baseball as a move to draw more women to the games.

A curling rink in Halifax, Nova Scotia, was temporarily used as a morgue for bodies recovered from the Titanic tragedy.

Flat-footed, as in slow

Stems from a base runner taking a lead and then getting picked off because of not being on his toes.

Off base, as in mistaken

Its daily use comes from a runner taking too large a lead off the base and getting picked off.

Right off the bat, as in immediately

Pretty obvious one here; the term comes from the speed at which a hit ball flies off the bat.

Root, as in applauding and supporting your team

This term comes from cheering fans stamping their feet, almost like they're trying to uproot something from the ground.

Screwball, as in someone who's a little crazy

The screwball pitch was around for years, but it was originally called the fadeaway. The term *screwball* didn't come about until a minor-league catcher tried to catch one and said, it was the "screwiest thing I ever saw." It's a crazy pitch.

Second-guess, as in doubting, questioning

Originated as lingo for all those fans who scream and yell, questioning a team or an ump's every move and call.

Showboating, as in a showboat, someone who shows off

Baseball took the term from riverboats, which often featured loud tunes and musical theater. Basically, a riverboat is loud and dramatic and so is anyone doing some showboating.

Smash hit, as in a success

Duh—a hard-hit ball is usually a success.

If swimming is good for your shape, then why do the whales look the way they do?
— George Carlin

COACHES SAY DUMB STUFF TOO

Hey, the guys in charge aren't excluded from the occasional verbal blunder.

"THIS TEAM IS ONE EXECUTION AWAY FROM BEING A VERY GOOD BASKETBALL TEAM."
—BASKETBALL COACH DOC RIVERS

"WE'RE NOT ATTEMPTING TO CIRCUMCISE RULES."
—FORMER STEELERS COACH BILL COWHER

"TOM."
—HOUSTON ROCKETS COACH TOM NISSALKE, WHEN ASKED HOW HE PRONOUNCED HIS NAME

"I DON'T CARE WHAT THE TAPE SAYS. I DIDN'T SAY IT."
—FOOTBALL COACH RAY MALAVASI

"IT ISN'T LIKE I CAME DOWN FROM MOUNT SINAI WITH THE TABLOIDS."
—FORMER INDIANAPOLIS COLTS COACH RON MEYER

"MOST OF OUR FUTURE LIES AHEAD."
—DENNY CRUM, LOUISVILLE BASKETBALL COACH

"THAT WAS THE NAIL THAT BROKE THE COFFIN'S BACK."
—KACK KRAFT, VILLANOVA BASKETBALL COACH, ON A KEY PLAYER FOULING OUT OF A GAME

Men's water polo was the first team sport added to the Olympics.

"I'VE GOT NOTHING TO SAY, AND I'LL ONLY SAY IT ONCE."
—FLOYD SMITH, TORONTO MAPLE LEAFS COACH, AFTER A LOSS

"WHEN WE'RE COMPETING FOR THE STANLEY CUP, THIS RECORD WON'T MEAN A THING."
—OTTAWA COACH RICK BOWNESS, AFTER THE SENATORS TIED AN NHL RECORD WITH 37 STRAIGHT LOSSES ON THE ROAD

Hank Williams Jr.'s *Monday Night Football* theme is officially called "All My Rowdy Friends Are Here on Monday Night."

LOST IN TRANSLATION

Some things just don't translate. To prove it, we've done a little experiment. Here's what happens when you take a classic call, translate it into another language, and then try to bring it back into English. Enjoy.

Jack Buck, 1985 NLCS Game 5: St. Louis Cardinals vs. Los Angeles Dodgers

The original: "Go crazy, folks! Go crazy!"
Chinese: "Changes crazy, waiter! Changes crazy!"

Joe Starkey, 1982 Big Game: Cal vs. Stanford

The original: "Oh, the band is out on the field! He's gonna go into the end zone! He's gone into the end zone! And the Bears! The Bears have won! California has won the Big Game over Stanford!"
Dutch: "Oh, the link are from in the area! In the end region he will go! He has gone in the end region! And the Roar! The Roar have won! California has won the large game concerning Stanford!"

Russ Hodges, on Bobby Thomson's pennant-winning home run against the Brooklyn Dodgers, October 3, 1951

The original: There's a long drive. It's gonna be, I believe—the Giants win the pennant! The Giants win the pennant! The Giants win the pennant! The Giants win the pennant!"
Japanese: "Has long-range. That goes to, if is, I believed—the giant won the signal flag! The giant won the signal flag! The giant won the signal flag! The giant won the signal flag!"

Al Michaels, 1980 Olympic Hockey: USA vs. Russia

The original: "Do you believe in miracles!? Yes!"
Japanese: "Miracle is believed!? It is!"

Johnny Most, Game 7 of the 1965 Eastern Conference Finals: Boston Celtics vs. Philadelphia 76ers

The original: "Havlicek stole the ball!"
Korean: "Havlicek it steals public affairs!"

Howard Cosell, 1973 World Heavyweight Championship: Joe Frazier vs. George Foreman,

The original: "Down goes Frazier! Down goes Frazier! Down goes Frazier!"
Dutch: "Below Frazier go! Below Frazier go! Below Frazier go!"

Mike Keith, Music City Miracle, 1999 AFC Wild Card between the Tennessee Titans and Buffalo Bills

The original: "10, 5, end zone . . . touchdown, Titans! There are no flags on the field! It's a miracle! Tennessee has pulled a miracle! A miracle for the Titans!"
Japanese: "Ended zone of 10 and 5 . . . ground and Titan! There is no flag in field! That is miracle! Tennessee pulled miracle! Miracle because of Titan!"

THE SPORTS NUMERIST 81–100

The games. By the numbers. Eighty-one through one hundred.

On January 22, 2006, Kobe Bryant scored **81** points in a 122–104 Los Angeles Lakers victory over the Toronto Raptors. It's the second-highest single-game point total in NBA history, trailing only Wilt Chamberlain's 100.

There are **82** games in the NHL and NBA regular seasons.

The 2006 St. Louis Cardinals finished the regular-season with a record of **83**-79—then went on to win the World Series. Their .512 regular-season winning percentage is the lowest of any World Series champion.

In 1985, Magic Johnson sets the record for assists in a six-game NBA Finals series with **84**.

Cincinnati Bengals wide receiver Chad Johnson wears No. **85**. In 2006 the NFL fined him $5,000 for wearing OCHO CINCO on the back of his jersey. To combat that, he legally changed his last name to Ocho Cinco in 2008.

86: number of years between Red Sox World Series titles (1918, 2004).

In 2003, Buddy Helms was the oldest living original NASCAR driver at **87**.

The classy John Rocker, who once referred to African-American teammate Randall Simon as a "fat monkey," recorded **88** career saves. Coincidentally, the number is also used as code among neo-Nazis to identify each other.

The best badminton shuttlecocks are made of feathers from the left wing of a goose.

Musher Joe Runyan won the 19**89** Iditarod Trail Sled Dog Race behind lead dog Rambo.

Major league baseball bases are set **90** feet apart from one another.

Joe DiMaggio had **91** total hits during his historic, 56-game hitting streak in 1941.

In 2007, 91-year-old former boxing "cut man" Roland Fortin challenged **92**-year-old fitness guru and onetime boxing champion Jack LaLanne to a boxing match. The match was intended to inspire old people to get into shape. LaLanne declined.

Estelle Frendberg ran in the Senior Olympics for 18 years. In 2005 she won 2 gold medals and set a world record of 7 minutes, 10.84 seconds in the 800-meter run. She was **93** years old.

An NBA court is **94** feet long and 50 feet wide.

In 1984, Magic Johnson set the NBA record for most assists in a 7-game playoff series with **95**.

Mike Tyson's highly anticipated comeback fight versus Peter McNealy grossed **$96** million on Pay-Per-View. The fight lasted just 89 seconds.

Don Larsen pitched a perfect game in Game 5 of the 1956 World Series. He threw just **97** pitches.

The highest jersey number allowed in the NHL today is **98**, as Wayne Gretzky's 99 was retired by the entire league.

Rick "Wild Thing" Vaughn, the head-case pitcher played by Charlie Sheen in *Major League,* wore uniform No. **99**.

What else could it be? Wilt Chamberlain scored **100** points in a 1962 win over the New York Knicks.

The first Winter Olympic Games were held in Chamonix, France, in 1924.

THEY'RE PLAYING MY SONG!

Can you match the baseball player with their introduction music? Use your noggin and you should be able to figure most of them out.

1. Hee Seop Choi	A. "Square Dance," by Eminem. This batter chose his music after breaking out of a horrible slump in 2004, and now has the song cued up to start playing at 11 seconds with the lyrics "People, it feels so good to be back."
2. Kaz Matsui	B. "Flash Gordon," by Queen
3. Xavier Nady	C. Unknown Korean Rap Song
4. Derek Jeter	D. "X Gon' Give It to Ya," by DMX
5. Tom Gordon	E. "Splurgin'," by Nelly. This hitter once became so annoyed at the low volume of his at-bat music that he pelted the DJ booth with baseballs.

There are between 300 and 450 dimples on the average golf ball.

6. *Mike Cameron*	F. Bruce Lee Theme
7. *David Dellucci*	G. "Sweet Home Alabama," by Lynyrd Skynyrd. Fitting for this Alabama boy.
8. *Mike Mordecai*	H. "The Godfather Waltz," by Nino Rota. This Italian-American player was hesitant about using the tune, but fans ended up loving it!
9. *Brad Wilkerson*	I. "New York City," by Jay-Z. This player was so excited to become a Met that he told the media at his signing press conference that this would be his song.

Turn to page 355 for answers.

China and Indonesia are the most successful countries in the world of competitive badminton.

A PING-PONG PRIMER

The least you need to know about Forrest Gump's favorite sport.

Why Not Table Tennis? Because Ping-Pong Sounds Cooler

Early paddles were simply pieces of parchment stretched around a wire frame. When hit, they made a "ping-pong" sound—hence the name. For a time, the game was also known as whiff-whaff.

Back in the Day

Table tennis got its start in England, where it served as amusement for the upper-class. It was a makeshift game: piles of books served as a net, a knot of string or a champagne cork would double as a ball, and cigar-box lids were used as paddles.

In 1901 English manufacturer J. Jaques & Sons Ltd. trademarked the name Ping-Pong and began producing serious table-tennis sets.

A Gripping Debate: The Penhold vs. the Shakehand

In the 1950s, wooden paddles, covered in a rubber sheet combined with a layer of sponge, similar to what's used today, made their debut. This spawned one of the sport's great debates: How do you hold the damn thing? There are two basic grips.

Shakehand grip, often referred to as the Western grip because it's most common in the United States and Canada.

Penhold grip, so-named because the player holds the paddle in the same way one might hold a pen. Used in the East.

Speed Glue

Though not overly familiar to amateurs, speed glue is a key aspect of the professional game. Speed gluing is the process whereby a new layer of glue is used to attach the rubber surface of a Ping-Pong paddle to the sponge and the blade of the paddle. The glue causes the paddle's middle sponge layer to expand, stretching the outer layer of rubber and resulting in a sort of "trampoline" effect that increases the speed and spin the paddle gives off. The effects only last for a few hours, though, so it needs to be continually applied.

The performance-enhancing glue was discovered by accident in the '70s when a player repaired his busted paddle with bicycle-tire-repair glue. It was then popularized by Yugoslavian player Dragutin Surbek in the early '80s. Today, there are only a few pros who play without it.

Pong

Besides being a damned awesome sport on its own, Ping-Pong also inspired Pong, one of the earliest video games, and the video-game industry's first breakout hit. Pong achieved success first in the arcades, then at home as a standalone console and later on the Atari 2600. The rules, printed on the machine, were pretty simple: "Avoid missing ball for high score."

Ping-Pong Diplomacy

Who knew ping pong could change the world? In the 1970s, Ping-Pong players from the United States and the People's Republic of China played in peace on each other's home turfs. It was an important symbolic event that worked to thaw the U.S. and China's tense relationship, and it paved the way for President Nixon's historic visit to Beijing.

The trip was most likely sparked by the touching and dramatic meeting of Chinese player Zhuang Zedong and American player Glenn Cowan. Cowan had been practicing with a Chinese player and missed the team bus. The Chinese player graciously invited Cowan to ride on their bus. It was then that Zhuang Zedong came over, introduced himself through an interpreter, and gave Cowan a gift: silk-screened portrait of the Huangshan mountains in the city of Hangzhou.

In a 2002 interview, Zhuang Zedong admitted he was torn, saying, "The trip on the bus took 15 minutes, and I hesitated for 10 minutes. I grew up with the slogan, 'Down with the American imperialism!' And during the Cultural Revolution, the string of class struggle was tightened unprecedentedly, and I was asking myself, 'Is it OK to have anything to do with your No. 1 enemy?' "

Glenn Cowan was touched and wanted to return the favor, but all he had was a comb. A comb wasn't much of a gesture, and Cowan said, "Jesus Christ, I can't give you a comb. I wish I could give you something, but I can't." So later on, when they met again, Cowan presented Zhuang Zedong with a red, white, and blue T-shirt emblazoned with the peace symbol and the words LET IT BE.

When Chinese dictator Mao Zedong, who had previously declined to extend an invite to the U.S. team to play in China, saw the story in the Chinese paper, he changed his mind. He later said, "This Zhuang Zedong not only plays table tennis well, but is good at foreign affairs, and he has a mind for politics."

The Table Tennis Terminator

These days, practicing against a wall isn't enough for some players. The serious ones turn to something a little more high-tech: robots. The Paddle Palace 989-E can fire nearly 100 balls a minute at speeds up to 111 mph; and even with that speed, still deliver pinpoint shots to 11 different spots on the table. Interested? Only $1,399.99! We know, a little expensive, but it comes with 120 free balls (the cool orange ones too!) and shipping is free.

Long Pong

In 2007, two-time Olympian Andrea Holt, joined by players Alex Perry and Mark Rosaller, set a new world record for longest Ping-Pong rally. They began at 8:57 a.m. and ended at 5:24 p.m.—that's an 8-hour, 27 minute rally!

Table Tennis Trivia

Jack-of-all-trades sportsman Max Woosnam, onetime captain of the England national football team and an Olympic and Wimbledon champion at lawn tennis, once beat Charlie Chaplin in a game of Ping-Pong using a butter knife as a racket.

Ping-Pong was banned in early-1900s Russia because people were convinced the game could ruin a player's eyesight.

According to the International Olympic Committee, which made Ping-Pong an Olympic sport in 1988, the game is now the world's largest participation sport: 40 million people worldwide enjoy the game.

Most folks assume Ping-Pong balls are made out of plastic. Well, most folks are wrong. They're actually made of celluloid—the same stuff used to make photographic film.

In 1935 the first ever Skee ball tournament was held in Atlantic City, New Jersey.

COBB

Stories about Ty Cobb, "the dirtiest player around."

Ty's Spikes

According to legend, not only did Cobb sharpen his spikes, he even did so in front of everyone, sitting in the dugout, eyeing the opposing fielders, letting them know what was in store for them should they block his slide. Now, whether or not Cobb really did sharpen his cleats remains a mystery, but either way, he didn't do anything to dissuade the rumor—he liked to intimidate.

Ty the Father

When Cobb's son, Ty Jr., dropped out of Princeton, Cobb traveled to the campus and beat him with a horse whip.

Ty the Racist

His sportsmanship was debatable. His parenting skills are open to discussion. What isn't questionable, however, is that Cobb was a brutal, violent, and despicable racist. Look at these four incidents.

> During spring training, Cobb attacked a black groundskeeper over the condition of the field. The groundskeeper's wife intervened, and Cobb choked her.
>
> He once slapped a black elevator operator because Cobb felt he was being "uppity." A black security guard intervened and Cobb pulled a knife and stabbed him.
>
> He refused to travel with his team on a tour through Cuba, saying "darkies' place is in the stands or as clubhouse help."

When a hotel chambermaid let it be known that she didn't approve of his use of the N-word, Cobb kicked her in the stomach.

Ty and the Heckler

Cobb was playing against the hometown New York Highlanders. Highlanders fan Claude Lueker was giving Cobb a particularly hard time, and by the end of the fifth inning, Cobb made it clear to the umps that if Lueker wasn't tossed from the game, there'd be trouble. In the sixth, Lueker called Cobb a "half-ni##er." The racist Cobb, inflamed, leapt into the stands and began to pummel the fan mercilessly.

Here's where the story gets really ugly. Lueker had no hands—he had lost them in an industrial accident. The crowd begged Cobb to stop, but Cobb didn't care and shouted, "I don't care if he's got no feet!" as he continued to beat the man.

Ty Stares Down Death with a Luger

By 1960, Cobb was dying, accompanied only by biographer Al Stump. He had no family with him—they'd all left him. Cobb, suffering from heart disease, diabetes, high blood pressure, kidney disease, and prostate cancer, traveled from hospital to hospital, carrying with him an envelope stuffed with millions of dollars in securities and a loaded Luger pistol. On July 17, 1961, he died. His first wife and a few other family members had come to be with him.

Ty's Funeral

Need more proof Cobb was one disliked son of a gun? Only three professional baseball players showed up at his funeral: Ray Schalk, Mickey Cochrane, Nap Rucker. Compare that to his contemporary Babe Ruth: More than 200,000 fans showed up to pay their respects to the Babe upon his death, and his casket was carried to his grave by former teammates.

There is an average of 2,000 demolition derbies held in the United States every year.

On Cobb

"Cobb is a prick. But he sure can hit. God Almighty, that man can hit."
—Babe Ruth

"He didn't outhit and he didn't outrun them, he out-thought them."
—Sam Crawford

"When he's at bat you can hear him gritting his teeth."
—Rebel Oaks

"Every time I hear of this guy again, I wonder how he was possible."
—Joe DiMaggio

"Few names have left a firmer imprint upon the stages of the history of American times than that of Ty Cobb. For a quarter of a century, his aggressive exploits on the diamond, while inviting opposition as well as acclaim, brought high drama. This great athlete seems to have understood from early in his professional career that the competition of baseball, just as in war, defensive strategy never has produced ultimate victory."
—General Douglas MacArthur

"The greatness of Ty Cobb was something that had to be seen, and to see him was to remember him forever."
—George Sisler

"Let him sleep if he will. If you get him riled up, he will annihilate us."
—Connie Mack

"COBB LIVED OFF THE FIELD AS THOUGH HE WISHED TO LIVE FOREVER. HE LIVED ON THE FIELD AS THOUGH IT WAS HIS LAST DAY."
—BRANCH RICKEY

For More Cobb

Writer Al Stump traveled with Cobb just before he died, working with him on an autobiography of his life. Just after Cobb's death, the book was published as *My Life in Baseball,* by Ty Cobb. It painted Cobb in a fairly sympathetic light. Then, some 30 years later, Stump wrote another book, *Cobb: A Biography,* which was a much more honest account of the man. Both are good reads and worth adding to your bathroom library.

The closest finish in Nascar history was .002 seconds on March 16, 2003, when Ricky Craven beat Kurt Busch.

ABC'S WIDE WORLD OF SPORTS

The thrill of victory . . . the agony of defeat . . . the story of the show.

ABC's *Wide World of Sports* was an extremely popular, long-running sports show that graced American TV sets from 1961 to 1998. *WWOS* introduced America to a number of sports that they didn't even know existed, and showed us, on our TVs, action from sports we'd only heard of, including jai alai, barrel jumping, cliff diving, logger sports, firefighter competitions, hurling, demolition derby, and surfing.

That Famous Intro

Jack-of-all-trades Stanley Ralph Ross (1937–2000) was the man behind the show's classic opening segment. He did voice-over work, wrote a third of the 1960s *Batman* episodes starring Adam West, composed over 200 songs, wrote for the Monkeys and *All in the Family,* and was an ordained minister. But his legacy is these words, played over a montage of sports clips and accompanied by dramatic narration courtesy of host Jim McKay:

> "Spanning the globe to bring you the constant variety of sport . . . the thrill of victory . . . and the agony of defeat . . . the human drama of athletic competition . . . This is ABC's *Wide World of Sports*!"

The Agony of Defeat

The "thrill of victory" line was illustrated by a number of images and clips over the years. But from the 1970s until the show went off the air in 1998, the "agony of defeat" line was accompanied by ski jumper Vinko Bogataj violently flipping, twisting, and crashing through a fence.

In Japan, Dodgeball is so popular that elementary schools compete every year for the Kuroneko Cup.

Once, Bogataj was on his way to an interview with ABC's Terry Gannon when he got into a fender-bender in the parking lot. Said Bogataj, "Every time I'm on ABC, I crash."

Comedian Rich Hall was the inventor of Sniglets—"any word that doesn't appear in the dictionary, but should." He defined *agonosis* as the "syndrome of tuning in on *Wide World of Sports* every weekend just to watch the skier rack himself."

Jim McKay

For more than 40 years, Jim McKay hosted ABC's *Wide World of Sports*. His finest moment as a broadcaster, however, was undoubtedly when he covered the Munich massacre at the 1972 Summer Olympics. After 14 straight hours on the air, Jim McKay came on the air and announced the news the world was dreading:

> "When I was a kid my father used to say, 'Our greatest hopes and our worst fears are seldom realized.' Our worst fears have been realized tonight. They have now said there were 11 hostages; two were killed in their rooms yesterday morning, nine were killed at the airport tonight. They're all gone."

When Jim passed away on June 7, 2008, Disney president and chief executive Bob Iger said, "Jim was a regular guy who wrote and spoke like a poet. He loved sports. To him, sports defined life—full of drama, adventure, accomplishment, and disappointment. The thrill of victory for some, the agony of defeat for others."

It's a Wide, Wide World

Need proof that *Wide World of Sports* was a true innovator? It was the first program to air coverage of the Indy 500, the NCAA basketball championship, Wimbledon, the X Games, the Daytona 500, the Little League World Series, the U.S. Figure Skating Championships, and the Open Championship.

Q: Where can you find the largest diamond in New York City? A: In Yankee Stadium.

In 2007, *Time* Magazine named ABC's *Wide World of Sports* one of the 100 all-time-best TV shows.

No More

In the mid-1990s, with the rise of the internet, cable television, and ESPN, much of *Wide World of Sports*'s appeal was lost. The show, in its standard anthology format, was cancelled in 1997, though ABC still uses the *Wide World of Sports* name for occasional events.

The longest recorded volleyball marathon by two teams of six was 75 hours, 30 minutes at Kingston, North Carolina, in 1980.

THE COSTANZA YEARS

What went down while George bumbled about the Bronx.

The House That Ruth Built (and George napped in)

As any real (read: obsessive) *Seinfeld* fan knows, George Costanza worked for the Yankees from May 19, 1994, to May 8, 1997, starting out as "assistant to the traveling secretary" and being promoted twice during his time there. During the "Costanza Years," the Yankees went a collective 234-181 and won one World Series (1996). Let's take a closer look.

The Costanza Years

1994

Record: 70-43 (44-31 with George on staff), finished first in division
Manager: Buck Showalter
Payroll: $44,785,334
Total home runs hit: 139
Team ERA: 4.34
Total runs scored/allowed: 670/534
Playoffs: No postseason in 1994 due to strike. George changes uniforms from polyester to cotton.

1995

Record: 79-65, finished second in division
Manager: Buck Showalter
Total payroll: $46,657,016
Total home runs hit: 122
Team ERA: 4.56
Total runs scored/allowed: 749/688
Playoffs: lost AL Division Series (3-2) to Seattle Mariners. George is suspected of stealing Steinbrenner's pills.

Ultimate Frisbee has been demonstrated to require a higher cardiovascular fitness level than any other field game.

1996
Record: 92-70, finished first in division
Manager: Joe Torre
Total payroll: $52,189,370
Total home runs hit: 162
Team ERA: 4.65
Total runs scored/allowed: 871/787
Playoffs: won the World Series. George coaches Bernie Williams and Derek Jeter on their hitting.

1997
Record: 96-66, finished second in division (19-15 with George on staff)
Manager: Joe Torre
Total payroll: $59,148,877
Total home runs hit: 161
Team ERA: 3.84
Total runs scored/allowed: 891/688
Playoffs: lost AL Division Series (3-2) to Cleveland Indians. George fake-streaks across the Yankee Stadium field.

Those are some pretty successful years, which is pretty much a miracle when you consider that George was running around the organization, doing his best to muck stuff up. Here's a bit more on the George contributions noted above, the very havoc that he wreaked during his years as a Yankee.

> Changed the Yankees uniforms from polyester to cotton, with disastrous consequences. Yankees announcer: "The new uniforms are too tight, they've shrunk. Oh my God, Mattingly just split his pants!"
>
> Gave batting tips to Bernie Williams and Derek Jeter: "Guys, hitting is not about muscle. It's simple physics. Calculate the velocity, *v*, in relation to the trajectory, *t*, in which *g*, gravity, of course remains a constant. It's not complicated."
>
> Was accused of stealing sports equipment (and all of Mr. Steinbrenner's pills).

The NY Yankees logo was designed in 1877—it was taken from a medal of honor for the New York City Police Department.

Coached Danny Tartabull on his swing, completely screwing it up and driving Buck Showalter nuts.

Had Jerry call in multiple bomb threats to the stadium in an effort to cover up his napping-beneath-the-desk trick.

Wore an authentic, game-used Babe Ruth jersey, then purposely got strawberry juice all over it.

Fake-streaked across Yankee Stadium in a skin-colored body suit, inadvertently becoming the fan-favorite "Body Suit Man."

Tied a World Series trophy to the bumper of his car and dragged it around the stadium parking lot while yelling though a bullhorn: "Attention, Steinbrenner and front-office morons! Your triumphs mean nothing. You all stink. You can sit on it, and rotate! This is George Costanza. I fear no reprisal. Extension 5-1-7-0."

Bye, George

Partway through the 1997 season, Steinbrenner traded George to Tyler Chicken ("a top-flight bird outfit," according to the Boss) for a supply of fermented chicken drinks for the concession stands. George's absence gave the franchise an immediate spark with the Yankees promptly winning back-to-back-to-back World Series.

William Leonard Hunt, aka "The Great Farini," invented the human cannonball in 1871.

NAISMITH, PEACH BASKETS, AND THE ORIGINAL 13

A bit about the early days of basketball.

It's a Peach!

Dr. James Naismith invented basketball in 1891 when he was charged with coming up with an "athletic distraction" for students at the School for Christian Workers, something to keep them busy during the long, cold New England winter. The sport was simple: Naismith nailed two peach baskets to opposite walls, gave the kids a soccer ball, and they started shooting.

Naismith didn't actually remove the bottoms of the peach baskets, however, so every time someone scored, they had to pull out a ladder, climb up, and take the ball out. Not a huge problem at the time—the final score of the first game was 1–0. Iron hoops and a hammock-style net appeared in 1893, but it wasn't until 1903 that the open-ended net made its debut. Hard to imagine that they went 20-plus years before realizing how much time they'd save by removing the whole "Hey-Jim-be-a-good-fella-and-get-the-ladder-out-someone-scored-again" aspect of the game.

The Original 13

When Naismith invented the game that he dubbed "Basket Ball," he came up with 13 rules.

> The ball may be thrown in any direction with one or both hands.
>
> The ball may be batted in any direction with one or both hands, but never with the fist.
>
> A player cannot run with the ball. The player must throw it from the spot on which he catches it, allowance to be made for a man running at good speed.
>
> The ball must be held by the hands. The arms or body must not be used for holding it.

According to an obscure law, all English males over the age of 14 are to carry out 2 or so hours of longbow practice a week.

No shouldering, holding, pushing, striking or tripping in any way of an opponent. The first infringement of this rule by any person shall count as a foul; the second shall disqualify him until the next goal is made or, if there was evident intent to injure the person, for the whole of the game. No substitution shall be allowed.

A foul is striking at the ball with the fist, violations of Rules 3 and 4 and such as described in Rule 5.

If either side makes three consecutive fouls, it shall count as a goal for the opponents (consecutive means without the opponents in the meantime making a foul).

A goal shall be made when the ball is thrown or batted from the grounds into the basket and stays there, providing those defending the goal do no touch or disturb the goal. If the ball rests on the edges, and the opponent moves the basket, it shall count as a goal.

When the ball goes out of bounds, it shall be thrown into the field and played by the first person touching it. In case of dispute the umpire shall throw it straight into the field. The thrower-in is allowed five seconds. If he holds it longer, it shall go to the opponent. If any side persists in delaying the game, the umpire shall call a foul on them.

The umpire shall be the judge of the men and shall note the fouls and notify the referee when three consecutive fouls have been made. He shall have power to disqualify men according to Rule 5.

The referee shall be judge of the ball and shall decide when the ball is in play, in bounds, to which side it belongs, and shall keep the time. He shall decide when a goal has been made and keep account of the goals, with any other duties that are usually performed by a referee.

The time shall be two 15-minute halves, with five minutes rest between.

The side making the most goals in that time shall be declared the winner.

6 foot, 5 inch Harlem Globetrotter Michael "Wild Thing" Wilson is in the *Guinness Book of World Records* for dunking a basketball on a 12-foot hoop.

Hank Luisetti and the One-Hand Shot

Before Angelo "Hank" Luisetti, the old "two-hand set shot" was the only way people shot. It was simply considered basic fundamentals. It was a young Luisetti that developed the running one-handed shot that's so common today. When he joined the Stanford University basketball team in 1935, Luisetti feared his coach would make him change his unorthodox shooting style. His coach pulled him aside and said, "Let's see a sample." Luisetti drained a one-hander from the corner and Bunn told him, "Stay with it, boy."

Not everyone was a fan, however. Coach Nat Holman, an important early figure in the game and once a great player, wasn't having it. He said, "I'll quit coaching if I have to teach one-handed shots to win." Fundamentals or not, it was hard to argue with the results, and it wasn't long before kids all over the country were tossing up one-handed jump shots.

Dribbling

Believe it or not, dribbling wasn't a major part of the game until the late 1950s. The game was based on passing and off-ball movement, with the occasional bounce pass thrown in. The asymmetrical, imperfect shape of early balls made consistent dribbling impossible; it became a fundamental aspect of the game only after the ball became better manufactured.

Shot Clock

Up until 1954, basketball games were actually pretty boring. Once a team took a lead, the game would often devolve into a big game of keep-away. The owner of the Syracuse Nationals, Danny Biasone, came up with the idea for the 24-second shot clock. What was once a slow, meandering game immediately became the fast-paced, up-tempo, speedy sport that we know and love today.

EXTRA INNINGS

Baseball Letter Equations (answers from page 50)

1. 3 Strikes and You're Out
2. Babe Ruth = First Person to Hit 700 Home Runs in a Major League Baseball Career
3. 6 = Outs in 1 Inning of Baseball
4. 162 games in a Major League Baseball regular season
5. 4 = Bases on a Baseball Diamond
6. 108 = Stitches on a Baseball
7. Cal Ripken Jr. = Played 2,632 Consecutive Major League Baseball Games
8. 90 Feet = Distance Between Bases on a Regulation Baseball Diamond

Tennis Trivia (answers from page 104)

1. b. Billie Jean King
2. a. 1896
3. a. Russian
4. c. Arthur Ashe
5. a. Ad court
6. b. Bjorn Borg

7. d. Chris Evert

8. c. Jimmy Connors

9. d. Bulgaria

10. c. Boris Becker

Athletes at the Movies (from page 126)

The Athlete	**The Line**
Dennis Rodman	"The last guy that made fun of my hair is still trying to pull his head outta his ass." [*Double Team*]
Hulk Hogan	"Rip 'em! Rip 'em! Rip 'em! Come on, Randy! Let's go, Charlie! We're gonna take on Jake Bullet!" [*No Holds Barred*]
Brett Favre	"I'm in town to play the Dolphins, you dumbass." [*There's Something About Mary*]
Brian Bosworth	[after knocking around a few would-be grocery store robbers] "You better clean up on aisle four." [*Stone Cold*]
Charles Barkley	"It was this girl, five-foot-nuthin'. Blocked my shot!" [*Space Jam*]
Roger Clemens	"You're trying to move in on my squirrel! I\ ought to stoot-slap your ass right now!" [*Kingpin*]
Shaquille O'Neal	"Hang on! I'm contagious, outrageous, spontaneous! You can't contain this." [*Kazaam*]
Dan Marino	"Hey, Ace, got anymore of that gum?" [*Ace Ventura: Pet Detective*]

NFL names first appeared on the backs of NFL jerseys during the 1960s.

Kareem Abdul Jabbar "The hell I don't. Listen, kid. I've been hearing that crap ever since I was at UCLA. I'm out there busting my buns every night. Tell your old man to drag Walton and Lanier up and down the court for 48 minutes." [*Airplane*]

Alex Karras "Mongo only pawn in game of life." [*Blazing Saddles*]

Riddle Me This (from page 233)

Q: In major league baseball, there are seven different ways a player can legally get to first base without getting a hit. What are they?

A: 1) Batter hit by a pitch, 2) catcher interference, 3) passed ball, 4) fielder's choice, 5) catcher drops third strike, 6) being used as a pinch runner, and 7) base on balls

Q: What is the minimum number of pitches that could be thrown in a major league baseball game?

A: 52

Q: There's one professional sport in which neither the participants nor the spectators know the winner or the score until the contest ends. What sport is it?

A: Boxing

Q: In which sport is the ball always in possession of the defense, and the offense can score without even touching the ball?

A: Baseball

Q: What is harder to catch the faster you run?

A: Your breath.

Q: My buddy Charlie can guess the score of a basketball game before the game begins. How can that be?

A: Because before the game starts, the score is always 0-0.

Q: A man left home one day, made three left turns, and was greeted by a man with a mask on. What was the first man's profession?
A: Baseball player.

The Baseball Movie Quote Quiz (from page 264)

Quote	Movie
"Quit trying to strike everybody out. Strikeouts are boring and besides that, they're fascist. Throw some ground balls. They're more democratic."	*Bull Durham*
"I love baseball. You know it doesn't have to mean anything, it's just beautiful to watch."	*Zelig*
"Those Yankees are real turds."	*Bad News Bears*
"When the bat meets that ball and you feel that ball just give, you know it's going to go a long way. Damn if you don't feel like you're going to live forever."	*Eight Men Out*
"Man, this is baseball, you gotta stop thinking! Just have fun."	*The Sandlot*
"There's no crying in baseball!"	*A League of Their Own*
"Remember, fans, Tuesday is Die Hard Night. Free admission for anyone who was actually alive the last time the Indians won the pennant."	*Major League*

Carlton Fisk was nicknamed "Frankenstein" because of his super erect posture.

"The one constant through all the years, Ray, has been baseball. America has rolled by like an army of steamrollers. It has been erased like a blackboard, rebuilt, and erased again. But baseball has marked the time. This field, this game—it's a part of our past, Ray. It reminds us of all that once was good and could be good again."	*Field of Dreams*
"Tonight, he will make the fateful walk to the loneliest spot in the world, the pitching mound at Yankee Stadium, to push the sun back into the sky and give us one more day of summer."	*For the Love of the Game*
"God, I just love baseball."	*The Natural*

They're Playing My Song! (from page 331)

1. Hee Seap Seop Choi	C. Unknown Korean Rap Song
2. Kaz Matsui	F. Bruce Lee Theme
3. Xavier Nady	D. "X Gon' Give It To to Ya," by DMX
4. Derek Jeter	A. "Square Dance," by Eminem
5. Tom Gordon	B. "Flash Gordon," by Queen
6. Mike Cameron	I. "New York City," by Jay-Z
7. David Dellucci	H. "The Godfather Waltz," by Nino Rota.
8. Mike Mordecai	G. "Sweet Home Alabama,"by Lynyrd Skynyrd
9. Brad Wilkerson	E. "Splurgin'," by Nelly

Do You Know Your Baseball Numbers? (from page 153)

1. b
2. c
3. d
4. c
5. a
6. c
7. a
8. a
9. d
10. c

Do You Know Your Football Numbers? (from page 203)

1. b
2. a
3. d
4. b
5. c
6. c
7. b
8. c
9. b
10. a

METRIC CONVERSION TABLES

Approximate U.S. Metric Equivalents

Liquid Ingredients

U.S. MEASURES	METRIC	U.S. MEASURES	METRIC
¼ TSP.	1.23 ML	2 TBSP.	29.57 ML
½ TSP.	2.36 ML	3 TBSP.	44.36 ML
¾ TSP.	3.70 ML	¼ CUP	59.15 ML
1 TSP.	4.93 ML	½ CUP	118.30 ML
1¼ TSP.	6.16 ML	1 CUP	236.59 ML
1½ TSP.	7.39 ML	2 CUPS OR 1 PT.	473.18 ML
1¾ TSP.	8.63 ML	3 CUPS	709.77 ML
2 TSP.	9.86 ML	4 CUPS OR 1 QT.	946.36 ML
1 TBSP.	14.79 ML	4 QTS. OR 1 GAL.	3.79 L

Dry Ingredients

U.S. MEASURES	METRIC	U.S. MEASURES		METRIC
1⁄16 OZ.	2 (1.8) G	2⅘ OZ.		80 G
⅛ OZ.	31⁄2 (3.5) G	3 OZ.		85 (84.9) G
¼ OZ.	7 (7.1) G	3½ OZ.		100 G
½ OZ.	15 (14.2) G	4 OZ.		115 (113.2) G
¾ OZ.	21 (21.3) G	4½ OZ.		125 G
⅞ OZ.	25 G	5¼ OZ.		150 G
1 OZ.	30 (28.3) G	8⅞ OZ.		250 G
1¾ OZ.	50 G	16 OZ.	1 LB.	454 G
2 OZ.	60 (56.6) G	17⅗ OZ.	1 LIVRE	500 G

The first World Series was played between Pittsburgh and Boston in 1903.

The NFL Pro Bowl has been played in Honolulu since 1980.

Emmitt Smith won the third Dancing With the Stars.

Princeton won the first college football championship with a 1-1 record.

The United States has won more medals at the Summer Games than any other country.

The NBA borrowed the idea for the 3-pointer from the ABA.

The champion of the Canadian Football League is awarded the Grey Cup.

About the Author

Max Brallier is the author of *Reasons to Smoke and Reasons to Drink*. He works for a major book publisher, reading manuscripts and writing copy — while on the toilet, of course. He lives in New York City.